FROM WEIMAR PHILOSEMITE TO NAZI APOLOGIST
The Case of Walter Bloem

Rodler F. Morris

Studies in German Thought and History
Volume 7

The Edwin Mellen Press
Lewiston/Queenston/Lampeter

Library of Congress Cataloging-in-Publication Data

Morris, Rodler F
    From Weimar philosemite to Nazi apologist : the case of Walter Bloem / Rodler F. Morris.
    p. cm. -- (Studies in German thought and history ; v. 7)
    Bibliography: p.
    Includes index.
    ISBN 0-88946-349-2
    1. Bloem, Walter, 1868-1951--Political and social views.
2. Bloem, Walter, 1868-1951. Bruderlichkeit. 3. Bloem, Walter, 1868-1951--Characters--Jews. 4. Judaism in literature. 5. Jews in literature. 6. Antisemitism--Germany--History--20th century.
I. Title. II. Series.
PT2603.L6Z75 1988
833'.912--dc19
                      88-14751
                          CIP

> This is volume 7 in the continuing series
> Studies in German Thought and History
> Volume 7 ISBN 0-88946-349-2
> SGTH Series ISBN 0-88946-351-4

Copyright © 1988 by Rodler F. Morris

All rights reserved. For information contact:

The Edwin Mellen Press

Box 450
Lewiston, New York
U.S.A. 14092

Box 67
Queenston, Ontario
CANADA L0S 1L0

Mellen House
Lampeter, Dyfed, Wales
UNITED KINGDOM SA48 7DY

Printed in the United States of America

This book is dedicated to my friend,
Dr. Thomas Payne,
whose intrinsic decency
has decisively furthered my own moral education.

ACKNOWLEDGEMENTS

I am grateful to the Earhart Foundation and the German Academic Exchange Service (DAAD) for funding my research and to the personnel of the Stadt Bücherei (Wuppertal), the Bundesarchiv-Militärarchiv (Freiburg/Breisgau), the Akademie der Künste (West Berlin), and the Deutsches Literaturarchiv (Marbach/Neckar) for opening their document collections to me and for the many other kindnesses with which they aided my work. I am thankful to Dr. Gerhard Weinberg who supervised my original work on Bloem and to the guidance of Drs. Ruth Angress, Henry Friedlander, and Sybil Milton in making revisions of the article summarizing chapters 1, 3-5 that appeared in volume 4 of the Simon Wiesenthal Center Annual (SWC). Professor Robert Heywood provided a helpful commentary on the preliminary version of the SWC article delivered as a paper at the 12th Annual Great Lakes History Conference, Grand Rapids, Michigan (April, 1986). Drs. Ralph Hancock, Warren Treadgold, Thomas Payne, Kendall Brown, and Daniel Hughes have provided insightful criticisms of the book manuscript. Appreciation is owed to Marsha Boemke and Jean McCaskey for their typing of original drafts; special thanks is due to my beloved wife Lynne for typing and editing the final copy. Naturally, I bear full responsibility for all the books's shortcomings.

Material (most notably chapters 2-5) from Rodler F. Morris, "Philosemitism on the German Right: The Case of the Novelist Walter Bloem." Simon Wiesenthal Center Annual. Eds. Henry Friedlander and Sybil Milton. Vol. 4. White Plains, New York, 1987, pp 203-259, has been reproduced with permission of Kraus International Publications: A Division of Kraus-Thomson Organization Limited.

TABLE OF CONTENTS

Acknowledgements iv

Introduction 1

Chapter 1: Bestselling Novelist of the Wilhelmine Twilight: The Road from Monarchist to Reluctant Republican 7

Chapter 2: The Mind and Character of Walter Bloem: Some Reflections 15

Chapter 3: The "Knight's Deed of the Spirit": The Genesis, Political Message, and Publication History of Brotherhood: A Novel 39

Chapter 4: The German Right and Brotherhood: A Novel: Political Impact and Critical Reception 49

Chapter 5: Liberals, Catholics, Socialists, Jews and Brotherhood: A Novel: Political Impact and Critical Reception 61

Chapter 6: The Erosion of Walter Bloem's Republicanism: 1922-1930 81

Chapter 7: Background to the Death of Walter Bloem's Republicanism: The Opposition in the Protective Association of German Writers (SDS) 97

Chapter 8: The Death of Walter Bloem's Republicanism: The Battle Within the SDS 115

Chapter 9: The Moral Suicide of an Honest Man: Walter Bloem as Nazi Fellow Traveler and Party Member 139

Conclusion: The Impotency of Walter Bloem's Philosemitism 155

Notes 167

Bibliography 229

Index 241

INTRODUCTION

In 1922, one of Germany's best-known nationalist writers, Walter Bloem, stunned his contemporaries with a political novel strongly opposed to racism, antisemitism, and extremism. Only a scant four years earlier, Bloem had been something akin to a novelist laureate for the Second Reich. Publication of Brotherhood (German title: Die Brüderlichkeit) was a singular event in the Weimar Republic. No other best-selling philosemitic novel by a prominent nationalist author appeared in the years 1918-32.

To be sure, other nationalist authors occasionally struck out against antisemitism in their fiction. Ernst Wiechert's short story, "The Gesture" (1932), was a powerful condemnation of antisemitism.[1] The self-styled Heimat and deutschvölkisch author Ernst Püschel even wrote a counter-novel, The Jews of Kronburg, to Arthur Dinter's Sin Against the Blood (1918), the prototype of all later racist novels which did much to fuel the antisemitic surge of 1918-23. "My novel," Püschel informed the CV-Zeitung in 1924, "demands nothing other than that the Jew who has proven his Germanness be ranked amidst the German Volk community." Püschel rejected the dogma of blood. He was convinced that völkisch-mindedness could "be living in a Jew just as well as in a Catholic or Protestant."[2] But, Wiechert's "The Gesture" was a short story with little or no impact; Püschel was little known and less read. Bloem, on the other hand, was quite likely the best-selling author on the German book market between 1912 and 1922. Brotherhood was, at least at first, a signal success, with ninety-thousand copies in print by the end of 1922.[3]

But the novel also became the focus of a passionate political controversy. On the right, Bloem's nationalist readers rejected his philosemitism and henceforth viewed him as a renegade; thereafter, his popularity slipped precipitously. On the left, liberals and socialists hailed his stand against antisemitism, but they in turn rejected his conservatism and nationalism. Jews themselves welcomed Bloem's assault on radical antisemitism and worked to bring his book to a wider audience. Their endorsement of Brotherhood, however, was not unqualified. They were troubled by Bloem's perpetuation of central aspects of the antisemties' image of the Jew.

Bloem more or less toed the unique political line laid down in Brotherhood until the end of the twenties. But the financial and psychological stresses born of the novel's aftermath helped to prepare Bloem for reconversion to antirepublican nationalism in the last years of the Weimar era. During the twilight before the dark night of the Third Reich, Bloem was elected head of both the German section of the PEN-Club and of the Protective Association of German Writers (SDS). Undoubtedly the legacy of Brotherhood furthered Bloem's election to these posts. All sides perceived him as being "between the stools." Ultimately, Bloem laid down his offices at the center of bitter political storms, which partly caused and partly stemmed from his realignment with the nationalist mainstream. Bloem's resignations were a turning point in the history of German writers' efforts to organize themselves professionally. Henceforth, these organizations were utterly politicized; they would soon prove an easy mark for Nazi efforts to transform them into instruments of totalitarian repression.

In the first months of the Third Reich, Bloem played a key role in transforming the independent Protective Association of German Writers into the Reich Literature Chamber (Reichsschriftumskammer), the lynchpin of Joseph Goebbels's literary dictatorship. Afterwards, Bloem served the Nazis with his pen. In writings tainted with the very racist poison that he had once bravely attacked, he strove to reconcile the "Old Nationalists" (whose chief literary mouthpiece he had once been) to Hitler. Ironically, Brotherhood kept Bloem from enjoying the fruits of his late attachment to the victorious Hitler juggernaut. Alfred Rosenberg never forgave Bloem for his philosemitic novel. Bloem remained something of an outsider under the Nazi regime, at least until 1938, when Goebbels's intervention enabled him to join the NSDAP.

During World War II, Bloem despite his seventy plus years went on active duty and helped the war effort as speaker and writer. He was conscience stricken by particular Nazi atrocities but did nothing significant to expose or stop them. He regarded the events of 20 July 1944, the great hour of the German resistance, as the work of traitors. The moral suicide of this once honest man was complete. After the war, he was acquitted by a de-Nazification tribunal, which was puzzled by the troubling question of how the author of Brotherhood had come to swim with the Brown tide. Bloem, once the nation's most popular entertainment novelist, died in 1951, partly scorned but mostly forgotten.

Walter Bloem has not yet received detailed scholarly scrutiny, though his dubious role in the writers' associations has been documented. The enormous circulation of his books and the storm over Brotherhood seem to justify an analysis of the genesis, contents, reception and effects of Bloem's philosemitic novel. Brotherhood's fate and its impact on Bloem's life illuminate the nearly insurmountable difficulties facing a national conservative yet philosemitic publicist in the Weimar era. Bloem's woes, moreover, underscore the dangers facing a politically committed writer without party ties or organizational backing. Bloem's career after 1922-23 will be given more than passing attention, partly because of its intrinsic importance, partly because it unfolded under the shadow of Brotherhood.

Bloem's case yields new perspectives on the moral dimensions of the German tragedy. His resistance to right-wing radicalism illustrates the freedom to resist the moral degradation of one's time. That he eventually succumbed, if not without reservation, underlines the insubstantiality of political commitments not firmly rooted in principle. Although Bloem was a political loner, he was also the representative author of an important component of German culture, the nationalist entertainment industry. As such, he was a mirror of what Moritz Heimann, the brilliant publisher's reader for Samuel Fischer, described as the "broad" provincial reading public "of pastors, doctors, judges, middle-level post and tax officials, teachers and estate owners."[4] Bloem's personal tragedy shows with especial clarity how hard it must have been for the German Everyman to choose wisely and ethically in the era of the world wars, yet how unwise, immoral choices resulted from a moral relativism that was not fated, but the product of personal, intellectual and character weaknesses, for which individuals carry responsibility. The moral roots of Bloem's temporary resistance and ultimate surrender to Nazi millenarianism will be examined with the aid of political philosophy on the assumption that his case history has much to suggest about how similar weaknesses led the German middle class (especially the Bildungsbürgertum) of educated burghers to Hitler.

The study of Bloem's abortive effort to stem the rising tide of antisemitism after World War I requires us to define philosemitism,[5] of which four types were found in his time. The first derives from the conviction that the Jews are the people chosen of God to prepare for the coming of His kingdom. This religious belief, rightly understood, does not ascribe to the Jews inherent virtue superior to that of other men, for the Jews have been chosen through God's grace, not their own merits (although if they accept the obligations imposed by their selection they will excel in righteousness). Yet, the special role of the Jews in God's plans cannot help but positively affect attitudes towards them. Belief in this special role is not only at the heart of Judaism. It is also accepted by non-heretical Christians whose belief is continuous with that of what they call the Old Testament. Christian love, moreover, has, when authentically expressed included Jews in its universal embrace. To be sure, Christian belief that the Jews have failed to recognize that with Jesus the kingdom has been ushered into this world has been misused to rationalize and even to generate anti-Jewish prejudices. Even Christian love has been perverted in anti-Jewish directions by requiring Jews to be force fed Christianity for their own salvation or to be removed from the community for the salvation of others.

The second type of philosemitism, implied in the very combination form, involves a love for Jews and things Jewish based on secular considerations, including a secular appreciation of Jewish religion. This love might be based on a realistic evaluation of the Jewish contributions to civilization, it might be an idealized image. Either way, such philosemitism like antisemitism works by judging individuals for the collectivity to which they belong (or seem to belong) rather than for themselves.[6]

A third type of philosemitism is basically equalitarianism, a belief that Jews must be accorded the same rights as others in society. Such a position, based on at least the residues of objective principle, becomes philosemitism only when forced explicitly to embrace Jews. This happens when antisemites either question the equalitarian principle or deny that it should be applied to Jews.

The final, minimal type of philosemitism involves some degree of opposition to antisemitism and some degree of sympathy for Jews subjected to antisemitic hatred or persecution. This type of philosemitism at its most diluted is little more than anti-antisemitism and might well be devoid of love for Jews or any conviction of their natural equality. Antisemites themselves, or those prone to think about Jews in unflattering sterotypes, have not rarely opposed anti-Jewish ideas or policies more radical than their own. Definition according to types that makes possible, at least under certain circumstances, the description of those corrupted by antisemitism as philosemitic is fraught with the peril of linguistic and even moral confusion. Yet there can be little doubt that to a degree philosemitism is relative to time and place. In this case, linguistic imprecision reflects the complex, blurred, ever-changing contours of human attitudes and sentiments and of the historical contexts in which they shape action. Obviously, "philosemitic" positions that do not see Jews with their heritage as they actually are and that do not protect their rights under all circumstances are much less reliable politically and much less sound morally than those that do.

Bloem's philosemitic statement of 1922 was to some extent colored by residues of Christian love and of the liberal principle that all people, since they are intrinsically equal, must have the same rights. Bloem also found aspects of the Jewish character explicitly admirable. Though his estimation of Jewish qualities had much in common with antisemitic stereotypes, Bloem differed in that he saw these traits, at least in certain contexts, as virtues rather than vices. He admitted, however, that when detached from national conservatism or driven to extremes, they become dangerous. Bloem's philosemitism was thus largely of the fourth kind, distinguished chiefly by opposition to <u>völkisch</u> racial antisemitism and sympathy for individual victims of unjust discrimination. For an American of the 1980s it may be hard to comprehend how Bloem can be considered philosemitic. But relative to the context of his times, when it was already unusual and politically risky for a person of the right to condemn hatred of Jews, he was certainly a philosemite, a term often applied to him by his contemporaries.

Something needs to be said about the meaning of the term völkisch, since Bloem was an author who attacked the völkisch movement of his times with weapons that owed much to the "vöolkisch idea." The word völkisch is an adjective derived from the noun Volk. This noun can be translated as people, nation or folk, although no such translation captures its full meaning in 19th- and 20th-century political usage, for Volk connoted a people organized along national lines and somehow organically fused together. Many political thinkers considered the Volk to be the ultimate political reality, a not unnatural development in a people that had to define nationhood in other than statist terms before 1871. Those who posited the Volk as the center of sociopolitical life--and who thus tended to call themselves völkisch--differed as to what was the cement of the Volk. Some saw the medium of fusion as blood (the racists), some as religion, some as culture, and some as shared ideals. Around 1912, a movement was born that called itself the völkisch, or German movement. This movement propounded a racist ideology and ultimately issued into Nazism. Indeed, it can quite properly be termed proto-Nazism. Since many others who did not adhere to this movement called themselves völkisch, I prefer (following Uwe Lohalm) to term it and its heir, Nazism, völkisch radicalism. Those who adhered to revolutionary conservatism, which posited the Volk as the ultimate sociopolitical reality but which rejected the primacy of race, might be termed völkisch conservatives. Bloem's reform conservatism of 1918-28 is völkisch conservative.[7]

CHAPTER 1

BESTSELLING NOVELIST OF THE WILHELMINE TWILIGHT: THE ROAD FROM MONARCHIST TO RELUCTANT REPUBLICAN

Walter Bloem was born at Elberfeld in the Rhineland on 20 June 1868 and raised in the adjacent, drab industrial city of Wuppertal. His parents came from the middle class--his father was an attorney and his mother was the child of manufacturers; Walter would always share, more or less, their bourgeois values and politics. Walter studied law (after a brief fling with philosophy) at the universities of Heidelberg, Marburg, Leipzig, and Bonn. But he was more interested in drinking and dueling than in his studies. Consequently, he emerged as a mediocre junior barrister, his face scarred by dueling, who just managed to pass his state and bar examinations.[1]

Bloem set up his own law practice in the autumn of 1895 in Barmen, a town near his birthplace. He quickly took on the burdensome responsibilities of a family although his financial situation was dismal due to the lack of success of his fledgling practice. Bloem married Margarethe Kalähne, the daughter of the director of the Elberfeld branch of the Reichsbank. Two children resulted from this union, a daughter, Margarete, in 1897 and a son, Walter Julius (who would one day himself become a famous right-wing novelist under the pseudonym Killian Koll), a year later.[2]

Writing helped Bloem dull the pain of a law career that he found as stultifying as it was unremunerative. In 1899 and 1902, his plays were produced at the Royal Theater in Berlin. Subsequent plays were just successful enough to convince him in 1904 to jettison his practice for a theatrical career. However, Bloem's plays were "beaten to death with cudgels" by the critics, a fact that he attributed to the disfavor in which nationalist authors were held by the arbiters of taste. Unable to break through to the private Berlin stage where fame and fortune were to be made, he survived on literary hackwork: lectures, badly paid novellas, and occasional feuilletons. In 1911, out of financial desperation, Bloem accepted the job of director and producer at the Royal Theater in Stuttgart. He held this post, with its 3,600 RM annual salary, until the outbreak of war in 1914.[3]

At the advice of his publisher, Bloem tried his hand at fiction. He experienced modest success with his firstling novel, The Freshman (German title: Der Krasse Fuchs; 1906), which presented a sympathetic, but somewhat critical, portrait of the German student.[4] After accepting the Stuttgart job, Bloem sold the rights to another novel, The Iron Year (German title: Das eiserne Jahre; 1911), to the Kölnische Zeitung for a pittance. This novel, the first of a trilogy about the achievement of German unity during the Franco-Prussian War, astounded Bloem's publisher by becoming a bestseller. The German public was ripe for a book wrapping nationalism and militarism into the pleasing package of a good story. The two sequels appeared in October 1912 and the fall of 1913. Each edition exceeded 100,000 copies by early 1914. The War Novel Trilogy of 1870-71 proved to be one of the greatest hits on the German book market in the twentieth century. By 1941, the total print run for the trilogy was 734,000.[5] An avid public turned back to earlier works in droves. The Freshman, for instance, had gone into a respectable but unspectacular 12,000 copies in the period 1906 to 1910. The total in print shot up to at least 50,000 by 1913, 112,000 by 1922, 176,000 by the fall of 1932.[6] After 1911 and until 1922, new novels by Bloem usually appeared in enormous first printings of 50,000 copies each; during these years, he was Germany's bestselling author.[7]

Greatly admired by the Kaiser, Bloem became the belletristic representative of the ruling elite and the broad provincial middle class. Yet his paeans to the Reich, the Kaiser and the German army were also lauded by the great left-liberal newspapers, since Bloem showed sympathy for defeated France and envisaged an all-inclusive Volk community. According to the Vossische Zeitung, for example, The Iron Year was "free from all chauvinism and full of justice even towards the enemy" and had to be "esteemed as a heroic poet's deed in the purest, noblest sense."[8] Book sales catapulted Bloem almost overnight from starving artist to millionaire. In the winter of 1915-16, he realized the conventional dream of the feudalized German middle classes and bought a genuine castle on the Sinn, a little river in Franconia.[9]

World War I awakened Bloem's interest in politics and helped prepare him for his postwar conversion to reluctant yet public support of the Weimar Republic.[10] In August 1914, Bloem marched into France as a 46-year-old captain of the reserve, in command of a company of the 12th Grenadier Regiment.[11] The August days were akin to a religious experience for Bloem because of the "sudden sinking of all inner-political, philosophical and religious differences."[12] On 13 September, Bloem was wounded in the battle of the Aisne during which his company lost 200 of its 250 men. Not for the last time, he showed exemplary bravery; by war's end, he had won 11 decorations including the Iron Cross First Class and the Iron Cross Second Class.[13]

On 27 December 1914, Bloem was assigned as press officer to Colonel General von Bissing, the Chief of the General Government of occupied Belgium.[14] An authoritarian militarist, Bissing was a "thoroughgoing annexationist," determined to incorporate Belgium into Germany. Yet he sought to understand the Belgians and to influence them to accept their role in enhancing German power. He fought, moreover, to protect the Belgians and their economy from ruthless economic exploitation. Bissing proved wiser than the highest German military and civilian authorities, whose deportation (over his objections) of Belgians to work behind the lines and in Germany proved to be an economic, humanitarian, and diplomatic disaster.[15]

With his assignment to Belgium, Bloem stood "suddenly in the focal point of a political life inflamed by war."[16] He reported to Bissing daily, accompanied the governor everywhere, and soon became a kind of clearinghouse through which the collective correspondence pertaining to Belgium reached Bissing. Bloem, as is often the case with men who control access to top leaders, even began to play a role in the decision-making process. Apparently Bloem was in agreement with the comparatively humane annexationism represented by Bissing.[17]

In the German press, Bloem took up the cudgel for the Bissing regime by countering enemy propaganda about German atrocities in

Belgium; he contended that Germany had painfully adhered to the Hague Convention in occupied territory. Enemy depiction of the Germans as Huns was so much nonsense meant to sway neutrals. Admittedly, villages had been burned and hostages, some innocent, shot as examples. These actions were, however, necessary discouragements to future criminal (i.e., partisan) outrages. While individual Germans had at times gone beyond the limits of justifiable self-defense or scare tactics, enemy propaganda had generalized and thus exaggerated these isolated incidents to an absurd degree.[18] Bloem did caution that the Belgians had to be won over to tacit acceptance and then voluntary collaboration. After the war, Bloem was listed by the Entente as a war criminal, partly for his justification of harsh measures to discourage partisans in an article in the Kölnische Zeitung, 10 February 1915.[19]

At his own request, Bloem was returned to combat, suffering new wounds at Mosty on the Nieman in September 1915.[20] Upon recovery he took part in the assault at Verdun, begun in February 1916.[21] The German supreme commander, Erich von Falkenhayn, had hoped to draw the French into a battle of attrition there that would break their will to continue. With the French sword struck from her hands, England, the chief enemy, would in turn give up the war. In the event, however, the battle proved a tragic holocaust, the "longest battle of all time" with the "unenviable reputation of being the battlefield with the highest density of dead per square yard that has probably ever been known." During the ten months of Verdun, German chances for victory evaporated.[22] The battle's carnage led Bloem to question for the first time the wisdom of Germany's military chiefs and, more generally, the rightness of the Wilhelmine order. Bloem would recall many years later: Verdun "was the most colossal military insanity that has ever been undertaken."[23]

On 10 March 1916, Bloem was transferred to the staff of the Chief of the General Staff of the Field Army. He was assigned to Section III B of the General Staff of the Field Army, commanded by Major Walter Nicolai. At the start of the war, Nicolai's Section III B collected intelligence reports abroad and conducted counterespionage at home. Soon, however, censorship and propaganda "came to be the most important activities of

Section III B." Nicolai ordered Bloem to set up a Field Press Office (Feldpressestelle) to guide opinion within the army and at home into channels desired by the Supreme Command. The War Ministry frustrated Bloem's plans to take over the job of countering enemy "atrocity" propaganda while the War Press Bureau stopped him from setting up a press agency for the civilian press. He did succeed in erecting an apparently effective agency for army papers, which provided them with suggestions and finished essays. The Field Press Office, staffed by officers who, like Bloem, had been partly incapacitated by wounds, supervised these papers by watching their content and maintaining written and personal contact, constant on the Western Front, sporadic on the Eastern. There were forty-six army papers, twenty-nine in the West. While these together might not use more resources in a year than one of the bigger provincial papers in a month, they filled among the troops the important niche occupied among the people back home by local newspapers. Bloem also founded a system of "war reporters" made up of army officers. This insured technically informed (and presumably politically reliable) news straight from the front lines, which found ready consumers among smaller newspapers on the home front; this innovation was retained by the German army in World War II.[24]

Bloem visited Kaiser Wilhelm II once or twice weekly in the great headquarters of Charlesville. Bloem did not hesitate to tell the Kaiser about the true situation at the front, much to the displeasure of Wilhelm's entourage. When the Great Main Headquarters was transferred to Pless, the Field Press Office was left behind. Bloem and his chief subordinates were convinced that this was done to separate him from the Kaiser.[25] More and more Bloem grew disillusioned with the Imperial leadership.[26] He was appalled by the Kaiser's friends, by the smothering camarilla, and by Wilhelm's isolation from hard military and political realities. He was also little impressed by the Supreme Command, disdaining Ludendorff and Hindenburg as much as Falkenhayn. Bloem still believed fiercely in the rightness of the German war effort. He savagely attacked the Reichstag deputies for their Peace Resolution of July 1917 in an article ordered by Ludendorff to be distributed en masse in the army. Slowly but surely, however, the negative impressions of the Second Empire's "great" germinated in Bloem's mind into recognition of the need for strictly delimited monarchy and finally into tacit acceptance of the events of November 1918.[27]

The war gave Bloem a new respect for the common man. In 1916, he recalled how the August days had fused the nation together irrespective of class, religion, profession or party affiliation.[28] At Stuttgart in January 1917, Bloem proclaimed that the true hero of the war was the nameless, common soldier at the front. In the trenches

> there are no castes, no social differentiations, there were only people who did their job and people who did not. The war has brought one lasting legacy: "We Germans will be permeated by a deepened feeling of brotherhood.[29]

After return to combat in early 1918, which led to new wounds and promotion to major, Bloem was reassigned (in October) to the War Press Bureau in Berlin with orders to deliver a series of lectures in major German cities.[30] He was directed to speak to the Colonial Society on 4 November in Berlin's Beethovensaal.[31] Bloem, who had long disapproved of the systematic deception of Kaiser and homefront as to the true state of the war effort, revealed that the war was hopelessly lost. He mentioned the possibility of abdication, although he hastened to add that he personally favored retention of Wilhelm. "We want to try it with one another one more time!"[32] Bloem's frank statements, above all his hypothetical discussion of abdication, appalled most of the ultra-nationalist, Pan-German "stock-reactionary" audience. A fourth reportedly walked out; there were expressions of rage by the officers present. The society's executive committee snubbed Bloem after the lecture.

The War Press Bureau immediately cancelled Bloem's speaking engagements in the provinces.[33] Right-wing papers like Der Reichsbote and the Pan-German Deutsche Zeitung lashed out at the speech. The Deutsche Zeitung reported, under the heading "Walter Bloem's Political Transformations," that the speech signaled Bloem's switch to the extreme left.[34] Later, Bloem had to submit to courts of honor by his officer's association and the old members of his two students corps on account of the lecture. Although he was "rehabilitated" in all three, rumors coursed through Germany about his "communist" lectures.[35] Bloem had taken his first step to distance himself from the nationalist mainstream; the bitter reaction from his erstwhile constituency was a harbinger of things to come.

Bloem had welcomed the constitutional changes of October (which had established a true parliamentary regime), Ludendorff's resignation, and the end of the Kaiser's Kommandogewalt (royal power of command). "This old Prussia," he confided to his diary on 27 October, "was outlived."[36] Yet, while he even accepted the necessity for the abdication of Wilhelm II,[37] Bloem's emotional ties to the old Reich ran deep. He was driven to thoughts of suicide by the news of the armistice conditions and the outbreak of revolution.[38] Years afterwards, despite his loss of faith in the monarchy, Bloem would describe the substitution of the Red for the Hohenzollern flags in Berlin as the worst moment of his life.[39] The indignities heaped upon officers by the revolutionaries in Berlin aroused his ire.[40]

Nevertheless, Bloem would brook no counterrevolution. He admitted to his diary on 10 November that the bloodshed stemmed not from the Red Guards but, as Vorwärts (the main organ of the Majority Social Democrats) correctly reported, "from the cracked columns of the old order . . . as indeed in the final analysis [had] the whole world catastrophe."[41] Bloem admonished his son, a rabid nationalist aflame with the honor of the officer class, that it was the duty of the time to support the new order.[42] On 13 November, Bloem signed his name to a declaration of support for the new regime drawn up by the "Berlin Artists and Writers."[43] This declaration was published in the 16 November number of Vorwärts.[44] The Great War and the revolution it bred had turned Walter Bloem, the widely read belletristic apologist for the Second Reich, into a reluctant republican. The war had also politicized his writing.

CHAPTER 2

THE MIND AND CHARACTER OF WALTER BLOEM: SOME REFLECTIONS

An evaluation of Bloem's art, thought and character should precede treatment of his post-war political writing and activity. Such critical examination may yield a more complete understanding of the genesis and ultimate inconsequentiality of this reluctant republican's attempts to function as a poetic, philosemitic praeceptor Germaniae. Bloem entered the Weimar era as the representative author of a particular segment of the German literature industry--that dedicated to quality entertainment literature.[1] While the Grethlein firm in Leipzig (a publishing house of indeterminate political direction) had the right of first refusal to Bloem's belletristic works, they also appeared with the Staackmann, Köhler, and Scherl firms, the chief publishers of nationalist Unterhaltungsromane (entertain- ment novels).[2] Bloem was fast friends with Rudolf Herzog, Karl Hans Strobl and Robert Hohlbaum, the leading authors for the L. Staackmann Verlag of Leipzig, the single most important outlet for such fiction.[3]

Staackmann authors and their ilk wrote the kind of novels designed to maximize sales by catering to the conventional tastes and nationalist sentiments of the German middle strata. Their fiction, while not altogether devoid of liberal residues, tended toward nationalism, social and moral conservatism, aesthetic traditionalism (expressed in a blend of romantic and realistic elements) and gripping, sometimes bathetic narrative. Readership of such novels far exceeded sales since they were the "classics of the lending libraries."[4] These libraries, which lent for a small fee, were patronized by blue-collar as well as white-collar workers; their standard fare was undoubtedly an important vehicle for implanting elements of the world view of the middle strata into the industrial working class.[5] Due to a more serious intent and more careful craftsmanship, writers like Bloem and Herzog marked a higher level of "Kitsch," of what sociologists of literature now call "trivial literature," than the likes of Hedwig Courths-Mahler, a one-woman literary assembly line who churned out annually eight to ten "stereotyped romantic novels" (which had much in common with today's supermarket romances).[6] On the other hand, writers of nationalist entertainment fiction were self-conscious, even proudly so, that they were neither aesthetic pioneers nor jewels in the diadem of high culture. Bloem wrote in 1928: "I stand outside any contact with the official and recognized, not to mention the 'high' literature."[7]

Bloem, however, sought to do more with his fiction than make money through diverting his readers. His novels, he wrote in 1916, have striven "to give broad culture portraits of some of the main areas of German society in the 1880s and 1890s (the life of students, the administration of justice, theater, and the way of reserve officers). My plan was to represent the great national experience in the form of the personal destinies of the Volk comrades and to build up out of these single destinies a picture of the great time."[8] Bloem's implicit purpose was to further the self-esteem, unity, and greatness of the German nation through his art. Being popular meant more to him than being a bestseller. It meant total integration with the Volk, sharing and giving voice to its experiences: "Only that which is attuned to the Volk becomes popular. Only one who has lived in tune with the Volk can write in tune with the Volk."[9]

Bloem's conception of a more serious, nationalist purpose to entertainment fiction became politicized during the war. The drama of the war itself must have made clear how much political decisions could affect life. His tour in Belgium gave him practical political experience and his command of the Field Press Office involved him in all levels of the business of using words for propaganda purposes. He actually committed himself to writing propaganda fiction (on enemy espionage activities) for the War Press Bureau. It should be noted that Bloem was merely one example of a general process that requires further study: the politicization of German (perhaps of Western) writers through direct involvement in the national propaganda machines generated by the war.[10]

After 1918, Bloem continued to infuse his writings with a political-educative content. Now he was prepared to address pressing current social and political problems in his novels.[11] Indeed, he began to write Tendenzromane, thesis novels designed to carry specific political messages. To be sure, Bloem refused to become the belletristic mouthpiece of a party, or to sacrifice characterization and story on the altar of propaganda. He remained convinced that it should be left to a novel's reader to draw its "teachings" from the concrete and living stuff of the narrative.[12] Thus, Bloem strove to remain an entertaining storyteller who nonetheless now slanted his characters, milieu and plot to deliver a political thesis.[13]

More lay behind Bloem's preference for pictorial-fictional machinery than the practical calculation that his popularity (and thus his income and political impact) hinged on the exciting, colorful diversion that had been demanded by so many book consumers since the late 1700s, when the Unterhaltungsroman had emerged as the leading item on the German book market.[14] Bloem's whole manner of apprehending and ordering human reality was largely pictorial. He used types, representatives, and personifications rather than abstract structures or universal principles to give unity and meaning to reality. Significantly, the changes in course in his political odyssey were determined mainly by personalities and concrete impressions. Thus, his political conversion during the Great War stemmed from personal contact with the Kaiser, his courtiers, and his generals.

Since Bloem's mode of cognition was essentially pictorial, it was only natural that he saw the main task of the writer to be the communication of images to his reader. The writer-poet (Dichter), he wrote in 1918, creates pictures intended to work on the reader by setting his soul into the motions known as artistic experience. In order to achieve this effect, the author tries to evoke in the reader's imagination or fantasy "a picture that coincides with that which hovers before his own soul during creation." This picture can either be pure fantasy or it can draw on experienced reality. In the measure that the writer nears reality he loses his imaginative freedom. He must put elements of reality in the portraits of his dreams. Otherwise the reader will sense a contradiction with his own memory or knowledge. In depicting the real world the writer must learn about the realities of the past and present.[15] Plainly, however, Bloem both perceived these realities and communicated them in his fiction in concrete, often personified form, rather than as abstract structures or as complexes of causal relations.[16]

Because his powers of observing and rendering the inside and outside of individual experience were not inconsiderable, Bloem's pictures of his times transcended the mere "politicized myths" found in the pot-boilers of a Courths-Mahler. His fictional depictions were (and are) useful sources for the texture of individual and social life in their times, and thus did more than mislead readers into substituting "black-and-white stereotypes for the challenging complexity of lived experience."[17] Yet Bloem fell far short of the great novelistic masters of the concrete. None could conceivably write of him what Isaiah Berlin said of Tolstoy: "The celebrated life-likedness of every object and every person in his world derives from this [Tolstoy's] astonishing capacity of presenting every ingredient of it in the fullest individual essence, in all its many dimensions, as it were. . . ."[18]

While influenced by the same realist tradition within which Tolstoy operated, Bloem of course lacked anything like the Russian's genius.[19] Bloem was, moreover, prone both to the entertainer's contrived pyrotechnics and the romantic's idealizing fantasy, two tendencies irreconcilable with apperception of the "concrete and multicolored reality of individual lives."[20] Most importantly, Bloem looked at empirical reality through conceptual spectacles that at once unified and distorted, creating pictures in his mind's eye (later committed to paper as fictional imagery) that were interconnected but imperfect replications of what he had observed.

The great Isaiah Berlin once divided writers and thinkers up into hedgehogs and foxes through figurative application of a line by the Greek poet Archilochus: "The fox knows many things, but the hedgehog knows one big thing."[21] According to Berlin, literary foxes are pluralists who grasp the manifold diversity of experience in all its individuality without striving for a "unitary inner vision," while intellectual hedgehogs are monists who "relate everything to a single central vision."[22] Berlin argued that Tolstoy was a fox by nature, which explained his extraordinary command of the texture of real life, although he was a hedgehog by belief who constantly quested for an inner meaning to the apparent chaos of history.[23] As for Bloem, if we might be permitted resort to Berlin's figurative distinctions, while his penchant for the pictorial and ability to learn from experience suggests instincts of the fox, his social conditioning and education turned him into a hedgehog whose "single, universal, organizing principle" was the nation.[24] When compared to the sources of the unitary vision of Berlin's greatest hedgehogs, for example the Good of Plato or the God of Dante, the nation was an impoverished lens indeed through which to focus the empirical. The resultant distortions affected not just the overall picture of the German reality, but the images of its individual facets, which lost their concreteness and blurred together into nationalist stereotypes.

The nation unified (and distorted) Bloem's inner vision in two ways. First, the nation was for him a world-immanent idol, the ultimate frame of reference by which all was to be interpreted and judged. What Bloem chose to see in the ocean of experience, how he pictured it, and what value he assigned to it was determined to a great extent by his nationalism. He explicitly admitted that the national experience was the integrating principle for his novels. Second, Bloem's vision was to his mind identical with that of the nation. For him, the Volk, the German people fused by language and culture, rather than the state was the nation. Residues in his thinking of the Romanticist and Idealist traditions, which had profoundly shaped the mentality of the 19th-century Bildungsbürgertum from which he sprang, were probably the source of his conviction that the writer-poet (the Dichter) was somehow a voice of the Volk, the medium by which the Volk achieved self-consciousness.[25] It is possible, although it cannot be proven, that fin-de-siècle historicism, which held all thought to be relative to the circumstances of time and place, legitimized in his mind the notion that the writer must voice the momentary standards of the Volk as the binding standards for the moment.[26] Conveniently for Bloem's conscience, his opportunism as entertainment novelist and political mentor (manifested by his fiction mirroring the shifting currents of public opinion and political reorientations almost precisely timed to coincide with the birth and death of the Weimar Republic) was rooted in conviction, in theories of the writer's purpose and of history.

Whether or not Rousseau was correct in arguing that the social contract must be an expression of the general will, it is clear that no nation in an industrial age of great social and intellectual diversity can speak with one voice. Bloem deluded himself into believing, however, that opinions prevalent in the Bildungsbürgertum, and more generally within the German middle strata, were the contents of the Volk mind. Integral, therefore, to Bloem's nationalism was an unreflective social conservatism. The social status quo was his subsidiary idol. Subordinate to his nationalism, since he was prepared to see it modified in the interests of the nation, the social status quo defined both the proper structure of the nation and who was qualified to voice its will.

Social conservatism came naturally to the scion of a social stratum like the Bildungsbürgertum which had formed part of the ruling elite in Germany since the 18th century. This was especially true for those like Bloem who had become lawyers, the most important segment of this stratum politically.[27] According to the great liberal sociologist Ralf Dahrendorf, lawyers in general possess a "conserving attitude":

> The law epitomizes the norms that hold, and thus, in a society, it is the incarnation of the status quo. Whoever administers it in whatever position is, in that capacity, chained to the status quo of social and political conditions. A certain conservatism is therefore not idiosyncrasy, much less personal default on the part of lawyers, but a necessary attribute of their role in society.[28]

Such conservatism has long run especially deep among German lawyers. Inexperienced with the adversarial system of justice, German lawyers were unfriendly to the idea that competition among viewpoints might yield truth and partial to the belief that true law is that which is codified and thus rigid. Moreover, during the Wilhelmine era, when Bloem established his temporary legal career, the identification of lawyers with the state was especially close. At all times, German lawyers were prone to what Dahrendorf calls the "fallacy of certainty."[29]

One might attribute what Dahrendorf sees as the "nostalgia for certainty, authority and synthesis" among German lawyers to a lurking allegiance to natural law.[30] Dahrendorf hints at as much when he writes of them: "If the regime is democratic in tendency, they do not hesitate to adduce natural law to remind it of its lack of authority; if the authority of the state is absolute, lawyers become its obedient servants."[31] That natural law is anything more for them than a polemical device is unlikely, however, given the preference for positive right implied in their passion for codification. Certainly perceptive observers of the German scene in Bloem's time believed that among the educated, the historical sense, which relativized all legal and moral principles, had taken the place of natural right and thus of "a standard of right and wrong independent of positive right and higher than positive right."[32] According to Dahrendorf, German lawyers have long been characterized by a combination of outer confidence in the social status quo and political authoritarianism with inner insecurity.[33] This combination bespeaks alienation from natural standards, not commitment to them. Bloem certainly did not rise above the blinkers of his time to a principled political vision. He was devoid of religious faith (a Calvinist upbringing notwithstanding); neither his neohumanist nor legal education had convinced him of the worth of the tradition of moral philosophy.[34] Thus, Bloem easily succumbed to a general tendency among Germans during his lifetime (mirrored and reinforced by positivism, literary and political realism and existentialism as well as historicism) to forego transhistorical standards for human action derived from canonical revelation or nature.[35]

That Bloem was neither a saint nor a philosopher might have mattered little if the ideologies of the German bourgeoisie had retained their pre-Bismarckian principled foundations. Unfortunately, however, in 1866, just two years before Bloem's birth, the National Liberal tradition in which Bloem would be raised had begun to renounce its ideals, its liberal principles, in gratitude for the victory of Bismarck-led Prussia over Austria.

At the end of 1866, the National Liberal historian Hermann Baumgarten was swept by enthusiasm over this victory to renounce the principled liberal fight of the early 1860s against "militarism and junkerism" in a statement that Hans Kohn regarded as representative: "The victory of our principles would have brought upon us misery, whereas the defeat of our principles has brought us endless salvation."[36] During the Second Reich, the trend among National Liberals was to become more nationalist and less liberal: the mature Bloem, a product of this trend although he probably never belonged to the National Liberal party, had no convictions resembling those of the pre-Königgrätz Prussian liberals much less those given their classic statement in the American Declaration of Independence: "We hold these truths to be self-evident, that all men are created equal, that they are endowed by their Creator with certain unalienable Rights, that among these are Life, Liberty, and the pursuit of Happiness."[37] When he focused on the American founding in a novel trilogy published during the Weimar era, he found the clue to the success of the new republic not in dedication to this proposition but in the great leader George Washington and the sense of nationhood he fathered.[38]

Nor did the German conservative tradition (to which Bloem was impelled by his social origins in an increasingly "feudalized" educated upper-middle class and by his legal training) provide him with a surrogate for liberal or Christian principle. Recently, Professor James Retallack has captured German Conservatism during the watershed Bismarck decades. Retallack modifies without rejecting the opinion common among scholars that the Conservative party during the 1870s and 1880s was Prussian in orientation, that it disregarded the importance of popular appeals, and that the Tivoli program of 1892 marked the arrival of antisemitism as a mainly political phenomenon. Retallack denies that the pentegram of elite influence in Prussia-- "the Prussian court, the Prussian state ministry, the two houses of the Prussian Landtag (the House of Deputies and the Herrenhaus), and the Prussian administration"--ensured conservative hegemony in late 19th-century Germany. Thus, Conservatives had to try to expand into west-Elbian Germany. This imposed the necessity to compete for popular support since Conservatives were outsiders in states like Bavaria, Württemberg and Baden. Especially prominent in this campaign was the Conservative national and regional press, which out of some combination of conviction with tactical considerations fused anti-liberalism with antisemitism while floating unsystematic proposals for social reform. Retention of elite influence entailed the loyalty of Otto von Helldorf (overall chairman of the Conservative party) to Bismarck's anti-socialist (Conservative/Free conservative/National Liberal) cartel although this necessitated constant trimming of conservative principle and reluctance to support west-Elbian Conservative efforts to wean National Liberals and Free Conservatives from their party leaders. Competition for popular support involved anti-liberal propaganda harmful to cartel harmony and social reformism alarming to Junkers. Even Conservative antisemitism was affected by this dilemma. Sufficient demagoguery to rouse the masses was irreconcilable with Christian ethics or the dignity of the social elite. Thus handcuffed, the Conservative press, which suffered even more from lack of business acumen and able contributors, was politically inefficacious and financially imperiled. Even Conservatives ignored or despised their own papers. Lack of success made Conservative publicists ever more susceptible to the myth of Jewish cultural predominance, and thus to anti-semitic cosmologies. Conservative publicists and west-Elbian agitators in the 1870s and 1880s spread antisemitism, made it respectable, paved the road to Tivoli (where antisemitism became part of the party program), and set in motion a radicalization process that led to the Pan-Germans of the late Wilhelmine period and beyond.[39]

What were the roots of the dilemma of German Conservatism and the sterility of Conservative politics, whether the party operated through the Prussian pentegram or strove for a popular constituency nationally? One possible explanation, it occurs to me, is to be found in an ongoing detachment from principle induced above all by Bismarck. Rudolf Stadelmann registered this decline when he observed that under Frederick William IV conservatism was a political world view, under Bismarck it had still embodied a spiritual tradition, while under Caprivi it had sunk to a mere interest group through its ties to the Agrarian League (Bund der Landwirte).[40]

In 1856, the English political essayist, Walter Bagehot, divided conservatives into three types: conservatives of enjoyment loyal to old ways; conservatives of fear; and conservatives of reflection. In Germany after 1871, conservatives of reflection, of principle judiciously applied to socio-political reality clearly seen, became ever rarer, and appear to have found their way to the Free conservatives, the Center, or even the National Liberals, if they did not opt for some apolitical inwardness. Few adherents of the German Conservative party could claim to have what Bagehot described as a "real mastery of the reasons, a real familiarity with the moral grounds--to say nothing of the political consequences--of the existing state of things!"[41] Among the principles which became increasingly obscure to German Conservatives were: belief in a transcendent moral order to which society ought to try to conform; commitment to social continuity tempered by readiness to make necessary changes; adherence to prescription; agreement with Plato that prudence is the greatest political virtue; affection for variety; and recognition of the imperfectibility of men and their institutions.[42]

Having lost contact with a principled basis for accommodating the economic, social, and political realities of the industrial world, German Conservatives became ever more Bagehot's "conservatives of fear."[43] This was true of those consummate Conservative insiders, the Prussian Junkers, who were transfixed by dread of losing their political influence, social privileges, and agrarian economic base, and of the impotent, pathetic Conservative outsiders across the Elbe, whose appeal apparently was largely to failed individuals and expiring social groups like the artisans.

Fear may be, however, a continuing source of mass appeal and cohesion only when transmuted into millenarian ideologies that promise a permanent release from insecurity, in for instance a Third Reich or workers' paradise.[44] While Conservative publicists were edging towards such ideologies by way of antisemitic cosmologies, Christian residues in their thought prevented conservatives on body from opting for the massively immoral means needed to achieve such "utopias" or even for the ends themselves, which posited a perfectibility to society dismissed by conservatives on principle (insofar as this was not completely attenuated) as beyond the reach of sinful mankind. To be sure, in the era after the Great War, conservatives would form catastrophic alliances with which the millenarian Nazis deluded that Hitler could be used for conservative ends. But, they themselves could not create a millenarian mass movement.

Perhaps only a principled, realistic political philosophy could have made the German Conservatives a national political party. Such a philosophy might well have enabled the Conservative party to absorb significant segments of Free Conservative, National Liberal and Center party support, and to out-compete both racial antisemites and Socialists for that rising new social stratum, the white-collar workers. A principled Conservatism of reflection might have generated a respected, influential conservative press and a politically engaged, but aesthetically elevated art. Surely such a conservatism would have been better placed to balance social continuity against the need to dismantle gradually the anachronistic remainders of the old Estates Society and of the Prussian pentegram while developing a systematic accommodation to the industrial world. In short, such a conservatism would have been the "reform conservatism" of Klaus Epstein's typology rather than the "reactionary conservatism" of the Junkers or the forerunner to völkish radicalism of the antisemites.[45] Reform conservatism might have removed the conservative party from the horns of its dilemma, making possible both retention of a Prussian citadel in which elite influence was exchanged in stages for popularity and expansion west of the Elbe.

In general, it should be observed, principle is prerequisite to authentic "reform conservatism." Principle provides the necessary touchstone for choosing between continuity and change. It is conservative principle that distinguishes "reform conservatism" from prudent progressivism (and not just, as Epstein argues, gradualist methods and the ultimate aim of preserving as much as possible of the past), from merely pragmatic accommodation to inevitable historical changes "dictated by objective, irreversible causes," and from cynical manipulation of new social forces for reactionary purposes.

That German Conservatism lost the principled foundation to reform conservatism seems attributable to Bismarck, an apparent paradox since he is often regarded as the epitome of flexible conservatism. Through partial fulfillment of their dreams in a new Reich dominated by the Prussia in which they wielded such great influence, the German Conservatives were no less than the National Liberals seduced by Bismarck into sacrificing principles on the altar of Realpolitik. Moreover, by not only retaining the Prussian pentegram but transmuting it into a cornerstone of the Second Reich, Bismarck lifted from German Conservatives the necessity of becoming a modern mass party in their Prussian citadel. Only subjection to relatively equal electoral competition could have forced Conservatives into what Bagehot called the "refinements of necessary reasoning," into "the complexities of political investigation."[47] Only necessity, the mother of invention, could have forced a healthy interplay between conservative principle and the realities of a rapidly modernizing industrial world.

Unfortunately, there was little such interplay in the German Conservative party of the Second Reich, in its chief post-World War I successor, the German National People's Party (DNVP), or among the partyless conservative men of letters. Thus, Bloem was in line with the general decline of the intellectual foundations of conservatism in Germany when he proffered his own "reform conservatism," his conservative republicanism, without a principled foundation constructed from tradition, reason, or canonical revelation. The lack of a principled conservative party or movement meant that there was no organization to correct his conservative vision, based on the false idol of the nation, or to promote it whether in original or improved form.

Condemnation of Bloem for being the wrong kind of hedgehog, one whose vision was united by worldly idols rather than principles accessible to reason or defined by faith, is likely to provoke resistance among scholarly readers today. Contemporary American social scientists, save for Catholic scholars or those decisively influenced by the great political philosophers Leo Strauss and Erich Voegelin, tend to be wary of so-called value judgments, and thus of admitting the possibility of objective standards much less the desirability of analyzing whether historical actors went wrong in failing to hold or to be guided by them.[48] Indeed, scholars who are themselves historicists, and thus convinced that standards are the subjective products of their times, or who are disciples of Max Weber, and thus convinced that facts are the only proper object of study for the social scientists whose values (while determinative of his questions) result not from scientific analysis but from existential (hence irrational choice), are especially unlikely to accept a critique of historical actors that mutatis mutandis might apply to them as well.

There is good reason to believe, however, that principles can be chosen rationally and that historical actors can be better understood if we take into account the wisdom and morality of their thought and action. Historicism contains within itself a logical contradiction. It asserts at least one transhistorical (i.e., eternal) truth, that all thought is relative to the historical situation in which it is generated. There appears, therefore, no way to ground historicism in reason, since it must contradict itself to assert itself. Nor does experience, whether drawn from life or historical scholarship, prove the total historicity of thought. Whatever experiential feeling we might have that all truth is relative seems outbalanced by a feeling at least equally strong that somehow right and wrong do exist, and not just as tablets of values cast up and shattered by the river of time.[49]

By the same token, exclusion of values from social science as necessarily outside the grasp of scholarly scrutiny seems arbitrary, a symptom of a decline in rationality. While rational selection of the proper values to determine how facts ought to be understood might be fraught with difficulty, there is no proof, rational or empirical, that it is impossible. There is good reason to believe (and we tend to act on the level of practical life if we do believe this) that we can make rational choices among values, that not all values are equal or to be ranked merely by the degree of authenticity with which they are held.[50]

As for the historian, it is doubtful that he can fully understand the motivations behind past thought unless he judges whether they included a quest for truth and morality. Nor can he comprehend the quality of such thought except by evaluating to what degree it successfully apprehended reality, including transhistorical measures of human action. Nor can we properly understand the impact of what people said and did in the past unless we understand whether or not they took into account realities, permanent and transitory, and tried to shape them to maximize human benefit properly conceived. Finally, history without regard to judgments about the rationality and ethical integrity of past historical choices is bound to be of little value in developing our capacity to make rational, ethical choices in the present. At most it can inform us as to means, improving our judgment about the inter-relationships within historical contexts and thus our expertise in changing other contexts, while leaving us in the dark as to the question of ends. One can only endorse John Hallowell in believing with Aristotle "that the social sciences can be most useful to our society when they are deliberately, consciously, and rationally directed toward making men better human beings--when they seek to discover the principles that make for a free and just society and encourage men by the best means at their disposal to put those principles into practice."[51]

Perhaps no subject requires attention to principle, both as a starting point for an object of interpretation, more than German attitudes toward Jews during 1918-45. The Holocaust, after all, marked history's most terrible violation of the natural right to "life, liberty and the pursuit of happiness." It was exactly what H. G. Schenk called it: "the greatest crime in world history."[52] Analysis of how Germans went wrong in reasoning about what was right and about the nature of things political appears crucial to comprehending both the genesis of German antisemitism and the ultimate impotency of German philosemitism, national conservative or otherwise.

It might be objected that the introduction of principle as an interpretive tool and object of study is to fall victim to the very "fallacy of certainty" that Dahrendorf saw as a cause rather than a solution of the "German problem." But, commitment to knowledge, as opposed to opinion, whether of moral and legal principle or other political things, does not entail dogmatism. There can be no denying that all men have a perspective limited by their historical horizon (as well as by their own multiple, individual limitations). Thus, reasoning about principle can never achieve full, final knowledge. Debate that constantly exposes false opinion in wrestling with the basic questions is thus fundamental to the pursuit of knowledge. The freedom to debate is itself part of the fabric of natural right. Debate must be predicated, however, on the conviction that there is a right answer, however far short we might necessarily fall in practice of finding it. Otherwise all battles of ideas must be "full of sound and fury, signifying nothing." Since utter lack of standards and guideposts is difficult to bear for those swimming in the stream of life, they may well react with dogmatism rather than a Humean suspension of judgment. Dogmatism logically appears more likely to result from relativism than from natural standards. (History apparently confirms logic, since the age of totalitarianism succeeded that of positivism and historicism, when liberalism became inimical to, rather than grounded in, natural right). Relativism, has moreover, no rational grounds for preferring tolerance over intolerance.[53] Only tolerance based on natural right, which on principle excludes intolerance, can therefore close the door to such historical abominations as antisemitism.

Bloem not only followed the educated mainstream in Germany in rejecting the philosophic quest for "the principles that make for a free and just society," but also remained innocent of the new social sciences that were the glory of his age. Neither the ideas of Sigmund Freud nor those of Max Weber had the slightest influence on him. His ignorance of Freud was especially telling at a time when many of Germany's best writers, including the conservative Thomas Mann, were influenced by the great psychologist. While the new social sciences might well be criticized for rejecting the possibility of a rational choice of first principles, there can be no doubt that they represent serious attempts to understand the structure and functioning of the human mind and of society. For Bloem, therefore, the nation was more than just a substitute for principle in the realm of ends. It replaced analytic procedures designed to show the regular causal relationships between psychological and social phenomena in the realm of means.

To sum up the argument to this point: Bloem's national conservative ideology, while unifying his vision, did not give him a principled standpoint for judging in the blinding flux of events during 1914-45 what was right and wrong politically. It provided him merely with questionable ends, the unity of the nation and the continued rule of traditional elites, that logically might be served with any means. Moreover, Bloem's image of the particulars of his time and their interrelationship was sufficiently distorted by filtration through the prism of this ideology that we might well follow Erich Voegelin in describing it as a "second reality," an imaginary world that was the more seductive for the verisimilitude it derived from Bloem's not inconsiderable powers of depiction.[54] It would be inaccurate to apply to Bloem Alfred Kazin's trenchant summing up of Ernest Hemmingway: "He brought a major art to a minor vision of life."[55] One can say, however, that Bloem's was a competent art in the service of a distorted vision of life. Furthermore, Bloem's national conservatism without principles distorted his image of himself as well as of his times.

To understand Bloem's utopian psychological identity, his deluded self-images, it might be fruitful to turn to James Rhodes. In his pioneering theoretical treatment of Nazism, which has been sometimes maligned and more often ignored, Rhodes translated the philosopher Hegel's notion of dialectical self-hood from the realm of spirit to that of psychology.[56] According to Rhodes, a dialectical self can be defined "as an insecure person who fabricates pleasurable self-images and demands that other people support these pretentious self-descriptions with servile praise."[57] The insecurity of those dialectical selves who would become Nazis was bred by experiences of rejection. Some were rejected by parents, others by society because of real or imagined failures, still others because they were handicapped. Perhaps, the most prevalent forms of rejection were social status discrimination and the failure to find "true comradeship."[58] The future Nazis responded to rejection by painting themselves in their mind's eye as one or more of a range of "great personalities."[59] A goodly proportion of Nazis, Rhodes notes, added to these individual utopian identities flattering "collective identities." The most important of these was the German nation, which was boundlessly idealized.[60]

It was not enough merely to create "satisfying subjective self-images";[61] confirmation was required from other people. "Having defined themselves as worthwhile subjects, the National Socialists looked for objects who would reflect their value back to them."[62] The chief problem with such dependence on other people as "magic mirrors" was that those imagining themselves to be great personalities had to "dominate every potential object whom they met because contradictions would have ripped their reflecting pools, distorting the self-images they wished to see." Indeed, the "dialectical Nazis" were swept up in a foredoomed "utopian enterprise." They could achieve neither full knowledge of their identities nor mastery of all objects and, since their assumptions about excellence were problematic, they opened themselves to self-doubt and mockery. They "were living in a dream world that was apt to be shattered at any moment" by the "resistance of troublesome objects." The main cause of their blindness of reality, of their picturing for themselves "an imaginary 'true existence'," was their vanity, although willful ignorance played a role too.[63]

Bloem was by no means as self-deluded as the Nazi dialectical selves described by Rhodes. Yet there can be little doubt that the nation, along with such conservative collectivities as the stratum of educated burghers, the student corps, and the army served as ego props for Bloem, helping to establish his sense of self-worth and direction. Military decorations, dueling scars and academic degrees, testimony to membership in and distinguished service to such collectivities, affirmed the personal worth of Bloem and his fictional heroes. Experiences like the August days of 1914 may have meant so much to Bloem partly because now the whole country confirmed the collective identity most important to Bloem, the German nation.

Bound up with his "collective identities" was a particular "great personality" that of novelistic voice of the nation. What might at first glance appear as modesty, Bloem's recognition that he stood outside the high literature of his times, was actually a manifestation of vanity. For high literature was not rooted in the Volk, not popular in the profound sense that his novels were. His fiction was bestselling precisely because it was recognized by the Volk as the best medium through which it could achieve self-consciousness. Thus, Bloem had transmuted what critics in his time and critics now hold to his discredit, that he was merely popular, into a proof of personal greatness masked as national service.

Why did Bloem generate these collective and personal identities? Rhodes's explanation of the genesis of dialectical self-hood seemingly contains part of the answer. Bloem surely was beset by a not unnatural insecurity following the twin "rejections" of an undistinguished legal career and the frustrating, impoverished years as a floundering playwright and hack writer. He did not blame his failures on his own inadequacies, on his irresponsible preparation for a legal career or on his incapacity as a dramatist. Rather he invented a fallacious cause of his theater failures, i.e., an anti-national theater establishment, remaining willfully ignorant of the real causes, which could easily be discovered by analysis of audience and critical reactions. To the end of his days, he vainly boasted, despite all the evidence to the contrary, that he was a "born playwright."[64] During his time of troubles, Bloem's insecurity (psychic and financial) was partly alleviated by his collective identities, reaffirmed by his career as a reserve officer and support by court theaters. Partly because of this insecurity, born of willfully misconstrued failures, Bloem latched onto a most flattering explanation of his success as a novelist. The applause of the populace, registered by massive sales, seemed objective confirmation of his subjectively chosen self-image as voice of the Volk.

As in his choice of the second reality of national conservatism, Bloem's delusions about himself were therefore rooted in a lack of genuine principle. Not only did he refuse to admit that his failures in certain worldly ventures were rooted in his short-comings while his successes in others were intrinsically shallow. He also failed to see that a principled quest for truth, beauty, morality, love and justice should have been his real aim. Such a quest would have gone far to preserve him from the moral transgressions (or sins) of willful ignorance and vanity (or pride).

On the other hand, history as well as moral theory is needed to explain Bloem's identities, for his socialization and formal education made it easy for him to choose them. The German class society, produced by industrialization, inherited from the estates' society it replaced, an even stronger propensity than is usual in human affairs to define oneself and others by social position, and thus in terms of a collective identity. The strata from which Bloem stemmed had been seduced by Bismarck's success in unifying Germany to forsake their liberal (or conservative) principles for nationalism. The waning of the educated burghers qua social stratum, who were challenged within their inner sanctum of the universities and by the emergence of free professions filled with social newcomers, was a source of insecurity, as was indeed the whole accelerated process of modernization in Germany. While God had not died for most in a modernizing Germany as Nietzsche had predicted He would, religious faith was declining, with the resultant vacuum often being filled by various worldly idols. German literary and philosophical traditions had bred the widespread notion of the poet as cosmic or national prophet. Historicism, positivism, even the vibrant new social sciences, agreed on the futility of rational, moral education. The apolitical nature of the German political elite, which was not irreconcilable with a penchant for authoritarianism, worked against the emergence of experienced, realistic, principled citizenship.

Whatever their derivations, Bloem's self-images were problematic from the point of view of maintaining a sound character and political orientation. They did not stem from genuine knowledge of the self or the self's place in the world, nor from any understanding of how steadfast character had to be grounded in principle. These self-images, which crystallized and thus closed off one's identity once and for all, shut the door to self-development, whether defined as self-creation or movement toward completion of one's essential nature. As a result, they did not give Bloem the resources to make himself a better man or to hold to the political course made ever steadier by increasing clarity as to principle that would have made him a worthy praeceptor Germaniae.

Worse still, dependence on self-images was a prescription for disappointment. The collective ego props of the nation or social elite could be kicked out from under Bloem either by the objective failures of such collectivities or their subjective rejection by all or part of the populace. By the same token, the self-image of writer as national spokesman could be jolted either by hostile critiques or a falling sales curve. The revolt of his readership, of the magic mirrors whom Bloem required to reflect back his imaginary great personality, would be especially painful. Disappointment would reignite insecurity, which in turn might have political consequences.

At worst, insecurity might lead to more radical reconstruction of the collective and individual identities, and of the national conservative idols with which these identities were joined, and thus to further distortion of Bloem's political vision. At best, he would be impelled to realign his opinions with the nationalist mainstream so that its component magic mirrors would reflect back his self-image as its fictional spokesman.

If Bloem's vision of himself and his reality was distorted, why did he for over a decade resist right-wing radicalism for a stance favorable to the Weimar Republic and the Jews? To understand why Bloem was temporarily a healthy voice, relatively speaking, on the German right, it might be useful to unfold in brief Rhodes's theory of Nazi millenarian radicalism (of which his concept of dialectical self-hood is but a part): in short to examine the most pathological form of German nationalism. Any critique or modification of this theory will be eschewed here.[65]

Rhodes argues that millenarianism was the root of Nazism's appeal, nature, and policies. Those who became millenarians experienced both estrangement from their societies and the formation of images of utopian existences that they imagined to be true being. These utopian existences were ideological, economic or psychological. The ideological existences postulated some form of perfect happiness or ultimate good that would bring salvation or absolute justice in its train. Those who generated them were motivated by pride, by a hubris unable to accept imperfect existence and thus prone to divinize man.[66] The economic existences imagined perfect security, stability and regularity in the material conditions of life. Such normalcy was sought by those in a state of willful ignorance who delude themselves into believing in a perfect economic state unattainable in this world.[67] The psychological existences, discussed above, involved dialectical self-hood, in which pleasurable (and totally unrealistic) self-images were generated by subjects who then demanded their confirmation by objects, i.e., by other people. These utopian identities, it should be recalled, stemmed mainly from vanity.[68]

World War I, with its August days and front experience, at first seemed to mark the fulfillment of these utopian existences, a metastasis or transformation of being. The ideologically deduced salvations seemed to be realized, the elimination of the few obstacles to normalcy achieved, the utopian self-images confirmed.[69] This paradisiacal order was dashed, however, as the Civil Peace disintegrated, the war was lost, and the old Reich toppled by the November Revolution. Rather than recognize the utopian nature of their existence, the soon-to-be Nazis reacted with a disaster syndrome characterized by total disorientation and fear of annihilation or slavery. Out of this dislocation of the rational side of the mind, emerged the other symptoms of millenarianism, each shaped by the fears and utopian aspirations that had contributed to the disaster syndrome in the first place.[70]

To cope with their disaster syndromes, the Nazis generated revelations, "derived from mystical movements in their souls," that explained their woes and promised redemption from imagined swords of Damocles. Such sudden unmasking of both the causes of disasters and means for escaping them was the second characteristic of millenial consciousness.[71] The third was the specter of hostile fiends which their revelations showed to be the root of their difficulties. The Jews were this "first principle of evil."[72] "Election" was the fourth characteristic symptom of millenial consciousness. Together with the knowledge of the demonic threat, millenarians "learned from their revelations that they had been chosen to fight and defeat the wicked forces, thereby saving themselves and the world from the satanic afflictions."[73] The notion that they were the chosen was coupled in the Nazis' minds with that of "eschatological wars," the final struggles of the good with demonic internal and external enemies. The millenarians, to quote Rhodes's description of the fifth millenialist symptom, "perceived that the demons and their minions were preparing to administer coups de grace to the good and, therefore, that the eschatological hours of destruction for the devils and salvation for the righteous were at hand. Accordingly, they desired to rise up and eliminate evil from the earth by smashing its existential representatives in short, titanic wars (battles of Armageddon)."[74] The eschatological wars would lead to heaven on earth, to a kind of secular millenium--i.e., to the Third or Thousand-Year Reich. The belief in a new order of being to be achieved in this life was the final millenarian symptom.[75] The Hitler elite saw man as a nontranscendent "God in the making."[76] According to Rhodes, "This passion for goods that never could be was the antithesis of their aversion to evils that never existed."[77]

Up to a point, Bloem's path paralleled that of the Nazi millenarians. Bloem, like Rhodes's millenarians in the making, formed deluded ideological and psychological existences. His successes on the eve of the Great War, the miracle of the August days, and his experience of brotherhood in the trenches resembled the metastasis described by Rhodes. His contemplation of suicide when the old Reich lost the war and crumbled has the earmarks of a disaster syndrome.

There appear to be at least five reasons why Bloem almost at once overcame despair and made a moral, realistic decision for the new republic instead of turning apocalyptic. First, Bloem's very commitment to mirror the popular will dictated republicanism at a moment when public sentiment was so manifestly determined to jettison Hohenzollern monarchy if that would bring peace. Second, Bloem was basically an emotionally balanced man. While Rhodes is probably right that the key to the Nazis' apocalyptic fantasy is not to be found in the unconscious, that the blow to the rational side of their mind stemmed from a conscious and immoral refusal to surrender their utopian existences, it is surely true that prior mental instability, somehow rooted in their physiology or the irrational side of their mind, weakened resistance to the millenarian pathology. Third, Bloem was a man of considerable character by nature or upbringing, with great physical (if less moral) courage, a sense of fairness, and sympathy for others. Fourth, residues of traditions with a commitment to objective standards had a considerable influence on his thought and action. From the Christian tradition he drew a lingering attachment to an ethic of love, from the liberal a commitment to the rule of law, from the conservative a disinclination to divinize man or to reject completely intermediary institutional, moral and legal checks to the power of the nation state. Finally, Bloem never lost entirely the instincts of the fox. His sensitivity to experience, his power of capturing the essence of its particulars in images, his willingness (however limited by his national conservatism) to learn from it, kept him from losing touch completely with true existence. Ideas, character, and aesthetic instincts intersected to evoke positions on the Republic and the Jews in the 1920s that were far healthier than those of most nationalists. Lack of principles to undergird his thought, to solidify his character, and to steer his actions, combined with the distorting effect of his unifying principle, made it impossible for him to sustain these commitments, or to refrain from becoming a Hitlerite fellow traveler in the 1930s.

CHAPTER 3

THE "KNIGHT'S DEED OF THE SPIRIT": THE GENESIS, POLITICAL MESSAGE, AND PUBLICATION HISTORY OF BROTHERHOOD: A NOVEL

That Bloem decided to defend the republic and assault antisemitism in a novel in 1922 stemmed from his liberal and Christian upbringing as well as his actual experiences. His father, clearly a liberal of the old school whose first wife had been Jewish, "considered antisemitism to be barbaric nonsense." The religious tradition of Wuppertal, where Bloem had been raised, viewed the Jews not only as those who killed Christ, but also as the people of the Bible. In the Berlin theater world, Bloem became a close friend of German nationalist Jews like Ludwig Fulda and Georg Engel. During the war Bloem was impressed by the bravery of Jewish soldiers. He was appalled when a young platoon sergeant in his former battalion, the son of Felix Holländer (a prominent writer and Max Reinhardt's leading producer), was denied promotion to the officer corps despite extraordinary heroism simply because he was a Jew. Young Holländer subsequently was killed in combat.[1]

The immediate impulse behind Brotherhood was the decision of one of the largest associations of university student fraternities, the Kösener Senioren Conventsverband (KSC), to exclude Jews.[2] In general, the corporations of university students saw themselves as the crucibles of the nation's future ruling elite. The student corps, or dueling fraternities, united in the KSC, were infused with an intense nationalism and a monarchistic tradition. They viewed themselves as the cream of the academics, a sort of an elite within an elite. Although the corps had traditionally been the most liberal, though apolitical, of the student corporations, they became after World War I both anti-republican and antisemitic.[3]

In 1920, the Kösener Congress passed an amendment to the KSC constitution obliging members "to serve the fatherland through cultivation of national usage and stock, through keeping away everything immoral and un-German." The Congress agreed unanimously to interpret this clause as precluding further admission of Jews. The racial fanatics in the corps were, however, dis-satisfied with this imprecise formulation. They pushed for a statute explicitly prohibiting acceptance of Jews defined by race.[4] Apparently, there was even a movement afoot to revoke the memberships of Jewish Old Boys (Alte Herren) and of those old members married to a woman of full or partial Jewish heritage.[5]

Bloem, an Old Boy of two member corps of the KSC, Teutonia in Marburg and Lusatia in Leipzig, was incensed by these racial demands. As a jurist he was particularly angered by the demands to expel Old Boys who had earlier married Jews and to block membership to the sons of such marriages. This "meant something judicially and humanely unheard of: a provision for punishment with retroactive force. . . ."[6] Significantly, Bloem's sense that the proposed statute was unjust derived from a procedural rather than a substantive view of the rule of law. The horror for him lay not in the impending violation of the principle of equality before the law but in the ex-post-facto quality of the projected measure.

A personal, emotionally charged experience crystallized Bloem's political stance. His corps brother, the well-known surgeon Wilhelm Schultheiss, had married an American Jew. They had three sons. Schultheiss was deeply involved in the affairs of the corps Teutonia in Marburg and had educated his boys "only in the thought that they would some day wear the blue-red-gold ribbon." His oldest son, ready to enter the university, would be barred from Teutonia if the KSC adopted the anti-Jewish membership clause.[7]

Bloem tried to thwart the move for a clear-cut "Aryan paragraph" in the KSC by direct action. He spoke on the Jewish question in Berlin before the collective board of the Association of Old Corps Students.[8] He lectured against antisemitism at several universities.[9] Finally in 1921, he stood up alone at the KSC Congress against the plan to exclude Jews, evoking bitter opposition.[10] But his efforts were in vain--the KSC Congress changed the statutes expressly to forbid admission of Jews by race to the corps. According to a further regulation, each freshman on demand had to produce proof that he "had no ancestor of Jewish heritage up to and including the line of his grandparents."[11]

The KSC adoption of an Aryan paragraph was the last straw for Bloem. Sharing the belief in the corps as training grounds for Germany's elite, he now decided to bring his case to the nation.[12] The action of the KSC Congress

> was finally decisive for me. Out of the whole structure of the old Reich, only the academic associations remained in existence after 1918 as protectors of the fatherland. And now these wanted to take a step, which let itself be answered before no court of honor and justice! I then, if ever, felt myself now called to a knight's deed of the spirit.[13]

For his "knight's deed," Bloem chose the literary genre most adapted to his talents and most likely to reach a mass audience--the novel.[14]

One last experience contributed to "the original material and punctum saliens of Brotherhood"--a meeting with Carl Sonnenschein, the Catholic theologian and founder of the Catholic-Social Student Movement.[15] Before the Weimar era, religion little concerned Bloem who, despite his Calvinist upbringing, was attached during his adult life to no church. After the collapse of the Empire, however, personal contacts in the strictly Catholic north Bavaria (where his castle was located) turned him into an admirer of the Catholic Church. His admiration affected the themes and messages of his fiction.[16] His pro-Catholic stance, however, stemmed from social-minded conservatism rather than from inner conversion.

Thus, Sonnenschein appealed to Bloem because the former aimed at harmony between the industrial workers and the rest of the nation. Sonnenschein saw the emergence of a social conscience among the academics as a prerequisite for fathering this harmony. Bloem incorporated some of Sonnenschein's central ideas in his image of a German "brotherhood" encompassing even those elements, namely the workers and the Jews, hitherto considered to be beyond the pale.[17] Sonnenschein himself, transparently fictionalized as the Catholic spiritual advisor Dr. Hohmann, plays a pivotal role in the plot of Brotherhood.

The novel, written in 1921, tells the story of two World War I heroes, the Aryan pilot, Hans Joachim Eichholz, who had won the famous "Blue Max," the highest possible decoration for an officer of his rank, and Ludwig Löwenstein, a Protestant of Jewish origin.[18] When Hans Joachim comes home from an English prisoner-of-war camp, he is afire to return to the university in Schafflingen where he intends to learn "what it means to be German" and to enjoy the comradeship of his old dueling fraternity, Franconia (which belongs to the KSC).[19]

He soon finds much awry in the corps, however. Franconia, indeed the student corporations generally, are bastions of privilege where tradition and trivial fraternity activities crowd out education about Germandom. Most disheartening is the anti-Jewish resistance to Ludwig.[20] Ludwig does have some flaws that Bloem clearly meant to be seen as typically Jewish. Sometimes boastful, Ludwig is inherently skeptical, innovative, and completely lacking in awe before secular tradition. These traits supposedly made the Jews agents of change. For Bloem, a moderate conservative, some change, both within the corps and within Germany as a whole, was necessary to adapt the old institutions to the demands of the present. "Jewish" traits, when constrained within the framework of a nationalist conservatism, were therefore an actual boon to society (although the equation of Jews with change approaches the antisemitic notion of Jews as the "ferment of decomposition").[21] Ludwig certainly has the right values: a man of great courage, he is the fraternity's best duelist; steeped in corps traditions, he reorganizes Franconia's finances and helps in all aspects of its administration.[22] In key respects, moreover, the Löwenstein family is the antithesis of antisemitic stereotypes. Ludwig and his sister, Ruth, with whom Hans Joachim falls in love, are physically beautiful and completely committed to Germandom.[23] Their father, a <u>Justizrat</u>, is a patriotic paragon of fiscal integrity who, much like the real-life Schultheiss, had longed for the day when his son would become a corps student.[24]

While Ludwig is the target of the traditional antisemitism of the fraternity's reactionaries, his deadliest antagonist is Hermann Ströbel, who represents the <u>völkisch</u> or racist movement of which the Nazis, then unknown to Bloem, would become the prime party-political representative. An insecure and unsavory bully, Ströbel compensates for his lack of a war record (the other Franconians are all veterans) by dueling unskilled freshmen.[25] Ströbel's hatred of Jews stems from racial theories, a sense of inferiority, and envy of Ludwig.

Hans Joachim (as Bloem's mouthpiece) agitates to reform the corps and through them the academic corporations and educated middle class generally. The corps, whatever their faults, are potential nuclei for German rejuvenation because they alone carry on the spirit of associative life, of community.[26] To fulfill their potential, they must cease to be citadels of "old interests and privileges" and temper respect for tradition with willingness to change.[27] Uncategorical opposition to the Weimar Republic must be dropped; however untimely and wrong in removing the Kaiser, the November Revolution swept away much that was outworn and was a natural explosion against "monstrosities" like "militarism, feudalism, antisemitism, mamonism. . . ."[28]

At any rate, Hans Joachim tells his peers, state form is second to national unity. The republic must be at least formally accepted as a bulwark against chaos and as the will of the working masses. These must be reconciled if the Bildungsbürgertum (the educated middle class) is to regain leadership and if all Germans are to become nationalists. Academic youth must take the lead in winning over workers by renouncing privilege and by responsible preparation for and execution of later public office.[29]

Reform of the corps must be coupled with a campaign against antisemitism. While conceding dangerous features to contemporary Jews, many of whom admittedly failed to do their part in the war, Hans Joachim argues that these are the product of the shameful repression of a race that had done nothing more than fail to understand a prophet of its own blood. Hatred of the Jews, which has been most pronounced in the corps and in the universities, has alienated them from the national movement.[30]

There are only two possible solutions to the Jewish question: pogrom until total expulsion or the removal of all barriers. Pogrom is out of the question for a multitude of reasons--it would be barbaric, un-Christian, and utopian, and it would isolate Germany among the civilized nations.

There is only one true Jewish policy: whatever harmful qualities the Jews may have must be educated out of them. The corps must take the lead in the job of schooling Jews of good will to Germandom; "only then do we have the right and duty to fight against the malicious with all means."[31] To reject Jews who come to a corps ready to accept its life style is more than just un-Christian, inhuman, and antisocial; it is stupid and politically harmful. Antisemitism is ridiculous in cases like that of Ludwig Löwenstein, a defender of the fatherland and a model corps student. Jews must be judged as individuals. Hans Joachim announces, therefore, that he will oppose any plans to ban Jews from the KSC "as medieval narrow-mindedness, worse than the burning of witches and the inquisition."[32]

The corps must become the bearer of true German unity through love, with brotherhood emerging the "fundamental truth of our life."[33] Love is the key to salvation and must embrace all Germans regardless of faith, class or race: "that love which also recognizes and honors the German brother in the political and economic opponent."[34]

Antisemitism in Franconia, which Hans Joachim is unable to defuse, breeds tragedy when Ströbel shoots Ludwig in a pistol duel.[35] Ludwig leaves behind a last letter glowing with love for the Germans and arguing that the corps students must take the lead in amalgamating the Jews. Germans must think national rather than <u>völkisch</u>, drawing proletarians and Jews into the fold.[36] Hans Joachim, who now feels a boundless hatred for hate, tells his followers in the corps: Ludwig "wanted to be German and therefore he was one. It is the heart that makes the German, and not the nose and not the blood."[37]

The <u>Justizrat</u> Löwenstein comes with Ruth to bury his son with honors provided by the corps. The old man quits Franconia when, at the corps function to mourn Ludwig, he sees through the formally correct veil of sympathy to the abyss of hate that killed his son. Father and daughter now see the absurdity of trying to be German. Ruth renounces Hans Joachim's love, raises the specter of the proletariat avenging the Jews and entertains the possibility of a new national pride, the Jewish.[38]

Dr. Hohmann (Sonnenschein fictionalized) intervenes to keep a desolate Hans Joachim from resigning from Franconia by enlisting him in efforts to create a social studentry as "bearer of the national unity--throughout all strata, classes, castes and races."[39] Hohmann reconciles the old Justizrat to the Franconians by asking: "Should Wotan, should Moses triumph--or Christ?" Ruth, who clearly will someday marry Hans Joachim, overcomes her father's hesitance by handing him his Franconian band. "The old man raised his glance. A light shone therein like the morning shimmer of a new day for humanity."[40]

The political message of Brotherhood, a brand of reform conservatism, was riddled by antisemitic misconceptions and a misplaced faith in the educated social elite. Ominously Bloem left the door open for future action against Jews (and others) who, after some indeterminate period of tolerance and reeducation, were deemed to be still outside of or opposed to the Volk community. Indeed, Bloem himself was beset with völkisch illusions, although for him shared ideals, common culture, national sentiment, and will, rather than race, were the cement of the Volk. The kind of Volk community projected by Bloem could tolerate all sorts of divergencies--political, economic, religious, racial--that were anathema to the völkisch movement and its chief heirs, the Nazis.[41] On the whole, for all its flaws, the novel was a powerful rebuttal of antisemitism. Bloem created Jewish characters (who while converted were seen as Jews by most actors on the Weimar stage) deeply loyal to Germany and humanly attractive in almost every detail. Furthermore, Bloem turned the tables on the antisemites by making his scurrilous characters reactionaries and völkisch radicals.

Bloem's Brotherhood was published by Grethlein in Leipzig, a politically unaffiliated firm that possessed the right of first refusal to Bloem's belletristic works.[42] It appeared around mid-June 1922 in a first printing of fifty thousand copies, standard for Bloem since 1912 but enormous for his times.[43] A publisher could afford such a risk only with a writer of unquestionably great marketability. The novel quickly went into new printings. By the end of 1922, there were at minimum ninety thousand copies in print.[44] These early figures were comparable to those for Bloem's popular war novels and marked Brotherhood as a bestseller at a time (1918-28) when the average book may have had a circulation of 3,000 copies and when high circulation was said to begin around 40-50,000.[45]   Sales of Brotherhood surely were helped by the fortuitous appearance of the novel almost at the moment of Walther Rathenau's death.[46]   Rathenau, the republic's foreign minister who was detested by extreme nationalists as a politically liberal Jew and exponent of the policy of fulfilling Germany's obligations under the Treaty of Versailles, was murdered by young men convinced that he was a leader of a Jewish world conspiracy.   His assassination, the most important antisemitic act in the early Weimar years, had multiple repercussions on German politics, galvanized those in favor of the republic to self-defense, and outraged millions of Germans.[47]   Reader letters in the Bloem literary estate in Wuppertal suggest that most readers fit into one of two categories: national-minded Jews and Bloem's traditional audience, the intensely patriotic middle strata.[48]

By the end of 1922, negative reviews in the nationalist press very likely discouraged further purchases among Bloem's traditional reader community. The novel may have also suffered from the general downturn in demand for books that set in around February 1923 with a "quiet buyer's strike" (born of the increasing financial decimation of the educated classes) and that continued with a vengeance after the stabilization of the mark in November.[49]   Currency stabilization made money scarce; book consumption plunged since people naturally used limited funds for material recovery rather than culture.[50]   Moreover, just as the book may have prospered in 1922 due to revulsion over Rathenau's death, it may not be entirely coincidental that Brotherhood withered in 1923 when the French occupation of the Ruhr, German passive resistance, and hyperinflation provided volatile new fuel for antisemitism and political extremism generally.[51] At any rate, the book does not seem to have been reprinted again until 1927, when "people's editions" of ten Bloem novels appeared.[52] One-hundred and ten thousand copies ultimately found their way to the bookshops.[53] The novel reached a further, although completely Jewish audience, through serialization in the Israelitisches Familienblatt.[54]   In 1928, the CV-Zeitung published an excerpt from Brotherhood.[55]   On at least one occasion, in the friendly environs of Elberfeld, Bloem read passages from the novel to a reportedly enthusiastic crowd.[56]

A publisher with greater economic clout or political commitment than Grethlein might have done better in sustaining the sales of Brotherhood beyond 1922 (and in preventing the subsequent dramatic decline in Bloem's marketability). Grethlein possessed neither right-wing credentials nor leadership; hence, the concern lacked the credibility, connections and leverage to counter hostile nationalist reviews. Also Grethlein did not have anything like the massive literary prestige of, for instance, the great S. Fischer Verlag or the tremendous economic clout and marketing expertise of the likes of the house of Ullstein.[57] Perhaps only such prestige or clout could have induced booksellers, whether directly or indirectly by generating a demand to which they would have had to respond, to push the book in the teeth of resistance. Far from being able to float Bloem above stormy seas, Grethlein appears to have begun a process of disintegration when Bloem's popularity, which had been so important to buoying the firm's finances, sunk like a stone after 1922. Retrospectively Bloem found Grethlein and its head, Kurt Hauschild, inadequate aids to his career even before the advent of Brotherhood: "The fact that I had to do without a great, supportive, and protective publisher during the years of my rise was one of the main accidents of my life." At any rate, Grethlein was a fragile reed for Bloem to grasp the moment he ceased to be a mere mirror of his constituents and tried to lead them where they resisted going. Partyless, Bloem was unable to compensate for Grethlein's weakness with the backing of a strong political organization.[58] This would render his völkisch conservative reformism impotent as the following detailed history of the novel's reception and impact shows.

CHAPTER FOUR

THE GERMAN RIGHT AND <u>BROTHERHOOD: A NOVEL</u>: POLITICAL IMPACT AND CRITICAL RECEPTION

There is evidence that Bloem's novel greatly influenced the political thinking of not a few German nationalists, especially in 1922. A good many more might have been swayed, but the right-wing press soon swung into action to warn potential readers of the book's seductive dangers. As a result, whatever hopes Bloem had had that his novel would work a far-reaching reform--whether within the narrower compass of the corps or in the whole German right--were doomed to frustration. Indeed, the novel aroused a storm of animosity, often quite personal, from the political directions and various associations that had hitherto viewed Bloem as one of their main literary proponents. These now rejected him with varying degrees of sharpness as a democrat, a republican, a pacifist and a philosemite. This was especially true of the main targets of his reform efforts, the student fraternities.[1]

To be sure, there were isolated voices among the student organs favorable to the novel. For example, Dr. O. F. Scheuer, in the <u>Deutsche Hochschul-Warte</u> in Prague, completely approved of Bloem's plan to educate the Jews to Germandom.[2] Dr. Karl Konrad was more reserved in the November/December 1922 issue of the <u>Burschenschaftliche Wege</u>. But Konrad did contend that even Bloem's opponents ought to be grateful for "the many inspirations and teachings in <u>Brotherhood</u>. The students will have to occupy themselves for a long time still with the novel."[3] In 1925, a critic for <u>Burschen heraus</u> left no doubt about his readiness to accept Bloem's program:

> Whoever approaches the content . . . [of this novel] . . . without prejudice and thereby keeps in view the pure intention of the author, who belongs to the best of the fatherland, must admit at the end of the novel: here a genuine German has told us where there is deficiency and how things should be done in the future.[4]

These favorable responses were only exceptions that underscored the rule. Völkisch tendencies had too deeply encroached into the non-Catholic associations for them to forgive, much less favor, a public critique of their antisemitism and traditionalism--even by an insider with nationalist credentials. The Kösener S. C. Verband was especially adamant in rejecting a novel that had been immediately inspired by the KSC decision to exclude Jews. In May 1923, the official KSC journal, the Deutsche Corpszeitung, blasted Brotherhood as a "bad book," totally dominated by a thesis out of touch with reality.[5] The KSC organ objected to Bloem's idealization of Jewish characters, "to whom some completely small failings and racial qualities are granted, presumably to make them at least somewhat more probable."[6] Bloem, the KSC mouthpiece insisted, does not understand the Jewish question at all; he fails to realize the incompatibility of the Jewish spirit with the essence of the corps. Bloem was wrong when he claimed that the corps had a responsibility to educate the Jews out of their dangerous features. His misrepresentations had much damaged the public reputation of the corps.[7]

Repeatedly, student organs alleged that Bloem had failed to understand the racial question and that he had spread a distorted image of the corps to the general public. For example, Die Volkshochschul-Gemeinschaft described Bloem's plea for brotherhood as tendentious while attacking the novel's idealization of Jews and its supposed failure seriously to discuss the race problem.[8] Similarly, the Berliner Hochschul-Nachricht would have no truck with Bloem's fight against traditionalism and anti-Jewish discrimination.[9] A review in the Akademische Mitteilungen denied the least value to Brotherhood, either as art or as message:

> The problems of the students in 1922 are not touched; those broached, the pre-November corps-student questions, are handled superficially (the Jewish question is not solved with an expenditure of sentimentality!)--The novel reads quickly, but is without deeper value.[10]

Not all academic critics of Bloem's novelistic diatribe against radical völkisch antisemitism were so unequivocally harsh in their judgment. Kurt Emig, in the 15 April 1923 issue of the Deutsche Hochschul Zeitung, found much good to say about Bloem's critique of tradition and praised Bloem's storytelling talents. Emig even concluded his essay with the view that the novel "will be much read, must be much read." Yet Emig also quarreled with Bloem's completely negative portrait of the racists and his idealized characterization of the Jews. Emig further contended that the book would not shake the determination of the corps students to exclude the Jews.[11]

Not every condemnation of the novel by active or old fraternity members was printed in the organs of the academic associations. One Old Boy, writing for the Hannoversche Landeszeitung, defended the corps's right to exclude whom they wished. The novel's inner tragedy, he proclaimed, stemmed from the misguided decision of the elder Löwenstein to force admission of his son.[12]

Bloem's book caused a furor in his own two corps, Teutonia in Marburg and Lusatia in Leipzig. True, Bloem was not without supporters in his own corps. Some expressed their backing privately, as did one Heinrich Speckert. In April 1923, Speckert wrote Bloem to express his appreciation for the novel--"I am pleased that you place human beings above party and above religion. I am no antisemite, no philosemite, but a philanthropist; I prefer a good upstanding Jew to a characterless Christian."[13] Other corps brothers did not hesitate to enter the public lists for Bloem and his novel. One fired off an open letter to the Pfälzer Corpszeitung, confuting at length a scurrilously ad hominem review of Brotherhood in that paper.[14] Of greater import was a review of the novel by Bloem's friend Georg Weiss in the house organ of the corps Teutonia-Marburg.[15]

Weiss's review appeared in December 1922 and described the novel's various characterizations as masterful. It is a wonder, Weiss exclaimed, "how Bloem is also able to put himself into the tragedy of the disunited, lonesome Semitic soul, forced as it is to hypercriticism!"[16] Weiss lauded the book for its struggle against the cult of tradition, "against the noble and cold isolation of the corps, against thoughtless, fanatic antisemitism and chauvinism, and for the timely rejuvenation of the original corps ideals." Weiss did admit that the novel had its exaggerations and omissions. He noted specifically the oversimplified identification of all antisemitism with the vulgar, rabid extremism of Arthur Dinter (author of the prototypal racial novel, the bestselling Sin Against the Blood) and Theodor Fritsch (honored by the Nazis as the "Old Master"). However, Weiss insisted, Bloem's motives were pure--Bloem's simplications stemmed from love of fatherland and the conviction of the need for unity with Catholics, Jews, and workers.[17] Weiss admonished his corps brothers to read the book with an open mind; "so much is required by brotherhood."[18]

But in 1922-23 the majority of corps brothers, both in Lusatia and Teutonia, appear to have been opposed to the novel and its program. As Weiss himself foresaw, the greater part of the Marburg corps brothers objected to his review.[19] The corps paper even printed a confutation by the Ministerialrat Rocholl.[20] Members of Teutonia in Heidelberg, as well as those in Marburg, reportedly took a hostile stance toward the book.[21] Hermann Münzel sarcastically described the reactionary mood behind the resistance to the novel in Marburg: "one celebrates the Kaiser's birthday on 27 January and waits for the war of liberation to break out in two hours. . . ."[22] The atmosphere in the Leipzig chapter of Lusatia was no less hostile. On 16 December 1922, an official commission of Lusatia resolved that Brotherhood had spread a false picture of the corps, "so that in wide circles false notions must develop and a great damage to the corps-student idea is to be feared. . . ."[23] In each of his two corps, Bloem was ultimately forced to face courts of honor. He was absolved in both cases, although his corps brothers certainly still differed from him on the Jewish issue. Much later, in his autobiography, Bloem would attribute the acquittals to the readiness of the corps to tolerate criticism and differences of opinion.[24] The chief factors in the acquittals were more likely Bloem's personal magnetism and reputation.

By the spring of 1923, Bloem had found it necessary to respond to criticisms from within the corps in the form of an open answer to Rocholl. Apparently, this open letter appeared in some five to six hundred copies.[25] In his answer, Bloem denied that the Franconia of the novel was modeled on the Marburg chapter of Teutonia. Bloem's letter also wrestled with the charge that he had damaged the public image of the corps by airing before a wide audience internal matters best discussed behind closed doors.

Bloem replied that he had addressed corps problems in a popular novel because corps-student assemblies had hitherto turned a deaf ear to his appeals. Besides, he wanted to reach all academics, not just the dueling fraternities. Moreover, corps-student problems are of crucial importance to the life of the nation, since the academic associations are the crucible of the country's future leadership. Thus he, whose entire life had been service to the fatherland, felt obliged to address the whole nation. Ultimately, Bloem asserted, the people as a whole, not any council of students, had to pass judgment on his novel, for his book was the cornerstone of a new academic edifice.[26]

Bloem seems to have won over in the long run those personally close to him to something like agreement with his views. Two corps in Würzburg--where perhaps not incidentally Bloem's son Walter Julius attended school--began to swing over to his stance on the Jewish question.[27] Bleuel and Klinnert, historians of the politicization of German students after 1918, report acceptance of a Jew by a Würzburger corps even after Hitler's seizure of power.[28] By 1928, Lusatia-Leipzig had come to accept Bloem's program for an evolutionary conservatism. The corps organ proudly reported that what Bloem had advocated for years had been transformed into the accepted goal of domestic politics through Hindenburg's example: "Loyalty toward other opinions and toward the state."[29] Such eventual acceptance of one or more of the main points laid out in Brotherhood was limited in corps circles to those who knew Bloem personally.[30]

Bloem's book was an attack on the radical völkisch movement in general, not just on its manifestations in the student associations. It was plainly designed to win over rather than just to polemicize against those susceptible to völkisch propaganda not just in the fraternities but in the nationalist middle classes as a whole. Brotherhood was just the kind of book, staunchly nationalist and saturated with völkisch ideas, likely to make converts on the radical right.[31] It proffered an alternative völkisch program, devoid of racism and violent attacks on the Weimar Republic. In the event, Brotherhood did lure even some völkisch activists away from antisemitism. The Montagsblatt (Prague) reported the pacification of some of the most hard-nosed anti-Jewish agitators in German Bohemia by Bloem's novel.[32]

As late as 1934, a Nazi poet and SA member named Winckler, who idolized Hitler, could suffer intense pangs of conscience because of Brotherhood. The novel reconfirmed Winckler's own happy experiences with Jews and made him doubt whether he could remain an active member of the SA.[33] Winckler was tormented by the hypothetical problem of Hans Joachim Eichholz's fate in the Third Reich. Hans Joachim, Winckler was convinced, would certainly have married Ruth Löwenstein eventually. Thus the young Germanic hero would have found himself a pariah in 1933, a Wahljude (a Jew by choice). Winckler was unable to do away with the notion of humanity raised in Bloem's books. He ended his last letter to Bloem in this vein: "For, not true, learned Herr Doctor, we must be able to sacrifice all for the fatherland except this one thing, if we wish to remain humans in the sense of the creator: we may not give up our humanity, our love and with these our souls?!"[34]

It is possible that Brotherhood might have made considerable inroads among the völkisch rank-and-file had it been left uncontested. However, völkisch organs recognized the seductive powers of the book and swung their critical artillery against it. In August 1922, a critic for the völkisch review, Heimgarten, expressed the fear that Brotherhood would convert many to philosemitism. He warned those who had read the novel not to draw general conclusions from the unique case of Ludwig Löwenstein. Ironically, the critic himself was susceptible to the novel's plea for a Volk community rather than racial hate. "Yet, unfortunately the problematic of . . . [Bloem's] . . . interesting novel loses itself ultimately with one-sided tendentiousness in the burning race question." Bloem is wrong when he says that anyone who wishes to be and feels German is German. Bloem had missed "the true core of the race problem."[35] Over a year later, Heimgarten plainly viewed the novel as still a grave enough threat to merit another long, hostile review. The author of this essay, Arthur Trebitsch, also described Brotherhood as an utmost danger to the völkisch cause. The book's powerful artistic qualities, Trebitsch insisted, insured it as far-reaching impact, especially on the young. As a counter to Bloem's central thesis, Trebitsch stressed the supposedly unbridgeable spiritual-corporeal differences between Jews and Germans.[36]

The Deutsche Zeitung, the organ of the Pan-German, radical völkisch wing of the German Nationalist People's party or DNVP, likewise deemed Bloem's book dangerous enough to warrant at least two substantial essays. On 12 November 1922, Hermann Engelbrecht lamented both Bloem's political conversion and his allegedly misguided idealization of the Jews in Brotherhood. "All in all: a glorification of the Jewish noble-race [Edelrasse], an abasement of the German! Bloem is one of the many who do not want to admit the racial teachings!" Engelbrecht felt it tragic that a man like Bloem, "who had earlier written good German, submits to the spirit of the time and slanders and denies his German Volkstum, to which he belongs by blood."[37] Another article, published in the same paper about two weeks later, expressed agreement with a number of Bloem's demands. But Bloem had gone beyond these points, transforming his fiction into a lead article for the Roter Tag. The fashion in which Bloem motivated the stance of the students toward the Jews was especially libelous.[38]

It is worth noting that Brotherhood made a bitter enemy for Bloem in the Nazi ideologist, Alfred Rosenberg. This emnity would cause Bloem considerable hardship in the early years of the Third Reich. Der Weltkampf, Rosenberg's journal for the international fight against Jewry, printed a vicious essay on Bloem in 1926 on the occasion of the novel's serialization in the Israelitisches Familienblatt. The essay's author, likely Rosenberg himself, advised Bloem to adopt a "beautiful little Jew or, in case he should have a daughter, to lay her in the bed of a rabbi as a wife. That would be the heroic confirmation of his brotherhood."[39] In his autobiography, Bloem reported how Rosenberg pictured him in the Völkischer Beobachter, with a Jewish woman on his right and a Negro woman on his left arm, extending a brotherly kiss to both.[40]

The press with ties to the DNVP (or to the far right of the German People's party or DVP) avoided this kind of base, ad hominem vituperation while reviewing Brotherhood. But German Nationalist organs generally rejected the novel's philosemitic intentions, its critique of the corps and of the Wilhelmine order, and its plea for acceptance of the republic. The Neue Preussische (Kreuz-) Zeitung, the journalistic citadel of old conservatism, described Brotherhood as convincingly written, but lacking in depth. According to the paper's critic, Bloem favored assimilation of the Jews, which made the book hard to enjoy for those of another opinion.[41] The Deutsche Allgemeine Rundschau accused Bloem of having written a demoralizing novel, based on an inaccurate, damaging portrait of academic life.[42] The Süddeutsche Zeitung made a similar judgment on Bloem's book, while also objecting to the "one-sided" idealization of the Jews and denigration of the antisemites.[43] The München-Augsburger Zeitung, "the house organ" of the DNVP in Bavaria, had no more use for Bloem's Brotherhood than for Dinter's Sin Against the Blood. The review, shot through with studied sarcasm, criticized Bloem's superficial handling of the problems and his portrait of the representative of the Völkische (Ströbel) as a coward.[44]

Important interest groups near to the DNVP were often even more hostile to the novel. The critic Stölting in Der deutsche Kaufmann im Auslande struck a racist note. Stölting insisted that a reader, despite Bloem's convincing prose, can feel the "yawning gap between the Aryan and Semitic races." Stölting found the novel's conciliatory ending to be contrived--an unprejudiced reader would lay the book down with the consciousness "that a civil truce is never the ideal of true brotherhood.[45] A newspaper tied to the Agrarian League (Bund der Landwirte), the Schwäbische Tages- zeitung, also condemned the novel from a moderate racist standpoint. The Stuttgart daily was "disgusted" with the book, which it regarded as no more a work of art, if better written, than its counterpiece, Dinter's Sin Against the Blood. Especially objectionable was Bloem's devastating portrait of Ströbel:

> Whoever has read this passage knows what stands in the whole novel. Each of the figures in the novel who steps in for Jewish-German "brotherhood" is boundlessly idealized, each opponent of this general intermingling of the races is drawn as a lout or as an idiot.[46]

At the best, German Nationalist organs damned the novel with faint praise. The Weser-Zeitung, influenced by nationalist-minded heavy industrialists, neither approved of nor criticized Bloem's position on the Jewish question. It simply quoted the passage in which Hans Joachim ruled out the possibility of a pogrom and demanded opening up the gates to Jews of good will. Bloem's description of the stultification of the corps was found to be somewhat exaggerated.[47] Of papers close to the DNVP, only the Schlesische Zeitung was reasonably sympathetic to the novel. This prestigious old newspaper pursued at least the semblance of independence, describing itself as "Christian national." Even the Schlesische Zeitung could not shake the clearly unpleasant impression that Bloem's sympathies "stand chiefly on the side of the Jews, in general as in particular." Yet, the SZ review ended on a fairly upbeat note:

> And yet the central thought of his [Bloem's] book is that of reconciliation, his intention the strengthening of the national idea. It means the artistic mastery of an exactly so difficult as timely material, and ranks in its literary value with that which Bloem wrote earlier.[48]

Aside from hostile reviews in the right-wing press, Bloem was, by his own account, subjected to a largely subterranean, mouth-to-mouth "counter-propaganda" campaign. This "negative oral propaganda," as Bloem described it, lasted long beyond 1922-23 and appears to have stamped Bloem as a renegade. The rumors soon took an ugly, personal turn. For example, when Bloem divorced and remarried in 1923, false rumors spread that his new bride was a rich Jew.[49] It is worth adding that Bloem was required to submit to a court of honor by his officer's association. As in the case of the Teutonian and Lusatian courts of honor, Bloem was absolved, but the affair left him with deep psychological scars.[50]

Brotherhood clearly failed in its goal of implanting a new outlook in the corps and in the German right as a whole. It did affect the thinking of individuals and small groups within nationalist circles. It might have been far more successful in weakening the grip of antisemitism on the right if it had won strong support from a nationalist party or association of weight.

Such support would have resulted in wider distribution and greater receptivity to the novel. The resultant success would likely have inspired imitators among writers and publicists. But the organs of the right were all but uniformly hostile to the novel. Readers of the novel were warned not to take its philosemitic message seriously; potential readers were scared off. Antisemitism of one kind or another and hostility toward the republic ran much too deep for any single book, especially one without organizational backing, to have much of a lasting impact.

Bloem's political avowal had a fateful, destructive effect on his own career. His unhappy experiences with Brotherhood were not likely to inspire other right-wing authors to try their hand at philosemitic fiction. These experiences contributed to Bloem's own reconversion after 1930 to extreme nationalism. Brotherhood permanently alienated from Bloem the political groups and social strata that had hiterto made up the bulk of his readership. The resultant financial and emotional strains were severe.[51] Bloem, in his unpublished, post-World War II autobiography, himself interpreted the publication of Brotherhood as "the great turning point" in his life.[52] Bloem felt that the novel had set the last half of his life on a precipitous downhill slide. It "hurled me with a jolt from the light to the shadow side of life"; it began the process by which Bloem was turned "from a favorite of the nation to a whipping boy."[53]

Brotherhood damaged Bloem's literary career and thus his pocketbook by incurring the lasting wrath of the nationalist circles from which he had drawn the readers (and hence buyers) of his books.[54] From 1912 to 1922, Bloem, clearly due to his appeal to the nationalist middle strata, was most probably the best-seller of the German book trade. His popularity on the book market made him a rich man. But the right-wing press and "whispering" campaign evoked by his novel turned off nationalist readers, book-sellers, and publishers.[55] As Bloem himself would later put it, "the part of my reader community, once numbering many hundreds of thousands, which had not fallen or been impoverished, now gave me up."[56] Bloem's earlier novels, including Brotherhood, had in most cases ultimately gone into printings of over one-hundred thousand. Apparently only one of his books first published after 1922 transcended forty thousand.[57]

Some of Bloem's novels printed in the years 1922 to 1933 appear to have been dismal failures on the book market. The Teutons (German title: Teutonen; 1926) may have attained only an incredibly low three-thousand copies.[58] Bloem regarded the failure of this novel, published by the nationalist K. F. Köhler Verlag and geared for Bloem's traditional nationalist audience, as especially ominous: "It would certainly have achieved a stormy success by my old community of readers. But it became always clearer: the subterranean sowing of mines by my slanderers had begun to work."[59] Bloem's Washington novels of the late 1920s were abysmal failures saleswise. Even Front Soldiers (German title: Frontsoldaten; 1930), which appeared during the war novel mania triggered by the unprecedented success of Remarque's All Quiet on the Western Front, reached only ten thousand in print. Only in 1931-33, when Bloem returned to the nationalist mainstream, did his books do fairly well, two going into editions of thirty thousand.[60] Even these last figures are far below those of Bloem's heyday, 1912-22.

There is also evidence of a de facto boycott of Bloem's plays and prose pieces by nationalist theaters and newspapers. His play, Heroes of Yesterday, for example, reportedly enjoyed a successful premiere. But the hostility of the right prevented it from being taken over by other stages.[61] In 1924, the Deutsch-Österreiche Tageszeitung refused to accept a Bloem article on the "national drama." The editorial staff, Dr. Karl Hans Strobl wrote Bloem, "does not wish to bring any contribution by you, because of your known stance in the matter of the Jewish question in the German corps."[62] Bloem was also turned down as a contributor, seemingly because of his political conversion, by the Bergisch-Märkische Zeitung.[63] As shall be shown, Bloem was especially hard hit by the drop in book sales and by the contracting market for his other literary pieces because the inflation and depression all but wiped out his earlier fortune.

The bitter antagonism, extending to Bloem personally, evoked by Brotherhood in right-wing circles also had severe emotional repercussions for Bloem. It was for these circles that Bloem had always written and in whose good opinions he put the most stock. Bloem's artistic creativity and peace of mind was obviously closely tied to a sense of integration with the nationalist middle strata in general and the <u>Bildungsbürgertum</u> in particular. Bloem was emotionally unprepared to assume the icy mantle of the writer as critical outsider. As he later admitted, Bloem craved love and friendship, particularly from those to whom he was bound by background and ideals.[64] In his autobiography, Bloem would write how he had been horrified by the "white glowing" animosity suddenly emerging, thanks to his novel, in groups of the population hitherto near to him:

> I am not suited at all to be a martyr! I did not think to be able to live in the thought that the world for which I had done so infinitely much viewed me suddenly as an outlaw, an apostate, a renegade and-- when it could do so without personal collision with me!-- also handled me as such![65]

Bloem was particularly appalled by the hatred for him aroused by his book among "the two anchors" of his life--the soldiers (veterans as well as active types) and the dueling fraternities.[66]

CHAPTER 5

LIBERALS, CATHOLICS, SOCIALISTS, JEWS AND BROTHERHOOD: A NOVEL: POLITICAL IMPACT AND CRITICAL RECEPTION

Bloem did not achieve a feeling of integration with nor did he build up anything like a compensatory audience out of the segments of the population loyal to the German People's party (DVP) or to the parties of the Weimar coalition. Bloem's Brotherhood was favorably reviewed by many newspapers and journals to the left of the DNVP, especially by the organs of the DVP and of political Catholicism (i.e., of the Center and Bavarian People's parties). However, neither liberals nor socialists nor Catholics felt entirely comfortable with Bloem's national conservatism. Those most enthusiastic about the novel were the Jews; the novel was actually reprinted in whole or in part in Jewish periodicals. Jewish critics were troubled, however, by the attenuation of the philosemitic thesis of the novel through antisemitic stereotypes and the portrayal of the central "Jewish" character as baptized.

Bloem's attitudes toward the republic and the Jews more closely resembled the position of the DVP (born 23 November 1918 when the National Liberals reorganized themselves) in 1922 than that of any other major party of the time. A key DVP paper, the Wiesbadener Zeitung, noted the close similarity between the program of the People's party and Hans Joachim's demand that the republic be recognized as the will of the masses.

> Brought from the novelistic German of theory into the wording of a real politician, this avowal coincides approximately with the attitude of our German People's Party, which, faithful to its principle of "the fatherland over the party," voted for the draft of the Law for Protection of the Republic, after it had addended a number of necessary changes.[1]

The Wiesbaden DVP paper acknowledged Bloem's credentials as Germany's most militaristic author, and expressed admiration for the nationalist sentiment and the love of the corps manifest in his novel. The review was critical on some points but finished up by declaring that Brotherhood "deserved to be raised to [the status of] a German book of warning and education, to the parole of the German reconstruction."[2]

Other papers linked to the DVP had a good opinion of the novel. The Magdeburgische Zeitung an independent newspaper close to the DVP and staunchly opposed to all political extremism, found the book's conclusion overly facile and contrived, but approved Bloem's goals and conceded that he had "laid bare the roots of the evil."[3] The Kattowitzer Zeitung agreed with Bloem's attack on racial hatred and disunity. The DVP organ did criticize what it saw as Bloem's probable overestimation of the corps's capacity for self-renewal. But the paper's review concluded with a glowing tribute to Brotherhood: "An inwardly true, strong and amiable book, born out of love for Germandom and filled up with hope for the inner rebirth of the German Volk!"[4]

Another major DVP organ, the Hildesheimer Allgemeine Zeitung (HAZ), devoted a giant front-page article to the book. The HAZ had dispatched Nathaniel Jünger's radical völkisch thesis novel, Volk in Gefahr!, in the same place only the year before. Now, the HAZ proclaimed, Bloem's book has appeared, whether by chance or destiny, at the very instant Rathenau's murder has shown the poisonous nature of antisemitism. Its purpose, the HAZ noted with approval, is, in contrast to that of Jünger, to heal the Volk from its deluded emnity toward the Jews. "Therefore a philosemitic book, friendly to the Jews, and its author is one of our most distinguished and at the same time most national German novelists: Walter Bloem." After quoting Hans Joachim's program for reeducating the Jews, the HAZ expressed the hope that Bloem's novel would find the widest possible following.[5]

Brotherhood was widely reviewed and well received in all branches of the Catholic press. Bloem's previous two novels (Gottesferne and Herrin), which had reflected Bloem's new sympathy for the Roman church, had already won him a sympathetic ear among Catholics.[6] His glorification of the Catholic social movement in Brotherhood predisposed Catholic critics toward this book too. Almost all organs of political

Catholicism, however, expressed reservations about parts of Bloem's program, especially about his confidence in the corp's potential for self-renewal. Theo Hoffmann, writing in Leuchtturm, alone among Catholic spokesmen shared Bloem's faith in the political vitality of the German fraternities. Hoffmann hailed Bloem's novel enthusiastically from the standpoint of the Catholic youth associations. Hoffmann insisted that the example of the Catholic corporations proved the capacity for renewal in the academic associations in general. The principles of the corporations remain valid; "What we fight against in them is indeed the unessential, the rubbish, the red tape."[7] Hoffmann also pointed to Bloem's "panegyric" (Hochlied) to Dr. Sonnenschein's social efforts:

> The book extols genuine völkisch work, not in the sense of a desolate antisemitism, which indulges itself in wild declamations and, directly blinded by the slogan "Aryan," lets like an animal breeder only race matter, only the blood, not spirit, not soul. . . . All in all, a book of genuine criticism, but full of optimism, with something to say to those of us who wish not to destroy but to renew the existing from within.[8]

The relatively conservative Bavarian Catholic press also endorsed Bloem's novel, although without completely identifying with Bloem's program. In the Bayerischer Kurier, the Munich organ of the BVP, the critic Georg Lutz insisted that Bloem's book had pursued a justified thesis in its attack on the antisemitic, calcified, and exclusive corps. "One is sympathetically impressed," Lutz continued, "by the recognition of the paradigmatic nature of the Catholic students in religious, scientific, and social life." Lutz had some (mainly aesthetic) reservations, claiming that Bloem had not completely succeeded in reconciling art and message.[9] The Augsburger Postzeitung was pretty much noncommittal, but it did praise the development of the novel until its close. The end was seen as illogical, but pleasing due to the pivotal role played by the Catholic spiritual advisor. The Bayerischer Volkszeitung described Bloem's portrayal of the Catholic student movement as positive and his treatment of the Jewish question as containing "some pertinent words." The Fränkische Volksblatt found the book's fight against the domination of the corps highly interesting and recommended it to others, especially to academics.[10]

The press of the Center party wished <u>Brotherhood</u> a wide circulation and a deep impact. The <u>Kölnische Volkszeitung</u>--along with <u>Germania</u> (notably silent about <u>Brotherhood</u>), one of the party's two truly supra-regional organs--considered the novel form to be especially suitable for tendency of Bloem's sort; fiction permitted a number of positions to be laid forth through dialogue. According to the paper's critic, Dr. Jos. Froberger, <u>Brotherhood</u> marked a great change in entertainment literature. He found it a slight loss to art and a great gain for the people when fiction was used for educational purposes:

> The pure idealism which speaks out of this work, fraught as it is with cultural-historical meaning, the great courage of the author in pursuit of the truth that lets him acknowledge without envy the high spiritual forces in the Catholic student and especially in the social student movement, the hot yearning for a cultivation of the rising intellectual generation in Germany, raise this novel high above that which one commonly calls entertainment literature.[11]

The regional press of the Center endorsed Bloem's stand in his fiction against calcified tradition and racism in the corps. The Bonn <u>Deutsche Reichszeitung</u> found Bloem's indictment of current corps life worthy of recognition.[12] The <u>Münsterischer Anzeiger</u> was far stronger in its approbation, hailing <u>Brotherhood</u> as "the" student novel. The paper's reviewer, a Dr. Contzen, adjudged Bloem's treatment of the Jewish question to be especially meaningful. "Might Bloem's suggestion," Contzen concluded, "fall on fruitful ground! That would be the finest success which could be allotted to the new Bloem."[13] Part of the review in the <u>Badischer Beobachter</u> was actually a reprint of an essay apparently first published in the left-liberal <u>Berliner Morgen-Zeitung</u>.[14] The remainder of the review, written by Dr. Gregor, was well-nigh ecstatic in its praise for Bloem's book, characterizing <u>Brotherhood</u> as a virtual apology "for us Catholics." <u>Brotherhood</u>, Gregor summed up, "is a signpost and brings clarity to all seekers. Written from life for life it almost loses the character of the novel. It is reality."[15]

Of the three main Catholic literary-political journals--<u>Hochland, Der Gral</u>, and <u>Stimmen der Zeit</u>--the last two reviewed <u>Brotherhood</u>. Dr. Georg Hayn, in <u>Der Gral</u>, described the novel as "doubtless a thesis novel in a good sense; it would like to do its bit to heal the wounds, to bring about reconstruction." Hayn was impressed both by Bloem's portraits of Dr. Hohmann and two Catholic coeds and by his tributes to Catholic religiosity and social work as the prerequisites for German rebirth. Hayn did wonder if the novel would make much of an impression on the circles at whom it was mainly aimed. He also doubted whether Bloem had penetrated deeply enough into the problems of the time. Clearly lacking Bloem's belief in the fundamental soundness of the corps, Hayn criticized the novel's end with its "reconciliation pathos."[16] Like <u>Der Gral</u>, the <u>Stimmen der Zeit</u> was largely positive in its evaluation of the novel, but also by no means identified itself completely with Bloem's standpoint. Bloem's position on the Jewish question, which opposed racism while imputing "certain congenital and . . . persecution-evoked failings to his [Jewish] hero," was implicitly approved by the journal's critic. This reviewer pointed out that the novel's notion of brotherhood was in the first line "national German." But he noted, with transparent satisfaction, the seeds of expansion to the wider community of nations envisioned by Christ.[17]

Reactions to Bloem's <u>Brotherhood</u> varied greatly in the left-liberal press. Indeed, there was universal approval for Bloem's stand against radical <u>völkisch</u> antisemitism and petrified tradition. But there was some disagreement as to the aesthetic worth of the book. More significantly from the political standpoint, left-liberal critics differed as to their degree of skepticism towards Bloem's national-conservative program. It is worth noting that the most influential democratic dailies were the least receptive to the art or message of <u>Brotherhood</u>. Neither the <u>Frankfurter Zeitung</u> nor the <u>Vossische Zeitung</u> appear to have even reviewed the novel.[18] The <u>Berliner Tageblatt</u> (BT), owned by the Mosse concern, applauded Bloem's handling of the Jewish problem, but disparaged his belief that the corps would lead the way to a halcyon future:

> Vividly and with a clear gaze, . . . [Bloem] . . . dwells upon the Jewish question, and with great seriousness he demands of academic youth that they engage themselves with understanding in the social and political sense. He hopes for fulfillment of his wishes--that a <u>Volk</u> brotherhood will develop from the corps brotherhood. We do not believe it. The rebirth will not ensue from above to below, [but] only from below to above. . . . The corps will, in spite of the encouragement of the dear Old Boy, Walter Bloem, continue to cut themselves off from below. They are ruins from the age of castles, decked out in colored ribbons. The street of the world passes them by. However, Bloem's optimism and manner of thinking remain welcome.[19]

Karl Würzburger took a similar stance toward <u>Brotherhood</u> in the January-February issue of the periodical <u>Vivos Voco</u>. This <u>Journal for New Germandom</u>, edited by Hermann Hesse and Richard Woltereck, was aimed more at inner than political renewal. Yet its orientation on moral and cultural matters was very much like that of the left-liberal organs. Würzburger, while reviewing <u>Brotherhood</u> at length, praised Bloem for valuable observations and judgments, while bowing to the latter's sincerity. But like the BT and in contrast to Bloem, Würzburger believed that the petrification of the academic associations was irretrievable. The corps were fated by their superficial "tautness [<u>Strammheit</u>]" and pride of place to play a destructive and decivilizing role in the life of the nation. Bloem's conciliatory ending was impossible because the corps were beyond reform; thus the conclusion resulted in a misrepresentation of the problem. The corps were inherently inimical to the very idea of brotherhood, and thus to both "spirit" and "love."[20]

On 23 June 1922, the <u>Berliner Morgen-Zeitung</u> published a sympathetic, if less than rave review of <u>Brotherhood</u>. By 1930 the most circulated daily in Germany, the <u>Morgen-Zeitung</u> (like the <u>Berliner Tageblatt</u>) belonged to the liberal-democratic Mosse concern.[21] The <u>Morgen-Zeitung</u> catered to a mass audience, and perhaps for this reason its review lacked the subtle political distinctions of the BT critique.[22] Indeed, most of the Berliner Morgen-Zeitung review was a rather straightforward plot summary. This summary was couched in language that implied total approval of Bloem's fight against antisemitism. For example, the book's "catastrophe," the death of Ludwig Löwenstein, was blamed on "antisemitism" in its "ugliest form." The critique ended with two sentences strongly suggesting the positive worth of Bloem's work.

> The Dichtung [poetic work] dismisses us with the hope of a development of our academic youth, which would raise them to bearers of the thought of the Volk community and of the recovery from inner strife. The work glows from the strong belief in Germany's indestructible life force, which is the main feature of Walter Bloem's production.[23]

This review--usually with deletions, additions, or reformulations--appeared in at least twenty newspapers.[24] Most of these, apart from the Berliner Morgen-Zeitung (where the review apparently first appeared), were regional or local papers, probably lacking in sufficient resources to maintain a fully independent feuilleton. By no means were all left-liberal, much less closely aligned with the DDP.[25] For example, both the Center party's Badischer Beobachter and the Socialist party's Bremer Volksblatt used the review as part of longer essays tailored to the needs of their respective parties.[26]

Almost all the provincial newspapers changed certain parts of the review to tone down its unmistakable disparagement of antisemitism. These papers substituted a sentence devoid of value judgments where the Berliner Morgen-Zeitung had attributed the novel's tragedy to "antisemitism" in its "ugliest form." "But the current emnity [Zeitläufige Feindschaft] with which the greater part of our contemporary youth regard the Jews, turns with vehemence against the corps brother of Semitic lineage [Ludwig Löwenstein]."[27] Some papers dropped the original review's last two affirmative sentences completely.[28] Two edited the review so heavily that there was no mention of the Jewish question at all.[29]

The prestigious, moderate-liberal Königsberger Hartungsche Zeitung (KHZ) approved the moral intent and the program of Brotherhood. However, Karl Herbert Kühn, who reviewed the novel for the KHZ, gave the book low marks as a work of art. Kühn even compared Bloem with the much-parodied Hedwig Courths-Mahler.[30] The KHZ, described by Thomas Mann as "the cultural paper of the Ostmark," plainly was unwilling to subordinate aesthetic considerations to political effectiveness.[31] Ironically, Ludwig Goldstein, the half-Jewish leader of the KHZ feuilleton, read and was enthralled by Bloem's novel, but only much later, after Hitler's seizure of power.[32]

It was the smaller, regional left-liberal papers that had the greatest appreciation of Bloem's art and message. The Neue badische Landeszeitung, the Mannheim organ of the DDP, praised the technical excellence displayed in Brotherhood as well as Bloem's efforts to combat the "senseless rages of the antisemites."[33] The Karlsruher Tagblatt described Bloem as a Dichter, a value-charged word connoting a high estimation of his art. The Karlsruhe paper dealt with the novel in a column dedicated to political affairs rather than in the literary supplement. It justified this unusual step by pointing to the especial relevance of the novel in the wake of Rathenau's assassination.[34] A long review in the Breslauer Zeitung (BZ) was even more generous in its accolades for Bloem's book. The BZ also mentioned the timeliness of the book's appearance in the light of Rathenau's murder. According to the BZ, the novel--due to its exciting plot, rich characterization, and multifaceted setting--was fascinating as well as educational reading. Brotherhood deserves the strongest attention, although "in particular one would gladly see some things handled differently." It would have been preferable, for example, if Bloem had unequivocally stressed the purely theoretical, unproven nature of the racial teachings. "But the discussion and the daring of the ideas give to the work a claim to a special place among recent belletristic literature."[35]

No newspaper had a higher opinion of the political importance of Bloem's novel than the apparently democratic Montagsblatt in Prague. The Montagsblatt played Brotherhood off against Dinter's Sin Against the Blood. In a long essay, Dinter's novel on racial shame, "the newest Bible of German-Aryan antisemitism," was attacked as a "miserable, clumsy piece of work . . . that merely on the basis of its hollow language scarcely merits being called a German book." Only the worst enemies of the German people could rejoice over the success of this book, which had poisoned the souls of thousands. As the great counterweight to Dinter's book, the Montagsblatt cited Brotherhood--"really one of the best German novels of the present"--by the "German National" writer Walter Bloem:

> A great question for the destiny of the tormented German Volk must be solved: Here Dinter--here Bloem! [Which] should triumph, the dark hatred of those who wish to erode the German Volk inwardly and to make [it] incapable of resistance against its enemy, or . . . the pure belief of those like Walter Bloem who wish to lead the German Volk through truth to brotherhood and a better future.

The Montagsblatt underlined the special relevance of Bloem's work for Germans in Bohemia, where the populace had turned on a part of itself, the Jews. Already, the paper reported, Bloem's book has converted a good number of the most recalcitrant anti-Jewish agitators in Bohemia. Everyone concerned with Germany's future must read and disseminate the book.[36]

Bloem's Brotherhood seems to have been largely ignored by the organs of the Social Democratic party (SPD) which like Germania and the great liberal dailies, the Frankfurter Zeitung and Vossische Zeitung, chose to ignore rather than pan a novel that embedded philosemitism and allegiance to the republic in a national conservative framework. Vorwärts, the central organ of the SPD, Germany's most potent democratic party, did not review the novel at all. Only in December 1924, on the appearance of another Bloem novel, The Land of Our Love, did Vorwärts note Bloem's readiness to support the republic.[37] The Socialist Volksstimme in Magdeburg, with a circulation of 45,000 in 1922, devoted a scant paragraph to Brotherhood, describing Bloem's attempt to work against engrained völkisch prejudices among the students. "The intention is in any case to be praised; whether it will succeed in reaching its goal one may doubt. The circles which Bloem wants to influence are not accessible to ethical admonitions."[38] The Socialist party's Bremer Volksblatt expressed similar skepticism about the likelihood of realizing the sunny future envisaged by Bloem. The völkisch movement had too strong a hold on academic youth. Yet, the Volksblatt wished the novel a great readership, "especially among the working youth."[39]

In the Deutsche Republik, Dr. Herbert Hirschberg welcomed Bloem's critique of the outmoded corps and defense of the Jews. Hirschberg also was impressed by Bloem's readiness to accept the fruits of the November Revolution--"In this recent poetic work the finally converted Walter Bloem--we ascertain it with joy--now also professes fully and completely [his loyalty] to the republic." Hirschberg noted the storm among the Pan-Germans aroused by Bloem's speech at the end of the war and commented that with more leaders like Bloem the war might have been won. Hirschberg also approved of Bloem's attractive portraits of the Löwensteins and his denigrating delineation of the Völkische.[40]

According to Bloem, neither he nor his book were supported by the republic's authorities. The Reich government, he reported in his autobiography, continued to view him as a militarist, nationalist, monarchist, and antisemite. As a result, his works were removed from the People's and school libraries.[41] There is no evidence that any republican party tried to distribute the novel.

It is worth briefly recording at this point the reaction to Brotherhood in politically non-aligned periodicals aimed at those with an advanced taste for or professional interest in belles-lettres. These periodicals were important because they influenced the middlemen of the literary business--critics, teachers, publishers, booksellers. The trade organ of the train station booksellers reprinted the basically positive review of Bloem's novel from the Berliner Morgen-Zeitung. The Literarischer Handweiser emphatically endorsed Bloem's fictional counter to antisemitism. One of the period's most influential literary journals, Das literarische Echo, published a summary of the novel by Arthr Brausewetter. Brausewetter clearly regarded Brotherhood as little more than cleverly contrived, crowd-pleasing entertainment. Less sympathetic still was the Deutsche Roman-Zeitung, an important purveyor of entertainment literature meant for the middle classes. The Roman-Zeitung found Bloem's "humane aims" admirable, but insisted that his oversimplified attribution of light to the Jews and dark to their enemies would be counterproductive. As hostile to the novel, although for totally nonpolitical reasons, was the Gross-Berliner neueste Nachrichten. This "Paper of the Berlin Society" demonstrated the total political irresponsibility of certain segments of the avant-garde by attacking Bloem's novel simply because its unflattering portraits of a pair of dancers had made artists "laughable."[42]

Jewish responses to Brotherhood were affected by how one balanced loyalties "to German nationalism and culture on the one hand and to Jewishness on the other."[43] Apparently, Zionists ignored altogether a novel that encouraged Jews to become fully assimilated German nationalists and that mentioned Zionism only as the option to which Jewish characters veered when they were most bitter and discouraged. Letters to Bloem from readers suggest, however, that his novel had a tremendous impact on the "national Jews." These Jews, no matter what their precise political or religious affiliation, stressed the high value of and their membership in the German nation. "National Jewish" readers closely identified with Ludwig Löwenstein, his deep love for Germany and his tragic fate. One such Jewish reader wrote Bloem that Brotherhood had touched her deepest inner life. "For I belong to those Löwensteins, who love their homeland with their whole soul and who are proud of their Germanness."[44] Another, having read the serialized version of the novel in the Israelitisches Familienblatt, wrote: "I feel as a Jew, who will never deny his Germandom, double occasion to preserve towards you a deep gratitude."[45] Erich Leyens, a much-decorated Jewish war hero, informed Bloem that Löwenstein was neither a fictional invention nor an isolated occurrence. Leyens gratefully reported to Bloem the enormous impact of Brotherhood. Leyens did warn that Bloem's attribution of anti-national qualities to the Jews might further rather than combat antisemitism.[46]

Even in the Third Reich, when Bloem himself had shifted his allegiance to Hitler, "national Jews" found Brotherhood a poignant statement of their own destiny. One Jewish youth recounted to Bloem how the coming to power of the Nazis had dashed his own career hopes and asked Bloem to take a stand for or against Brotherhood. "But why is Franconia today the whole of Germany, and why are there no more Eichholzes? Are the hundreds of thousands of Löwenstein destinies no longer worth having German men fight for them?"[47] Ludwig Goldstein, a half-Jew and for many years the feuilleton leader of the Königsberger Hartungsche Zeitung, read Bloem's book only after 31 January 1933. In late 1934, Goldstein wrote Bloem that

> already in the middle [of the novel] the deepest emotion gripped me, as I have only rarely experienced during the reading of a novel, and it became all the stronger the further I hurried to the end. . . . Permit one, who has always felt German to the core, but who is now tossed to the un-Germans as a half-caste, to say with hearty assertion that your book has made the deepest impression not only on him, but on his whole environs.[48]

One "national Jewish" organ was not as unequivocal in its reaction to Brotherhood as these enthusiastic individual readers. The K. C. Blätter, the organ of the "Kartell Convent," reviewed Brotherhood in August 1922. The "Kartell Convent" was the roof association of the Jewish student corps. Its very statutes demanded combat against antisemitism and for the political and social equality of the Jews. The Jewish corps united in the K. C. defined themselves as "national Jewish," and thus rejected both total assimilation and Zionism.[49] The K. C. was closely tied with the Central Union of German Citizens of the Jewish Faith (C.V.) "both in membership and ideology."[50] The K. C. Blätter welcomed Bloem's novel as an aid in the battle against antisemitism, saying "It is a warning for those tumbling into the abyss, a call to awaken for the indifferent."[51]

However, the K. C. Blätter added, there were single places from which one could wring a false meaning, and which therefore had to be criticized. The national Jewish-minded K. C. Blätter was particularly displeased by Bloem's contention that the Jews must be educated to the German "state idea." In reality, the K. C. organ scolded, the Jews have a far deeper love for the fatherland than the Völkische. Umbrage was also taken at Bloem's insistence on the full amalgamation of the Jews. Assimilation is only possible so long as it does not mean dissolution--differences and unique traits must be acknowledged and accepted.[52]

The organ of liberal Jewry, the Jüdisch-liberale Zeitung, reviewed Brotherhood at least twice. The first essay on the novel was written by Rabbi Dr. Dienemann and appeared on 1 September 1922. Dienemann took pleasure in the fact that a well-known author had dealt humanely with problems so often taken up in fiction by völkisch fanatics. Dienemann described Bloem's portrait of the corps as largely accurate and praised the novel's vision of a brotherhood based on will and desire rather than on race. Nevertheless, Dienemann contended, "praise and recognition may not make one blind to weaknesses and deficiencies. Some things are seen wrongly." Dienemann pointed to residual prejudices in Bloem's thinking and quarreled with the choice of a baptized Jew to represent Jews in general. The rabbi also criticized some of the psychological motivations attributed by Bloem to the Löwenstein family, such as the "yearning of the son of the desert, of the nomad for Germanic rootedness, limitation, and form." Dienemann refused to believe that a family like the Löwensteins, who had given up Judaism, would feel any obligation to stand up for Jewish rights. Above all, the rabbi was dismayed by Bloem's explicit contrast of Christ with Moses and Wotan, which smacked of the age-old identification of Judaism with hatred and revenge. Although Dienemann spent a great deal of ink on the novel's shortcomings, he did wish that it and many more like it could be spread to every Christian house.[53]

In February 1923, the monthly supplement of the Jüdisch-liberale Zeitung published a second endorsement of Brotherhood, less adulterated by qualifications. This second essay, by Alfred Auerbach, admitted that "it is painful to the Jewish reader, that Bloem represents the young fighter just as baptized." Yet Auerbach went on to explain away this defect as a novelistic technical necessity, for only a Christianized Jew could believably gain admittance to the antisemitic corps. Auerbach paid glowing tribute to Bloem the man, lauding the latter's healthy, Rhineland warmth. "We all have reason to thank our fellow German citizen in the best sense for his deed."[54] It should be added that the editorial staff of the Jüdisch-liberale Zeitung, shortly after Brotherhood's publication, actively sought a novella by Bloem on a Jewish theme for its feuilleton.[55]

Least sympathetic to Brotherhood among the Jewish organs was the Israelitisches Wochenblatt für die Schweiz. This Swiss weekly did credit Bloem with good intentions. It also gave its imprimatur to Bloem's fight against un-Christian racism and class superiority. But the weekly's reviewer, identified only as "M.," dwelt on the demerits rather than on the merits of Brotherhood. According to "M.," Bloem, like all non-Jewish writers since Freytag, had drawn impossibly blurred Jewish characters. "M." was also disconcerted by the way Bloem had played off Christ against the symbols of revenge, Moses and Wotan. But "M." was most concerned about the alternative set up in the novel by Hans Joachim--either pogrom to the end or total acceptance of the Jews. While Hans Joachim (and Bloem) saw the first alternative as immoral and impossible, "M." feared that the Völkische might well come to the opposite conclusion.[56]

The Israelitisches Familienblatt paid Bloem's novel the ultimate compliment by reprinting it in 1925-26. Earlier, in October 1922, the Familienblatt had carried a generally sympathetic review by Rabbi Dr. Dienemann. The Familienblatt occupied a neutral position among the Jewish factions.[57] As in his earlier article in the Jüdisch-liberale Zeitung, Dienemann found some things wrong with Bloem's novel: the representative role of a baptized Jew; the unrealistic flirtation of assimilationist Jews with Zionism. Yet, Dienemann again hoped that the book would be widely read. "In spite of [the defects], the noble way of thinking, which speaks out from the book, is splendid; it is humanity and love of fatherland."[58]

The Familienblatt serialized Brotherhood but only after the novel had been purged of the "defects" marked by Dienemann and other Jewish critics. On 24 October 1925, the Familienblatt informed the Grethlein concern that Brotherhood had to undergo some editing before it could be reprinted. The especial mentality of the paper's exclusively Jewish readership was given as the reason for these "unessential" changes.[59] Bloem, in a letter dated 28 October agreed to bow to the special needs of the Jewish paper, but insisted on being informed and allowed to approve of any changes in advance.[60] On 5 November 1925, the editors of Familienblatt sent Bloem a copy of Brotherhood with the projected changes penciled in. An accompanying letter explained and justified the changes.

The Familienblatt insisted in striking the depiction of Ludwig Löwenstein as baptized. "Otherwise the entire novel cannot be published by us. We stand upon the position that anyone who is baptized no longer belongs to Jewry [Judentum]." The Familienblatt also wanted to strike what it rightly regarded as essentially negative, stereotypic phrases and character traits. For example, the editorial staff asked to have a phrase describing Ludwig Löwenstein, "Jewish vanity and assumption of airs," changed to read simply "vanity." "It would certainly injure our readers very much if we would blame all Jews for the vanity of Löwenstein." The Familienblatt further demanded cuts and rewording that would spare the religious sensibilities of readers, "many of whom are strict orthodox [Jews]." The editors apparently found Bloem's continual identification of Christianity with brotherhood, combined as it was with the juxtaposition of Jesus with Wotan and Moses, to be especially likely to offend Jewish readers. The Familienblatt pointed out that the changes were minor, little affecting "the course, content, tendency [thesis], and style of the novel." Yet, the editors made it clear that their suggestions were "unconditionally necessary."[61]

Bloem seems to have accepted the changes without protest. In early December 1925, the Familienblatt announced the impending appearance of the novel in the next issue of the "Jewish Library," the paper's literary supplement. The editors hoped that Bloem's work would contribute "to overcoming the disastrous splintering predominant in the German Volk."[62] Shortly before, the Familienblatt had published a short essay by Bloem in letter form, entitled "A Word to Brotherhood," specially written to introduce the novel's serialization.[63] This letter reached a further audience when it was reprinted (on 24 December) in the CV-Zeitung, German Jewry's major organ for self-defense.[64] Oddly enough, the Nazi Der Weltkampf also printed the letter verbatim as proof of Bloem's political apostasy.[65]

In his letter to the Familienblatt, Bloem stressed his commitment to securing unity for the whole German Volk. Bloem underscored his own deep love for Germany. But he criticized the one-sided emphasis on nationalism, which had been carried to absurd extremes in the (First) World War.

> I am determined to develop my special quality as a German just as strongly and consciously as my [uniqueness] as . . . [a native of the Rhineland] . . . But beyond the national borders, I have learned to feel since the war and through it to be a member of mankind as well as of my collective Volk, and indeed first of all to be [a member of humanity's] . . . "western" culture group.

Reflecting the impress of Oswald Spengler's ideas on his thinking, Bloem added that all white men, not only the Germans, "must stick together in the struggle for our cultural goods against the threatening subversion through barbarism." Bloem proclaimed his animosity to antisemitism as a "retrogressive confusion, detrimental to culture and development." Indeed, everyone who took part in German spiritual and moral life was German, no matter what his faith or religion.[66]

The serialization in the Familienblatt ran to the spring of 1926 and reportedly was positively received by all camps of German Jewry.[67] The paper's editorial staff informed Bloem, on 1 April 1926, of its readiness "to publish a further work by you, insofar as it concerns itself with Jewish problems." The editors suggested to Bloem that he incorporate their changes in later editions of Brotherhood, geared for general consumption. In this way, the novel "would really deserve to be subscribed to by all circles of the German Volk, also by the Jewish. Such occasional sentences, which must be interpreted as unfriendliness, are however likely to make Jewish readers shy."[68] In the event, Bloem actually tried to incorporate the revisions made by the editorial staff of the Familienblatt in a new edition of Brotherhood planned in 1927. Only the tardiness of the Familienblatt in responding to Bloem's request for a listing of these revisions seems to have prevented the "people's edition" of 1927 from incorporating them.[69]

The reprint of "A Word to Brotherhood" in the CV-Zeitung (December 1925) inaugurated a period of mutual respect and friendly cooperation between Bloem and the Central Union of German Citizens of the Jewish Faith which was committed in equal measure to defense against antisemitism and "loyalty to Germany." Already in August 1924, the paper had praised Brotherhood, contrasting it with antisemitic novels like Fritz Halbach's Genosse Levi.[70] In July 1927, the CV-Zeitung solicited an article from Bloem for a special issue on the theme, "Influences of Jewry upon German Culture."[71] Bloem had to decline this invitation, since he had just returned from a trip around the world. But, in a letter of 18 July, he expressed his support for the goals of the Central Union. "Indeed you know that your statutes have my full approval and that I have the most lively interest in the final opening-up of a relationship between our Jewish and non-Jewish fellow citizens that will be worthy of both parts."[72] As a substitute for the solicited article, the Cv-Zeitung asked for and received permission to publish this letter by Bloem.[73]

On the occasion of Bloem's sixtieth birthday (which took place on 20 June 1928), the chairman of the Central Union sent a particularly warm congratulatory letter. Bloem replied in a fairly long note of gratitude: "On my way I have had to experience so much rejection and emnity from the various sides that it was a true refreshment of the heart for me to receive on this day of looking back so many voices which prove that I have not worked and struggled in vain." Bloem vowed to fight on against divisive forces and remarked that German Jewry had contributed to and would continue to further the German idea.[74] Two days after the birthday, Herbert Eulenberg (a novelist of some note and a convinced democrat) paid tribute in the CV-Zeitung to Brotherhood, with its "new German ideal for the future, the 'will to Volkheit,' that is the selfless love for all German citizens, whatever estate or belief they might be, to whatever class or race they might belong."[75]

Ironically, during the next months Bloem became embroiled in two disputes in the pages of the CV-Zeitung, the first triggered by the Eulenberg tribute. Eulenberg described how Brotherhood alienated part of Bloem's former public. Mistakenly, Eulenberg also reported that Bloem's own corps had taken back his ribbons (symbolizing revocation of membership).[76] A Jewish corps member, Fritz Josephtal, wrote Bloem asking whether Eulenberg's report was correct.[77] In a reply of 10 July, Bloem denied that either Teutonia at Marbug or Lusatia at Leipzig had taken away his ribbons. Bloem's letter to Josephtal explicitly affirmed a continued belief in the corps idea. Bloem also reconfirmed his readiness to stand by the political program outlined in his novel. Bloem authorized Josephtal to send this letter to the CV-Zeitung for publication.[78]

The CV-Zeitung sent the Josephtal letter to Eulenberg, who was quick to answer.[79] Eulenberg wrote that he was glad that Bloem had not lost his corps ribbons on account of Brotherhood. His mistaken report, Eulenberg explained, stemmed from rumors widely current in the Rhineland. However, Eulenberg stood by his condemnation of the antisemitic corps, and made known his doubts about Bloem's confidence in their capacity for brotherhood.[80]

Bloem replied to Eulenberg in a letter of 27 July to the CV-Zeitung. In this final epistle, Bloem justified his faith in the inner vitality of the corps; he attributed the unsavory features of the academic associations to time-bound, passing aberrations. He stated his hope that in the long run Brotherhood would plant the seeds for internal reform of the fraternities.[81] On 3 August, the CV-Zeitung published Bloem's letter to Josephtal, Eulenberg's reply, and an abbreviated version of Bloem's last word of 27 July.[82] The whole affair is of more than passing interest, since it stemmed not just from a mistaken report, but from fundamental political differences. In the final analysis, the dispute arose from completely opposed attitudes toward the corps and the social strata from which these fraternities drew their membership.

Also during the summer of 1928, Bloem published an article in the CV-Zeitung that drew fire from within Central Union circles. On 18 June, the CV-Zeitung asked Bloem for an article on his stance toward the Jews.[83] Bloem quickly wrote an essay entitled "Das Judentum im Weltbild." Bloem sent the essay to the CV-Zeitung on 23 July.[84] In a cover letter, he expressed his readiness to consider rewriting objectionable parts.[85] His article appeared, apparently unchanged, in the later summer.[86] In it, Bloem proclaimed that common ideals, not race or citizenship in a state, were the determinants of nation. Thus, Bloem contended, Jewry was itself a nation, since it was based on shared ideals. While a person could not change his race or culture, he could adopt a new nation by adhering to its common ideals.[87]

On 16 November, the CV-Zeitung published an article by Dr. H. W. Placzek, which was at least in part a confutation of Bloem's "Judentum im Weltbild." Placzek accused Bloem of a confusion of concepts.[88] Like the Eulenberg dispute, the argument over Bloem's essay stemmed from deep-seated political differences. Bloem's definition of nationhood--based on an idealist but not racist völkisch standpoint--was at variance with the liberal, statist definition of German citizenship. To the best of this author's knowledge, Bloem never again contributed to the CV-Zeitung. Quite possibly Bloem's experiences with the CV-Zeitung in the summer of 1928 heightened his awareness of the fundamental disparities between him and both the bourgeois democrats and liberal Jewry.

At any rate, Bloem was painfully aware of mixed reviews of his "brotherhood" novel in the republican and Jewish press.[89] He had unrealistically expected the book to be hailed with uniform enthusiasm by the press left of the DNVP. The actual reception bitterly disappointed him. On a number of occasions after 1933, he described with transparent displeasure how the "Ebert circles" had failed to support him.[90] He was enraged when the republican authorities, attacking him as "an antisemite, a monarchist, and a war-monger," took actions against his works. Bloem felt betrayed and isolated by the failure of the democratic press and authorities to push Brotherhood without reservation. "So I, who had bravely taken up the gauntlet for . . . [the German democracy], lost any protection from behind and ultimately stood abandoned and isolated, at least in public."[91] Bloem had striven to reconcile nationalists to the republic; he was appalled to find himself, "between the two stools." "From both sides," he wrote in answer to Rocholl in 1923, "I am in part spit upon, in part killed by silence."[92] In the long run, Bloem's discontent with the critics' reception of his book helped to weaken his resistance to the most virulent of right-wing viruses, anti-republicanism and antisemitism. In 1933, Bloem justified his renunciation of his own novel in a letter to a young Jew victimized by the Third Reich:

> My novel, Brotherhood, found in its time in no way the kind of reception among Jews which it might have expected. The great Jewish press [i.e., the great liberal dailies] as good as killed it by silence; the press of the rabbis [the actual organs of organized Jewry] made it clear to me that I understood nothing of Jewry, for baptized Jews were in general not Jews at all.[93]

Ironically, then, a book aimed at winning the German right for the republic helped ultimately to win its author for Hitler. The democratic press showed a characteristic lack of publicistic imagination in not pushing Bloem's novel hard. Only such a book was likely to convert völkisch and German Nationalist rank-and-file away from antisemitism and to at least tacit recognition of the republic.[94] Moreover, a golden opportunity to cement the allegiance of the nation's then most popular author to the republic had been missed. For his part, Bloem was shortsighted and politically immature in his failure to foresee and to accept criticism from groups and parties that did not share his faith in national conservatism, and hence in the future benign role of the fraternities. But the roots of the misunderstanding go deeper than publicistic unimaginativeness on the one side and hypersensitivity on the other. Neither Bloem nor the republican feuilletons fully understood that policy, class, and ideological differences were secondary to agreement on a constitutional framework that was, however imperfectly, grounded in and protective of certain fundamental moral and legal-political principles, including the proposition that men are created equal and endowed with certain inalienable rights. Neither side completely recognized that these important but secondary conflicts could be managed successfully within a social partnership dedicated to defending civilized public order.

CHAPTER 6

THE EROSION OF WALTER BLOEM'S REPUBLICANISM, 1922-1930

A series of personal and financial difficulties made Bloem all the more vulnerable to the storms unleashed by <u>Brotherhood</u>. Soon after the war's end, Bloem had made his home at the castle on the Sinn. Here he played the role of the "petty sovereign" with no little relish and was even looked upon by his neighbors as something of an aristocratic patriarch.[1] However, Bloem was soon disappointed in his dream of an idyllic country existence, given over to worry-free creativity. Especially depressing to Bloem was the effect upon his wife, Margarethe, and his two children, of her congenital hearing defect. Matters only worsened when Bloem's increasingly senile mother was taken into the household. Bloem's vital nature was unable to flourish under the pall of sickness.[2] A further source of unhappiness was the troubled marriage of his daughter, Eta (Margarete), to a Swiss newspaperman, the one-time editor of the <u>Deutsche Allgemeine Zeitung</u>. Ultimately (in 1928?), Eta would commit suicide; this would be a terrible blow to Bloem, who loved his daughter above all else.[3] By 1923, Bloem felt a deep sense of isolation at his castle:

> Therefore not much became of the "little kingdom." Even deeper the feeling of a gruesome alienation pressed upon my soul. In Berlin, I would have hoped to have been able to escape this accursed domesticity.[4]

This oppressive situation changed somewhat in 1923. Bloem's mother died in the spring. Soon afterwards, he divorced his wife Margarethe and married his cousin, Judith, whom he had long secretly loved.[5] Judith provided Bloem with the happy marriage for which he had long thirsted.[6] Yet the fact remains that Bloem's personal difficulties came to a head in 1922-23, preventing him from finding psychological refuge at home during the tempest aroused by Brotherhood. This lack of emotional security undoubtedly heightened the sense of isolation born in the wake of Brotherhood.

At the same time (1919-24), Bloem was plagued by financial troubles. When he bought his castle during the war, Bloem had a fortune of something between 1,000,000 and 1,500,000 marks in securities. Bloem had hoped that this money, earned by his pre-war novels, would forever free him from the need to write for monetary rather than purely artistic and moral--political purposes. But the inflation ate up his savings and all the more quickly because he had invested in paper rather than in real values. Even the castle was more a white elephant than a sound investment, since it was not readily resellable. Besides, Bloem had sunk huge, irretrievable sums into modernization of the castle. An attempt to create a rentable farming estate around the castle failed.[7]

Once more, Bloem had to write for his bread.[8] But the inflation undoubtedly reduced the earnings on his books. Sometime during the inflation (likely in early 1922), Bloem agreed to a temporary modification to his contract with Grethlein. According to this "supplementary contract," Grethlein no longer had to pay him for an entire edition as soon as it was printed. The honorarium on a printing was to be paid only when enough copies had been sold to warrant an order for a new printing. Only those copies already sold had to be paid for when a printing was not sold out by the balance day (30 June of each year).[9]

No doubt Bloem lost heavily in this arrangement. He received a percentage of the retail price fixed by the publisher, but some time after the book was sold. Thus his honorarium was greatly devalued during the interval between the book sale and the payment to Bloem. Bloem, like other provincial authors, probably suffered further loss due to the time span necessary for his check to arrive from Grethlein. There was much justice in complaints voiced by writers during the Weimar era that they had been harder hit by the inflation than either the booksellers or the publishers. Authors, unless paid in advance, simply received their cut later and thus after much devaluation.[10] By the time the currency was stabilized, Bloem's marketability had plummeted, largely on account of the after-effects of <u>Brotherhood</u>.

Bloem blamed the Weimar Republic for his monetary woes. As shown above, Bloem held the lack of support by the republican regime and its constituent parties partly accountable for his declining sales. Moreover, like most of his contemporaries, Bloem was unaware that the seeds of the great inflation had been sown by the wartime financing of the German government. He regarded, to the end of his days, the Weimar regime as responsible for inflating the currency to pay its debts at the cost of the Reich creditors.[11]

In the long run, these various troubles helped to undermine Bloem's resistance to the political mythology of the right. Yet Bloem adhered to the course charged in <u>Brotherhood</u>, at least until 1930.[12] As late as October 1929, Bloem could still write that "I uphold even today my novel <u>Brotherhood</u> completely, in every connection."[13] A letter of 2 April 1925, succinctly sums up the main features of Bloem's reluctant republicanism between 1922 and 1929. His experiences during the war at the head of the Field Press Office, Bloem wrote, had given him insights into the essence of the old, imperial regime. These insights had changed his political thinking. Thus he had welcomed the revolution, if not in its actual form, at least as an act of demolition of the Bismarckian Reich, as a necessary transitional stage of German development. The war had shown that only a strictly centralized nation headed by leaders of its choice could compete in the modern age. True, the Weimar constitution and the republic based upon it are insufficient and therefore in need of radical improvement. Furthermore, there is a need for outstanding "personalities," driven by an inner "call," to lead the nation. Yet, Bloem insisted, polemics against the existing system in favor of necessary changes should never go so far as to make government impossible by the constitutionally chosen leaders.[14]

Clearly, Bloem's loyalty to the republic had thin intellectual roots, completely aside from the pressure of personal difficulties and events. His republicanism had grown out of nationalism rather than out of an intense love of or enthusiasm for democracy. Bloem advocated cooperation with the Weimar Republic as the most expedient way to assist the resurgence of the Reich. But for him, the republic was a stage on the road to a more nationalist, more dynamically led state, rather than an end in itself. From 1918 on, there was an ever-present danger that Bloem would turn on the republic if it seemed to forsake the pursuit of national greatness or if a new, promising nationalist pied piper appeared on the scene. As early as the summer of 1922, just after the publication of Brotherhood, Bloem revealed the priority of nationalism in his thinking and his readiness to submit to the "superior leader."

> For my person, I may really claim that I, after all that I have done in life and creation for our fatherland, remain free from suspicion of wishing to favor any movement that follows other goals than the reconstruction and future greatness of the Reich. This fundamental engagement commands me not to make the task [of government and reconstruction] more difficult unnecessarily for those personalities of average stature with which the age has had to help itself for some time now. In the moment when the superior leader emerges, then believe you me, I will be the first who raises his banner in word and deed.[15]

Bloem remained politically isolated throughout the period 1922-30.[16] His political position did not coincide exactly with that of any major party or organization. And he was repelled by the top leadership of the few organizations with a platform roughly in line with his own views. Bloem had no knowledge of National Socialism or of Hitler before 1921.[17] The Beer Hall Putsch of 9 November 1923 had left him cold. Bloem did recognize that the Nazi program, which occasionally came to his attention after 1921, had a number of points in common with his own political outlook. But, Bloem would later recall of this period, the Nazi stance "toward Jewry naturally precluded any rapprochement of my efforts to the further development of this movement."[18]

Bloem did seriously flirt with the idea of joining the Young German Order (Jungdeutscher Orden or Jungdo).[19] Founded in 1920, the Jungdo was led by Arthr Mahraun. It was permeated with völkisch ideals, although

Mahraun explicitly rejected the antisemitism of the DNVP. "It was," Professor George Mosse writes, "structured along the lines of a medieval order of Germanic knights and sought to perpetuate itself as the future German nation, founded on principles of community and leadership." By the mid-1020s, the Jungdo had well over 130,000 members. Mahraun, in contrast to many of the Jungdo rank-and-file, ultimately agreed to parliamentary involvement, fusing his organization with the DDP in 1930 to form the State party.[20] The Jungdo actively tried to recruit Bloem. Mahraun sent one of his co-workers to Bloem with a multitude of political statements. Bloem signed these almost without change; he was temporarily enamored of the Jungdo. He even went so far as to meet with Mahraun in Berlin. However, two hours with Mahraun, whom Bloem found personally repellent, were enough to "cure" Bloem of his desire to join the Jungdo. The Stahlhelm also extended feelers to Bloem. Again, personalities played a greater role than ideology in keeping Bloem from ending his political isolation: "a chance meeting with Herr Seldte was sufficient for me to stay away from the Stahlhelm."[21]

Bloem, unable to play a role in any political organization, continued to seek to exert political influence through his pen. After publication of Brotherhood, Bloem agreed to write a popular history of the Great War for the Verlag Reimar Hobbing, the publisher of the Deutsche Allgemeine Zeitung. It took Bloem only four months to finish the voluminous manuscript of his The World Conflagration (German title: Der Weltbrand). The book, illustrated by Ludwig Dettmann, appeared in two large volumes in 1923.[22] Bloem's history balanced admiration for the embattled German nation with measured criticism of the wartime Reich leadership.[23] In his conclusion, Bloem addressed the problems of the early republic. He denounced hereditary monarchy for its dangerous concentration of power in the hands of a man chosen by the coincidence of birth. And he declined to support dreams of revenge. "For if we want to live, we must work together, that means live together, with the other peoples of the earth, therefore, with our enemies." German national feeling cannot depend on outer power or magnificence or on "the state form of hereditary monarchy."[24]

In his closing paragraphs, Bloem reiterated the chief themes of <u>Brotherhood</u>. Bloem would write much later that these paragraphs "included in all brevity a representation of the great transformation of my whole world view as the experience of the war had brought it to me."[25] Bloem contended in <u>The World Conflagration</u> "that the Germanization of our German-speaking but international-feeling proletariat is the prime mission of the immediate German future." Any attempt at national reconstruction without the workers "is an atavism, a fumbling back into a sunken past, is reaction in the most evil sense of the word, is as politically unwise as it is un-Christian and inhuman."[26] Once again, Bloem mixed a hard blow against antisemitism with uncritical acceptance of the notion that the Jews somehow lacked in national sentiment:

> And finally still another group of German citizens stands up, till now outside of the spiritual bonds of Germandom: the German Jew. The destiny of the proletariat is scarcely a century, the tragedy of the German Jews two-thousand years old. A nation--which through such a long history stamped an element of its <u>Volk</u> and economic body living and working in its midst with the stigma of an alien parasitism, and yet then still wonders that this element leaves something to be desired in national community feeling and sense of sacrifice--exhibits a political and human immaturity that has a parallel only in the naivety with which the representatives of the same backward opinion demand from the proletarian the joyful sacrifice of his blood and life without providing him in brotherly fashion, gladly and as a matter of course, with a full share of the goods of national freedom and civilization consonant with his national performance in peace and war.[27]

<u>The World Conflagration</u> was Bloem's last considerable success in the Weimar period. Forty-thousand copies went into print, despite the very high price of forty marks.[28]

Bloem continued to pursue political education in his novels and plays. He spent the winter of 1923-24 in Hamburg, where he witnessed a Communist uprising. Here he wrote <u>The Land of Our Love</u> (German title:

Das Land unserer Liebe). The novel was printed in the Hamburger Nachrichten before Grethlein put it out as a book in 1924. Bloem once described the book as a witness to his "socialist convictions."[29] The major theme of the novel was the need for reconciliation between the Bürgertum and the proletariat as the first step in national rebirth.[30] Bloem's attempt to further sublimination of political and social differences even prompted a favorable comment in Vorwärts.[31] However, the novel did not sell nearly as well as Bloem's earlier fiction, probably because its combination of nationalism and reconciliation pathos fit none of the Weimar Republic's political pigeonholes.[32]

In 1924, Bloem also published a play about the Great Elector, entitled Der Kürfürst. Bloem explained the motivation behind this play in his unpublished autobiography: "I wanted to show at least once how a writer [Dichter] could announce his protest against the war leadership of the late OHL [Supreme Command] without sinning against the genius of the nation." The play was something of an aesthetic experiment, combining rhymed verse and prose. The book version contained a dedication, "To the German Republic," in which Bloem exhorted the republic to remember the heroes of the German past. Reportedly, Bloem again drew fire from both supporters and opponents of the republic. Nationalists were incensed by the transparent attempt to play off the effective wartime leadership of the Great Elector against that of Ludendorff. Democratic critics looked upon Bloem's opening admonitions as opposition. Initially, the play appeared only at the City Theater in Rheydt, a small-town stage. Even after the play was rewritten entirely in prose, it appeared only on minor stages for one-night stands.[33]

In 1926-27, Bloem took a trip around the world, armed with a diplomatic pass from the German foreign office.[34] The immediate product of this journey was the travel book, Face of the World: A Book of Present and Future Humanity (German title: Weltgesicht: Ein Buch von heutiger und kommender Menschheit), which appeared in 1928.[35] The book described Bloem's itinerary to Soviet Russia, China, Japan and the United States. But its purpose was, at root, political.[36] Weltgesicht was the highwater mark of Bloem's republicanism; its leitmotif was "all men are becoming brothers."[37] Brotherhood was now posited as the goal of all mankind as well as that of Germany. According to Bloem, the machine age had bound the world together with a network of communications and a common experience. Now the world had to be unified politically and economically. "The fact [of] humankind must be ratified through a conscious decision and be set into effect through organization." Each state must give up a great part of its sovereignty.[38] Each man must become a good citizen of "the coming world state, All Menschland [literally, Pan-Humanityland]."[39] Christianity, freed of its confessional bickering, can provide the spiritual basis of a united humanity: "In Christianity, the world views of both hemispheres are accepted, reconciled, bound to the highest unity and perfection."[40]

Armed conflict between nations, as the Great War demonstrated, has become too terrible to contemplate. "Whoever experienced this war and did not become a 'pacifist'--he is incapable of working together in the coming humanity-state." Not that the Germans unilaterally have to give up the idea of self-defense. German disarmament must be contingent on a general renunciation of military hardware. "Therefore: pacifism if the others go along. So long as the others build tanks and bombers--so long militarism to the very bones!!" Bloem even confessed a love for the glory and romanticism of the wars of yore. "But," he hastened to add, "I lack the organ for the romanticism of the gas war." Thus, he felt, any attempt to overcome war, whether through the League of Nations or anti-war pacts, must be supported. Nor was domestic political violence to be tolerated. The clash of ideas and interests, whether within or between nations, had to be carried on without violence.[41]

Bloem's vision of international brotherhood by no means entailed the sacrifice of his national conservatism. He insisted that national peculiarities ought not to be buried in the world state, just as individuals should not be submerged in the various Völker. In his first chapter, Bloem gave his own definition of nationhood. Nations are not bound together by blood; that idea is "romantic illusion." Nor are they founded on a common culture. Rather, nations are communities of ideals pointing toward the future.[42] Such nations, Bloem wrote in his conclusion, "are personalities.

They will remain so eternally." Depersonalization is to be opposed whether it affects individuals or nations.[43] Internationalism is necessary in areas which can be safely standardized without loss to the inner life of men and Völker. But independent, unique modes of housing and clothing, national customs and art, along with the different ways of life and happiness, must be preserved. "Nationalism to the extreme, where personality values of the Völker are in question, which mean a piece of the soul, and therefore cannot be given up without the world thereby becoming poorer."[44]

Bloem's conservatism was reflected in his continued belief in the need for leadership by an elite dedicated to educating the masses. "It will not be possible in the long run to lead a nation without a nobility." Yet, this must be a nobility of talent and of spirit, not a caste or class. And this nobility must never forget its obligation to the people. It must never become hereditary, nor close itself to new members rising out of the whole Volk. The lower classes must be given the economic basis for a good life and the educational opportunities necessary for ascension into the elite.[45]

Germany will play a key role in the realization of the world state. Mankind's ideal must be the transformation "from the particularism of races, classes, petty nations, national states, confessions, continents to the unified state, humanity. . . . And this ideal--we want to acknowledge without any sense of superiority, but yet also with joyful pride--this ideal is a German, is the German ideal." German classic poets and idealist philosophers first dreamed of a united humanity.[46] However, this dream was initially disappointed by the Napoleonic conquests and most recently by the World War. As a result, German idealism had been split into three warring, ideological camps--the nationalist, the republican, and the Communist. "Each party encompasses and recognizes a part, a splinter . . . of the universal German idealism of our classical thinkers and poets."[47] Now Germans must find their way back to one another, reassembling exploded German idealism. All sides must sacrifice: "This also demands the sacrificium intellectus, the sacrifice of a part of our convictions deeply grounded as they still may be."[48] Hindenburg provided the greatest paradigm of such a sacrifice, "when he, the most faithful of all to king and Kaiser, not only swore the oath to the constitution of the republic, but has held [to it] with unheard-of and exemplary faith to the present hour." Germany, once it has created order in its own house through the "spirit of brotherhood," will be able to spread the glad tidings at the heart of German idealism to the whole world.[49]

Bloem's visit to the United States on his world trip also provided him with the inspiration and material for a projected novel trilogy about George Washington. The first volume, Son of His Land (German title: Sohn seines Landes), was completed during the winter of 1927-28 at his castle. It was published in 1928 by the nationalist Köhler concern. The second volume, Hero of His Land (German title: Held seines Landes), appeared in 1929. Bloem viewed Washington through the prism of national conservatism. For him, Washington was the leader qua hero, at once the finest product and father of his nation. Son of His Land was translated into English and published by Harper and Brothers. Harper ultimately pulled out of a contract for the American editions of the second and third volumes. Much later, Bloem rather absurdly attributed this to what he called the then growing alliance between England and the United States.[50] At any rate, this experience helped convince Bloem that nationalist German authors were being purposely hindered from finding a market abroad.[51] Failure to find an American publisher for his last two Washington novels may have made Bloem susceptible to the myth of Jewish cultural hegemony. In late 1929, a lecture by Bloem, "German Dissension and Jewry," revealed that this myth had crept into his thinking about the Jewish question.

Indeed, the years 1928-29 were disappointing ones for Bloem, completely aside from the fate of the Washington trilogy. Bloem was disappointed by the national response to his sixtieth birthday on 20 June 1928. "The agitation of my enemies on the right and left had done its work," he later complained.[52] The controversies with contributors to the CV-Zeitung, described in the preceding chapter, must have added to Bloem's discomfiture.

More significant was the fact that Bloem's declining income made it necessary to sell his castle. Perhaps in mid-1929, Bloem sold his castle to a government-backed consortium, which turned it into a youth hostel. Bloem estimated that he retrieved about only one-tenth of his investment.

Only 150,000 marks remained of the 1,500,000 brought in by Bloem's books "until the great turning point of <u>Brotherhood</u>." The move out of the castle on the Sinn meant a precipitous decline in Bloem's standard of living. He had to sell off much of the art used to decorate the castle, as well as half of his six-thousand volume library. Unwisely, Bloem put the proceeds from the castle into I. G. Farben stock. A few weeks later, Germany was engulfed by the general world depression heralded by the crash of the New York Stock Exchange in October 1929. The tattered remains of Bloem's once considerable wealth plunged from 270 to 90 marks per share.[53]

Bloem's disappointment in 1928-29 by no means immediately undermined his republicanism. Indeed, he reaffirmed his allegiance to the program laid down in <u>Brotherhood</u> on 25 October 1929.[54] But a lecture given just over three weeks later bore witness to Bloem's growing susceptibility to right-wing propaganda. On 17 November 1929, Bloem spoke on the Jewish question at the tenth anniversary celebration of the Hamburg local of the "Patriotic Association of Jewish Front Soldiers." Grethlein published the lecture shortly afterwards as a book, <u>German Dissension and Jewry</u> (German title: <u>Deutsche Zwietracht und Judentum</u>).

Bloem's speech discussed the interconnections between the "Jewish question" and what he saw as the prime political requirement of the time, German national unity.[55] The lecture was a criticism and admonition to both sides, the antisemites and the Jews. On the one hand, Bloem detailed the disastrous effects of anti-Jewish discrimination. On the other, he raised a series of criticisms of Jewry drawn from the arsenal of the antisemites. Of course, Bloem had mixed defense of the Jews with antisemitic modes of thought even in <u>Brotherhood</u>. But in the novel, the philosemitic tendency was predominant. Now, however, Bloem's emphasis had shifted. In "German Dissension and Jewry," he placed the burden of blame for the allegedly unsatisfactory German-Jewish symbiosis on the Jews. Unwittingly, Bloem had fallen victim to and was now propagating the myth of Jewish cultural, economic and political hegemony.

Bloem opened his lecture with a discussion of the need for national unity. Disunity, he claimed, had been Germany's Achilles's heel for many centuries. The Jewish problem was inextricably bound up with the larger, vital question of national unity. Anti-Jewish discrimination was largely responsible for the failure to liquidate the Jewish problem as a cause of dissension during the nineteenth century. The Jews would have melded without friction into the German nation if cultural, social, and human equality had followed formal emancipation.

True, the invisible ghetto walls disappeared temporarily in the glorious days of August 1914. The Jews volunteered en masse for combat. But they were soon disillusioned by the unjust continuation of discrimination denying them equality of treatment and promotion. One can readily understand why the Jews lost enthusiasm for military service, why they gravitated to safe base camps, why they may have been guilty for the final collapse.[56] Thus Bloem rendered his condemnation of earlier anti-Jewish measures all but worthless by coupling it with an uncritical parroting of some of the most damaging antisemitic charges.

Bloem explained to the Jewish war veterans why he had defended the Jews in the past, even though this had left him open to attacks from the whole spectrum of non-Jewish Germans. Genuine national-mindedness, he proclaimed, does not mean rejection of everything that does not coincide with one's own nationalist program. Rather, it manifests itself in the struggle against everything that separates different groups of the Volk from one another. "What I wrote and said against unjust slighting of Jewish fellow citizens and comrades, what I am saying today, that I said and am saying from national-mindedness!"[57] Bloem stated that he was neither a philosemite nor an antisemite. "I am a German and only from this standpoint do I regard the problem of the German Jews."[58]

Bloem addressed the Jewish war veterans as comrades, as paradigms of what he wanted all Jews to become. "Whoever acknowledges your association, also acknowledges by this very fact the great German fatherland."[59] Now, Bloem told the veterans, he would openly say "what we non-Jews have on our mind against the German Jews."[60] At the same time, he cautioned that his comments did not apply to his present audience and expressed the hope that his listeners would "carry this way of thinking out into the Jewish souls still standing far from our viewpoint."[61]

The Jews as well as the Germans, Bloem argued, had contributed to the failure of total amalgamation. The Jews had developed, during the long years of suppression, certain qualities (like the lack of moderation) that are undesirable if understandable. After all, the great wave of antisemitism must have grounds. The Jews, often the victims of national passion, have with some reason been drawn to internationalism. Admittedly, the effort for international reconciliation is vital to the future of the human race. But, there are--and the Jews must never forget this--national values that the German Volk cannot give up without betraying its inner self. The Jews are working too quickly and with tainted weapons even in respect to those national values that will ultimately have to be sacrificed for international fusion.[62]

At the heart of Bloem's argument was his final acceptance of the myth of Jewish cultural predominance. Undoubtedly, Bloem's own failures on the stage, the declining sales of his books, as well as his inability to find publishers abroad had worn down his hitherto relative immunity to this myth. "You all know," he told the Jewish veterans, "in how strong a measure the Jewish intellectuals have intruded themselves in all the leadership positions of our public life." This cultural hegemony stems partly from a high level of accomplishment. But reciprocal aid by Jewish intellectuals and suppression of non-Jewish culture has played a major role. The theaters of Berlin and hence of the nation are almost without exception in Jewish hands. Jewish overlordship has resulted in a stage repertoire made up mostly of foreign works. Jewish cultural predominance poses a threat not only to the national spirit of Germany, but also to that of all Western peoples. Sooner or later, these peoples will be driven to fearful counter-measures.[63]

Bloem also echoed the explosive antisemitic charge that the Jews had come up best in the "general collapse of German well-being" after the war. The widest circles of the Volk believed that only the Jews had benefited from the war. Bloem conceded that such generalizations were not altogether just. "However, it is hardly necessary to emphasize that such a mood of the Volk is not merely to be attributed to demagogic agitation." Bloem also charged individual Jews, if not Jewry as a whole, with being perhaps chiefly responsible for the sinking of public morality made manifest by recent, gruesome cases of corruption.[64] Perhaps Bloem's financial woes, capped by the incipient depression, had made him receptive to the antisemitic image of the Jews as immoral profiteers.

Bloem did not exactly defend monarchism in his lecture. Yet, he accused the Jews of wounding the sensibilities of those worthy groups of Germans for whom the birth of the republic had been an inutterable catastrophe. These groups were incensed by the fact "that this whole development had been intellectually founded by Jewish theoreticians, frequently led by Jewish leader-personalities, and greeted with enthusiasm by the great majority of the Jewish Volk comrades." Small wonder that great segments of the German people regarded the November revolution as the work of the Jews.[65]

What, Bloem asked rhetorically, can the one-time Jewish front soldiers do? First, he answered, you must understand antisemitism. "You must grasp that it represents a defensive movement, which must be taken very seriously, of the German Volk-soul against an exaggeration of the Jewish power of expansion unchained through the emancipation."[66] The swastika is more than the symbol of vulgar, demagogic bullies. It is the symbol of a spontaneous uprising by Germans determined to protect the goods of the nation. A movement like this could not have arisen without guilt on the Jewish side.

Having grasped the essence of antisemitism, the Jewish war veterans must continue to do exactly what they are doing, with their total "allegiance to Germandom [Bekenntnis zum Deutschtum]."[67] You, Bloem told the veterans, must forbid other Jews from carrying on their undermining activities. You must renounce those Jews who have only hatred and scorn for the pious love of the German Volk for its great past, its heroes, and its heroic world view. Ultimately, all Jews must become Germans inwardly. This does not mean renunciation of Judaism, but commitment to German culture, history, and destiny. "Then, however also only then, will you and your racial companions succeed in overcoming antisemitism in the whole world. It will disappear because no defense, no counter-measures will be necessary any longer." If Germans are to be saved from the present state of confusion, a spirit of understanding, of pardon, of compromise, and of sacrifice must stem from your circles. Prove, Bloem pleaded, through good will and loyalty to Germany that his rejection of antisemitism has been the right course.[68]

Thus Bloem had stepped across the thin, blurred line dividing his earlier brand of philosemitism from cultural-political antisemitism. Aside from his continued rejection of anti-Jewish legislation, there was now little to distinguish his position from the national conservative antisemitism of men like Wilhelm Stapel, Gustav Pezold, and Hans Grimm. Except for racism, Bloem had accepted the whole panoply of antisemitic charges and stereotypes with only marginal reservations. And he had even conceded the rightness of the worst kind of antisemitism, that of the Hakenkreuzler (i.e., that of the Nazis). The Jewish problem could only be resolved if Jewry became national conservative. Clearly, this approximation to the dominant völkisch conservative position on the Jewish question cleared away a chief barrier to Bloem's realignment in the next few years with the nationalist mainstream. This process was hastened by the neglect of the published lecture by the liberal press and by the hostility toward it in Jewish organs. Bloem took this as proof that national-minded Jews were and would remain a small minority. Thus he could rationalize his switch to support of virulently antisemitic parties.[69]

CHAPTER 7

BACKGROUND TO THE DEATH OF WALTER BLOEM'S REPUBLICANISM:
THE OPPOSITION IN THE PROTECTIVE ASSOCIATION OF GERMAN WRITERS (SDS)

Walter and Judith Bloem moved back to Berlin after the sale of their castle. At first, they rented a small apartment in Potsdam. Later, in the fall of 1932, they found more suitable quarters in a five-room story in the Budapester Strasse in the Old West section of Berlin. The return to the Reich capital marked the beginning of a new period of political involvement for Bloem, culminating in a decisive turn to the right.[1] In late March 1933, Bloem would point to the move from the castle on the Sinn as a watershed in his post-war struggle to solve the riddle of German destiny:

> So long as I lived at my castle in Franken, the final understanding of the German development remained closed to me. About 1930, the darkness of this lonesome struggle began to lift. I returned to Berlin. A new, stubborn struggle set in. I <u>gradually</u> had to understand that the second enemy of our future was "internationalism." The reconciliation of Völker is a utopia, until we Germans have completely unified ourselves within, secure in form and thought, and determined on the most unbending self-preservation.[2]

The key word in this passage is "gradually." For Bloem publicly entered the lists for the anti-republican right only in mid-1932. Of course, Bloem's philo- semitism and stance toward the radical völkisch movement had been watered down even before 1930. Moreover, his reintegration into the upper-middle classes in Berlin helped to reawaken dormant nationalist ideas and prejudices. Pre-war friendships were reopened in 1930-32. Once more, Bloem could attend the monthly meetings of the alumni associations of his old student corps. Bloem again became active in the four officers' associations to which he belonged. Through a friend, he even gained admittance to the socially prestigious Christlich

Brandenburgische Tischgesellschaft von 1817. Bloem formed contacts at the society's monthly gourmand meals with noted representatives of the most variegated professions. Yet, even in January 1932, Bloem was still regarded as a man between the political stools. Experiences within the leading writers' associations proved decisive in Bloem's turn to the antirepublican right in 1932. It was within the narrower compass of the writers' organizations that Bloem became enmeshed in the political maelstrom of depression Germany.[3]

Bloem had been a leader before World War I in the pioneering efforts of writers--increasingly aware, as Roy Pascal puts it, of their professional solidarity as a distinct "social grouping"--to organize in defense of their economic and legal interests.[4] Bloem had been a cofounder and the first General Secretary of the Association of German Playwrights. Indeed, he had coauthored the associations's statutes with Arthur Dinter. Bloem had also helped to found the Protective Association of German Writers (Schutzverband der Deutschen Schiftsteller or SDS) in 1909. He had been an original member of the main Executive Committee, the governing body of the SDS. Now, almost immediately after his return to Berlin, Bloem resumed his activities in the writers' associations. He accepted an invitation to rejoin the Main Executive Committee of the SDS, the most important of these organizations. Bloem also assumed leading positions in the Cartel of German Lyricists and the Association of German Novelists. Moreover, he soon joined the German section of the international PEN-Club.[5]

The Marxist literary historians, Friedrich Albrecht and Alfred Klein, have, through a combination of documentation and commentary, traced the internal struggles within the most important of these writers, organizations, the Protective Association of German Writers. Their "Der Kampf der Opposition im Schutzverband Deutscher Schriftsteller (1931-1933)," chapter IV of Aktionen, Bekenntnisse, Perspektiven, pictures Bloem as an agent of the coming Third Reich in the SDS. Their selection of documents conveys the impression that Bloem, at the head of a nationalist opposition of Arbeitsgemeinschaft, pursued a single-minded, right-wing program within the SDS, consciously designed to render the association impotent in the face of rising fascism. The conservatives and reactionaries in the SDS, with Bloem playing a pivotal role, joined with the republican parties to frustrate the Communist-led opposition's attempts to turn the Protective Association into a truly democratic, anti-fascist union. Claims by Bloem and his ilk to be defending the original, purely professional and thus unpolitical character of the SDS were part of a smokescreen meant to hide fascist political aims. In short, Albrecht and Klein have resurrected for the special case of the SDS the Communist notion of a "fascist front," extending from the Nazis to the SPD (the so-called Social Fascists).[6] Old socio-political myths, like old soldiers, never seem to die; sometimes they even fail to fade away. This tapestry of the internecine battles in the SDS--woven out of documents, comments, and an introductory narrative--has been taken over virtually intact by the West German Hans-Albert Walter in the first volume of his monumental Deutsche Exilliteratur.[7] The Klein-Albrecht interpretation adopted by Walter is faulty in several respects. Therefore, a fresh sketch of the history of the SDS opposition is necessary for a more accurate picture of Bloem's political activities and development.[8]

The Protective Association was established, with Bloem as a cofounder, in 1909 as a professional organization of writers. It was the first comprehensive writers' organization in Germany, including novelists, poets, dramatists, journalists, translators--in short, all those who made a living with their pen. The SDS immediately set out to draw all possible men of letters into its ranks. By 1918, its organization extended almost everywhere in Germany. Headed by a Main Executive Committee, the SDS was divided into Gaue (districts) and Ortsgruppen (locals). Yet, Berlin remained the Protective Association's center of gravity. Both the business office and the largest Ortsgruppe were located in the Prussian and Reich capital.[9] By late 1931, the Berlin Ortsgruppe had 900 out of a total Reich membership of 2,500.[10] The goals of the SDS, laid down in its statutes, were the protection, representation, and furtherance of the economic, legal and spiritual interests of its members. In November 1918, the Protective Association, reacting to the growing power concentrations in the realms of the production, sale, consumption and censorship of literature, began to style itself a union: the Protective Association of German Writers, e.V. (Union of German Writers).[11] In the early republic, this writers' union vigorously battled against the censorship instituted by reactionary bureaucrats and police officials.[12]

The SDS was founded as a politically neutral organization. It was set up to protect all writers, whatever their philosophical, religious or political persuasion. Even a writer like Alfred Döblin, who advocated political activism for intellectuals, opposed turning the SDS into a political forum.[13] Kurt Tucholsky criticized the SDS in the <u>Weltbühne</u> during 1921 for too close ties to the government and for failing to come to grips with the basic conditions underlying the misery of writers. Yet, even he upheld the unpolitical tradition of professional solidarity. According to Tucholsky, "a publishing house contract of the Count Ernst zu Reventlow and one of mine are legally and economically one of a kind. What we create by the lamp is another thing. Outside we are pushing wares." Writers, so ran Tucholsky's argument, have identical economic interests; thus to win their rights they must hang together regardless of their various ideological orientations.[14]

Tucholsky and the founders of the SDS were probably right. Retention of the purely economic and professional character of the Protective Association was the <u>sine qua non</u> of a unified front of writers. To be sure, the SDS had to enter the political arena as an organization to battle censorship and to influence legislation affecting writers. This kind of intervention would inevitably be colored by political tactics and philosophy. For example, a commitment against censorship would inevitably draw on the ideas and formulations of liberalism. An effective fight against censorship would require cooperation with particular political parties. Nonetheless, the SDS could not pledge permanent allegiance to a particular political party or ideology. Such politicization of the politically multicolored SDS meant inevitable fragmentation. Arnold Zweig, chairman of the SDS in the late twenties, foresaw such a fate for the SDS in 1930, just when the political struggles within the association were beginning to gather steam. Zweig was one of the great political novelists of his age, and he insisted on political activism in the public arena. However, he rightly pointed out that such activism had to be restrained enough within the association to permit the cooperation of its differentiated membership: "to politicize it [the SDS] means to paralyze it."[15]

Yet political controversy raised its head in the SDS in the mid-twenties. The vanguard of politicization within the SDS was a group of Communist writers. Their base of operations was Berlin. Berlin, the cultural heart of Germany, was the center of Communist belles-lettres. Most of the writers in Berlin aligned with the KPD had begun to involve themselves in the Berlin Ortsgruppe of the Protective Association about 1924. Within the Ortsgruppe and at the annual main assemblies of the SDS, the communist literateurs pushed their standpoint. According to them, the iniquities of the German literature industry stemmed from the existing social and economic system. Only the proletarian revolution could overthrow the existing social structure and thus alleviate the distress of men of letters. "Not less," the Communist writer Leo Lania wrote in 1926, "but more politicization is necessary in the SDS."[16]

The first relatively successful offensive of the Communists within the SDS seems to have taken place in early 1926. At a demonstration to protest the distress of German writers, Ernst Toller and Berta Lask pointed to the objective social conditions underlying the poverty of writers and charged the "bourgeois ideology" with blocking a unified front to end this misery. The majority of the demonstration accepted, over the objections of the SDS chairman, Theodor Heuss, a resolution against the idemnification of the former ruling princes. This was a clear violation of the Protective Association's tradition of political neutrality; the referendum on compensation for the expropriated properties of the princes, scheduled for 20 June 1926, was then a hotly contested issue.[17] Leading elements of the executive committee of the Berlin Ortsgruppe tried to mobilize a front against this transparent attempt to force a partisan stance on the SDS. "We can," they proclaimed on 2 March, "only stop the falsification of the true mood of our Ortsgruppe, we can only conquer the minority who wish to press the SDS to give up its political neutrality, if all friends of this neutrality stand by us."[18]

Tension between the writers grouped around the Communists in the Berlin Ortsgruppe and the Main Executive Committee continued to grow. Something akin to a storm broke out when Heuss, chairman of the SDS, foolishly voted in his capacity as a DDP Reichstag deputy for the Schmutz- und Schundgesetz (Filth and Trash Law). This measure was ostensibly aimed at the protection of youth from pornography. Many German writers, including some of the most prominent, opposed the Schmutz- und Schundgesetz as a deadly step against freedom of the press. These fears were well founded; right-wing officials during the early twenties had often moved against politically or philosophically uncomfortable literature on the grounds that it endangered public morality. Heuss's vote in the Reichstag did not affect the stance of the SDS. The Protective Association joined a front of writers' organizations against the law. Nevertheless, Heuss's failure to vote against the law infuriated many in the Berlin Ortsgruppe. On 10 December, the Berlin local demanded not only Heuss's resignation as chairman, but also his expulsion from the SDS. Heuss did resign, but the Main Executive Committee, pointing to a member's right to defend his personal opinion, refused to expel him. Communist members of the Berlin Ortsgruppe seem to have played a significant role in the attack on the law and thus on Heuss's Reichstag vote.[19]

The Heuss affair was the high point of Communist-led efforts to politicize the SDS before 1930. The deep-rooted aversion to political conflict within the Protective Association proved too strong in the relatively stable late twenties. Besides, the Communists seem to have had no program for the SDS in tune with writers' needs during these years.[20] Politicization of the SDS could come about only if (1) writers aligned with the KPD formed a tighter organization; (2) if the Red authors could devise a program meeting the actual needs of writers; (3) there was a downward turn in the economic and political climate.[21]

During the late twenties, the Communists did lay the organizational basis for an effective Literaturpolitik both within and outside the SDS. Communist artists, including literati, had begun to organize as early as 1924, when a Red Group was formed. This Red Group was dedicated to making propaganda through literary works, pictures and stage productions. Among its goals were the ideological and practical education of Red artists, the undermining and neutralization of bourgeois writers, the utilization of bourgeois art exhibitions for propaganda purposes, and the fight against counter-revolutionary culture.[22] Communist writers would pursue the same or similar goals in the SDS right up to 1932. KPD efforts to turn various art forms to political account bore fruit even in the mid-twenties. By October 1927, for example, the Reich Commission for the Supervision of Public Order and News could report that "the proletarian stages . . . represent an uncommonly effective propaganda and agitational means for the KPD and the Communist world view."[23]

Yet, a new stage in the history of communist belles-lettres began with the formation of the League of Proletarian-Revolutionary Writers. In March 1927, the 11th Party Congress of the KPD showed a heightened interest in literature as a political weapon by passing a resolution encouraging belletristic contributions to the Communist press. At the same time, a Proletarian Feuilleton News Agency was authorized as a "press service for the cultural pages of the party's publications." Johannes Becher, who rocketed to prominence among Communist circles during his trials for literary high treason (1925-28), headed the agency until its demise in 1929.[24] In November 1927, Becher attended the First International Congress of Revolutionary Writers at Moscow. There the International Office of Proletarian and Revolutionary Writers was founded. Becher became a member of the Executive Committee. Plans were laid at Moscow for organizations of Communist writers in the various countries represented in the Third International. In Germany, these plans were carried out by an Action Council of Proletarian-Revolutionary Writers to which Johannes Becher, Kurt Kläber, Egon Erwin Kisch, Karl Grünberg and Berta Lask belonged. On 19 October 1928 their efforts bore fruit with the foundation of the League of Proletarian-Revolutionary Writers.[25]

The league was styled a supra-party organization, but it pledged allegiance to the political line of the KPD.[26] According to the founders, the league should represent a

> comradely association, an abode of criticism, of clarification, [should] be a defensive means against censorship and

justice, and [should] give advice and help in questions of the field of impact and of sales; above all, it should also create a very tight relationship to the working masses.[27]

The league, while not disregarding economic problems altogether, refused to be a "substitute union [Gewerkschaftsersatz]." Indeed, it expected "from all its members that they organize themselves professionally as well as politically." In short, "Proletarian-revolutionary" writers were encouraged to join or remain active in organizations like the SDS. The league itself would concentrate on its main, cultural-political mission.[28]

The proletarian writers' association included middle-class intellectuals and even products of the upper class, as well as real proletarians. "Proletarian-revolutionary" was synonymous with Communist rather than with working-class origins:[29] By late 1931, the league was the second largest group in the International Vereinigung revolutionär Schriftsteller, with 350 members. Economic privation seems to have been a common denominator of the membership. Only 1 percent were true writers with a passable income. Twenty percent were unemployed; of the remaining 80 percent, the greatest part had an income considerably below the minimum needed for existence.[30]

In the summer of 1929, the League of Proletarian-Revolutionary Writers decided to publish its own literary monthly, Die Linkskurve. "The editorial board, headed by Becher," Werner Angress reports, "consisted of writers fully committed to Communism: Kurt Kläber, Ludwig Renn, Erich Weinert, Andor Gabor (until April 1930), and his replacement, Hans Marchwitza." The Linkskurve aimed to create a mass literature as a propaganda weapon for the KPD.[31] Becher spelled out the journal's purpose in the first issue. He condemned the bourgeois writers for degrading literature to "a harmless parlor game." The middle-class Dichter has declined "to create history." Each artist must take a stand in the class struggle; even silence is a form of commitment. As for proletarian-revolutionary literature, it "sings class love and class hate." This literature has its own special political impact. "Art is for us a highly responsible and dangerous thing. It is a breakthrough, it pierces and drums upon people there, where, often untouched by the political struggle of the day, the emotional masses lay concealed."[32] Such literature, Becher wrote a few months later, must be put into as many hands as possible.[33] Linkskurve achieved a circulation of seven thousand copies by 1931 and seems to have been rather widely read.[34]

The proletarian writers' league and its journal did make a concentrated effort to encourage the consumption and production of Communist belles-lettres. High priority was given to creating a "proletarian mass novel." In May 1930, Kurt Kläber outlined in Die Linkskurve a program for developing widely circulated, politically effective fiction. Kläber exhorted Communist writers to fill a crucial gap in proletarian letters by producing "the novel of the factory and the novel that lies not more than eight till ten years behind the events of the moment." An even more important problem than producing Communist Zeitromane is to find buyers for them. Workers must be made aware of the value of the novel as a political weapon. Then they will value content more than appearance, buying cheaper paperback rather than expensive bound editions. This will enable them to afford more books, increasing circulation, and thus lowering prices. Once the proletarian novel becomes cheaper, it can be a useful tool in breaking the ranks of Catholic and SPD workers. Kläber announced at the end of his article that cheap proletarian "mass novels" were already being prepared. "Therefore, the attacks upon the new and old proletarian reader strata can already begin in one or two months."[35]

In line with Kläber's program, monetary prizes were used to stimulate the creation of proletarian novels.[36] Communist publishing houses--led by the Internationaler Arbeiterverlag, the Malik Verlag, and the Agis Verlag--strove to fill the order for cheap Red novels. The Internationaler Arbeiterverlag put out two especially influential novels series: the "International Worker's Novel," which relied heavily on translated Russian fiction; and the "Red-One-Mark Novel," which proffered a native German ware. Linkskurve introduced the latter series with much fanfare.[37] The first "One-Mark Novel," Sturm auf Essen by Hans Marchwitza, appeared in late 1931 and within four weeks reportedly sold a healthy fifteen thousand copies.[38] The series planned to offer a new work of fiction every month.[39] Linkskurve made every effort to stimulate demand through reviews and advertising. Proletarian novels, like other Communist literature, were disseminated at party meetings and educational gatherings as well as through reprints in newspapers.[40] Such books likely stocked the Marxists Workers' Library in Berlin, founded with four-thousand volumes in the summer of 1930.[41] Efforts by the League of Proletarian-Revolutionary Writers to expand the circulation of Communist literature were a great success, if we can believe the figures given in Die Linkskurve. While the total production of German books dropped from 1928 to 1931, proletarian book production rose from ca. 1,200,000 to ca. 10,900,000.[42] In October 1931, Becher could report: "The proletarian-revolutionary literature of Germany has achieved great things: it has constituted itself as literature; from a literature of single comrades, a literary movement has emerged in the course of a relatively short time (1927-1931)."[43]

Were these efforts to organize writers and to create a mass, "proletarian-revolutionary" belles-lettres dedicated to blunting the rise of National Socialism? The answer to this question will go far in establishing or disproving the Marxist theory that politicization of the SDS along Communist lines was the best hope of turning that organization into a dynamic instrument in the fight against fascism.

In 1928-29 the Soviet dictator Stalin broke with Nikolai I. Bukharin and the right wing of the Russian Communist party. This brought about a sharp leftward turn in the Comintern (the Communist or Third International). In Germany, this new course seemed vindicated by the onset of the Great Depression, which seemingly spelled the impending end of capitalism. "The Third International [and thus the KPD] maintained . . . that world capitalism had entered its final crisis, which would automatically drive the masses toward Communism."[44] Allegedly opposed to the imminent victory of Communism was a united "fascist" front, extending from the Nazis through Heinrich Brüning to the SPD. The SPD was now branded as the worst enemy of the proletariat, since the Social Democrats "were delaying the process of capitalist disintegration" by defending the bourgeois state. Once again, the Social Democrats were tarred by the KPD as "Social Fascists." The Communists, rather than cooperate with the

SPD leadership against the Nazis, sought to win over the Socialist rank-and-file in a so-called united front from below.[45] The "National Fascists," the Nazi movement, were marked out as enemies of the workers. Yet, the threat posed by Hitler was obfuscated by the practice of labeling any group disliked by the KPD as fascist. Indeed, the KPD even subscribed to the fatal theory that Hitler's appointment as Reich Chancellor was necessary, since it would automatically bring about the collapse of the old order.[46]

The "literary movement" centered on the League of Proletarian-Revolutionary Writers did even less than the KPD to combat the true fascists. As Istvan Deak puts it, Die Linkskurve "outdid its own party in ignoring the 'National Fascists,' in other words the National Socialists, and used all its venom against the 'Social Fascists.'"[47] According to Linkskurve, the struggle against the Nazis was itself "bound with the front against the Social Fascist leaders, who represent a decisive weapon in the faschistization of Germany."[48] Social Democracy was a prime force in the coming of "culture fascism."[49] It is worth noting that the first two volumes of the "Red-One-Mark" novel series, Hans Marchwitza's Sturm auf Essen and Klaus Neukrantz's Barrikaden auf Wedding, were incendiary attacks on the republic and the SPD. Other proletarian novels, like Adam Scharrer's Der Inflationsroman: Der grosse Betrug, also focused their polemics against the Social Democrats.[50]

Linkskurve also attacked left-wing and progressive intellectuals, especially the Die Weltbühne circle.[51] "We will," Johannes Becher explained, "win over the best among the 'sympathizers' only through relentless and open battle, not by hiding our face and going along with them in order to placate them."[52] From reading Die Linkskurve, one might conclude that Alfred Döblin's great novel, Berlin Alexanderplatz, posed the greatest of threats to the workers' movement. "The book confirms for us," one reviewer declaimed, "the proof of the fact that the so-called 'left-bourgeois' writer poses a political danger for the proletariat against which we must turn with the sharpest watchfulness."[53] The Communist literary journal had only utter contempt for Thomas Mann's plea for a united democratic front against the Nazis.[54]

Only occasionally did the organ of the League of Proletarian-Revolutionary Writers concern itself with the Nazis or their literature.[55] Racist novels, the most characteristic form of völkisch literature, were generally ignored as beneath criticism. "However," Hans Jäger wrote in early 1931, "it is not worth the effort to lose even a few words over Die Dithmarscher by [Adolf] Bartels or over [Arthur] Dinter's Sünde wider das Blut."[56] Indeed, Nazi racism and antisemitism were attacked only rarely.

Thus it is true that the Communist literati had created the organized basis for a concerted Literaturpolitik by 1929-30. Yet, the Communist literary machine was far from being consecrated to any holy war against the true fascists, the Nazis. One should not expect to find efforts by the Communists to politicize the SDS motivated by the desire to create an anti-Nazi front.

Communist writers had not originally viewed their league as a substitute professional organization. But, they remained aloof when opposition to the Reich leadership of the SDS reemerged in the Berlin Ortsgruppe in 1929.[57] The origins and make-up of this opposition are at present obscure. Yet, it was partly motivated by the financial dislocation of the association accompanying the takeover of the business leadership by Werner Schendell. The Berlin-based opposition obviously wanted a more dynamic unionism, demanding that personalities like Müller-Jabusch, who held prominent positions in financial institutions, not be tolerated in responsible posts in the SDS. Linkskurve expressed no confidence in these fledgling efforts to transform the SDS and posed the proletarian writers' league as an alternative: "Transformed--fundamentally transformed--it [the SDS] can be only after the proletariat has seized power. Therefore we place the organization of proletarian-revolutionary writers up against the SDS."[58]

However, the League of Proletarian-Revolutionary Writers shifted its position when opposition began to surface in the provincial organizations of the SDS. The birth of a provincial opposition owed much to a recent wave of censorship, directed largely at Communist organs. A group of leftist writers, headed by Hermann Kesser and Ernst Gläser from the district Rhine-Main, voted with the opposition from Berlin at the national assembly of the SDS, 30 March 1930. The assembly passed a resolution introduced by the opposition demanding the release of thirty-two arrested Communist editors. A fund (proposed by the Rhine-Main district) was established to support writers persecuted by the state for political or philosophical reasons. An "Action Committee" was set up to govern expenditures of the money. Communist writers, encouraged by the growth of the opposition and its stand against anti-Communist measures, now begin to play leading roles in the opposition. Egon Erwin Kisch and Ludwig Renn were elected to the Main Executive Committee of the SDS as representatives of the opposition. Another communist, Karl Grünberg, sat on the executive committee of the Berlin Ortsgruppe. Linkskurve reflected the new attitude of the proletarian writers' league to the SDS opposition in May: "Now it is a matter of recruiting allies in the struggle against the cultural reaction from among the self-dissolving ranks of the writers and of bringing to them the clear solutions of our struggle and structure."[59]

The Communists, despite their limited numbers (forty to sixty out of a Berlin Ortsgruppe numbering 900), rapidly became the "core" of the opposition in Berlin.[60] As early as March 1931, Linkskurve could report that the opposition was now grouping itself around the Communists.[61] Apparently, the meetings of the Berlin Ortsgruppe were often lightly attended. This gave the Communists--with their tight organization, discipline and single-mindedness--a decided advantage.[62] Calculated mayhem at the Ortsgruppe meetings by the Communists may well have scared off some writers hostile to the opposition.[63]

Yet, the bulk of the opposition remained non-Communist, even in 1931-32. According to Alexander Roda Roda [Sandor Friedrich Rosenfeld], the opposition was politically multicolored, "held together by discontent with the economic situation." Diverse elements blamed the Reich leadership of the SDS for the desperate financial straits of writers and closed ranks with the Communists.[64] One important component of the opposition in the SDS was the left-wing intellectuals grouped around Die Weltbühne. These intellectuals had moved far to the left after 1928-29. They did not become Bolsheviks, "but the KPD became what the SPD had been for their counterparts in the early Weltbühne: that party with which they basically identified and which they vigorously criticized for not living up to its program."[65] The Communists, for their part, remained ambiguous toward the Weltbühne circle. On the one hand, they blasted the left-wing writers; on the other, they welcomed their collaboration, whether in the publicistic empire of Willi Münzenberg or within the SDS. It is noteworthy, as Istvan Deak points out, "that no one in the KPD called the left-wing intellectuals fascists, which made them the only 'nonfascist' group in Germany outside of the Communist party."[66]

The Weltbühne circle supported Communist-led efforts to turn the SDS into a dynamic union dedicated to the fight for writers' interests and against government attempts to curtail freedom of speech.[67] In July 1931, Weltbühne published an article by Erich Mühsam, "Union of Writers," attacking the Reich leadership of the SDS. Mühsam supported efforts by the opposition to free the Berlin Ortsgruppe from the oppressive control of the Main Executive Committee. He condemned the committee's willingness to take subventions from the state which, he alleged, vitiated the association's stand against government measures. The SDS, Mühsam insisted, must be transformed into a dynamic, completely independent union.[68] Mühsam's program for the SDS was in many respects quite sensible. Yet, both he and others in the Weltbühne circle clearly misunderstood the real motivations of the Communists. Those around the Weltbühne remained blind to the fact that the Communist core of the opposition was merely using issues like unionism and freedom of the press to pave the way for a Red dictatorship. They failed to see that the Communists' true aim was a regime that would be the very death of their most cherished values: democracy; freedom of the press; independent and dynamic unionism.

Democratic liberals were also often sympathetic to the opposition. Some (though not all) of the political/literary commentators for the Berliner Tageblatt approved of opposition demands for a staunch defense of freedom of speech, for a vigorous unionism, and for democratic practice within the SDS. During the late republic, the Tageblatt fought a tenacious rear-guard action against government interference with the free distribution of journals, newspapers, and books.[69] Dr. Lutz Weltman, for example, condemned the prohibition of books as "a step to fascism," pointing to the war against censorship as liberalism's great mission.[70] Writers for the paper like Dr. Apfel lamented the fact that the organizations of "intellectual workers" had accepted the confiscations of books almost without protest.[71] In this context, it is not surprising that key writers for the Berliner Tageblatt like Rudolf Olden and Friedrich Burschell gravitated to the opposition.[72] Olden, long a key figure in the SDS leadership, resigned from the Main Executive Committee and joined the Berlin-based opposition in the winter of 1930-31. Olden had no wish to politicize the SDS and distanced himself from both the revolutionary program and obnoxious, disruptive tactics of the Communists in the Berlin local. Yet, Olden had no use for the blatantly anti-Communist measures of the Main Executive Committee of the SDS. He lamented the lack of democratic procedure within the SDS and favored a more dynamic leadership.[73] As for Burschell, he was convinced of the need for a staunch unionism within the SDS as the only antidote for the miserable situation of the free writers brought on by the depression. Burschell welcomed the opposition as essential in transforming the SDS into a combative writers' union. He disparaged the idea that the opposition was a purely Communist operation. "The struggle is therefore of a union-political and not of a party-political nature."[74]

Writers opposed to the politicization of the SDS and far removed from the League of Proletarian-Revolutionary Writers supported individual measures put forth by the opposition. It is important to note that Walter Bloem was one such man. At the main assembly of the SDS in late March 1931, Bloem cosigned, along with leaders of the opposition, a protest against the emergency decree of 28 March 1931.[75]

The campaign against the opposition was directed by the Main Executive Committee of the SDS, backed by most of the association's Ortsgruppen and Gaue. East German historians have characterized those determined to stop politicization as "reactionaries."[76] Hans-Albert Walter has made this interpretation his own: "bourgeois and conservative-nationalist writers tried (with the support of social-Democratic authors) repeatedly to bring the association under their control, [and] to silence or to expel radical democratic and Marxist members."[77] It may or may not be true, as Walter maintains, that the provincial organizations supporting the national leadership of the Protective Association contained a large proportion of national conservative and even Nazi writers.[78] But the dominant elements in the Main Executive Committee were convinced republicans, and thus only "fascists" or "reactionaries" in the misleading terminology of the KPD of the early 1930s. The chairman of the SDS in 1931 was Artur Elösser, a literary historian of note and the theater critic for the left-liberal Vossische Zeitung.[79] Robert Breuer, perhaps the most influential member of the Main Executive Committee and a cofounder of the SDS, was a prominent Social Democrat.[80] Theodor Bohner, who often worked closely with Breuer, was a DDP deputy in the Prussian Landtag.[81] In fact, the nationalists were, as Walter Bloem notes in his autobiography, the most poorly represented political faction.[82] Bloem himself was the leading nationalist in the Main Executive Committee and he remained a republican, however reluctant, until mid-1932. There is little evidence that the anti-republican right made a serious effort to subvert the SDS before 1933. Writers close to the DNVP and the NSDAP preferred to set up their own, alternative authors' organization, the National Association of German Writers, in October 1931.[83]

The predominant group in the Main Executive Committee--the so-called "group Bohner-Breuer-Schendell"--fought to keep the SDS a political neutral, reformist writers' union. The SDS was to protect the interests of writers, as Robert Breuer put it, "from case to case." The mission in the economic sphere was to increase the authors' share of the literary industry's income. As a reformist union, the SDS could safely accept financial aid from the government.[84] In short, the Main Executive Committee was deadset against any attempt to turn the SDS into a politicized union bent on revolutionizing the structure of the literary industry in particular and of society in general. This position was likely partly dictated by the political affiliations of the "Bohner-Breuer-Schendell" group. According to Rudolf Olden, this predominant group in the Main Executive Committee (led, he implied, by Breuer and his fellow Social Democrats), was determined to restore the unity of the German working class by stirring up, attacking, and outvoting the Communists in the SDS.[85]

Yet, the fight against politicization was no mere mask for naked SPD or DDP politics. Breuer, Bohner and their followers were undoubtedly sincere in their belief that only political neutrality could save the SDS. In 1926, the Social Democrats Robert Breuer and Bruno Schönlank had sacrificed their party's interests to the unpolitical tradition of the SDS by opposing the attempt to commit the Protective Association against the compensation of the princes.[86] It is worth noting that Breuer tried to stop any SDS protest on his behalf when he was arrested on 23 July 1932 by the Papen regime.[87] Even as convinced and independent-minded a democrat as Roda Roda, also a member of the Main Executive Committee, stood up against the opposition's plan to politicize the SDS:

> The Protective Association may not choose in things of world view and politics. For what reason would it do so anyway? Neither the existence of God nor the excellence of Hitler's politics can be proven or refuted by union resolutions.[88]

The ban on politics within the SDS may have been necessary to keep it from splintering along party lines or from becoming a pawn of the KPD. But it had the unfortunate effect of preventing the Protective Association from taking a stand against the National Socialists. The majority of the Main Executive Committee and its backers saw the Nazis as just another party. They failed to recognize the totalitarian nature of the NSDAP--and thus that Hitler's triumph would mean the death of free literature and of the SDS itself.[89] Theodor Bohner epitomized this false estimate of the situation in an article published in the summer of 1932 to justify his actions as chairman of the SDS. Bohner rejected attempts by the opposition to commit the SDS against the Nazis:

> it was immoral according to the opposition that the executive committee remembered that it has National Socialist as well as Communist members; . . . that there are fascist as well as

Communist writers of rank. The executive committee concludes that it has to fight for the free word under every regime, but not that it has to affirm or to deny a specific political direction.[90]

Bohner had not the slightest inkling that there would be no SDS to defend freedom of the press under a Hitler regime.

CHAPTER 8

THE DEATH OF WALTER BLOEM'S REPUBLICANISM: THE BATTLE WITHIN THE SDS

At first, the national leadership of the SDS tried to defuse the opposition through control of the executive committee of the Berlin Ortsgruppe. Both Robert Breuer and Theodor Bohner were elected in 1930 to the Berlin executive committee, with the latter becoming chairman. Bohner tried to keep a lid on the opposition by parliamentary manipulation. He set the agendas for the local assemblies months in advance, permitting action on opposition proposals only if no one objected (Breuer usually did). Bohner also tried to mobilize the provincial organizations of the SDS against the Berlin-based opposition.[1] These high-handed techniques were very likely counter-productive in the long run. Rudolf Olden, for one, was put off by such violations of democratic procedure.[2] Bohner's methods helped to provoke tumultuous scenes in the general assembly of the Berlin local in early March 1931.[3]

The opposition's Fronde in March was fueled by a second incendiary ingredient added to the boiling SDS caldron in the preceding months. The Protective Association's syndic, Dr. Fluhme, had accused (wrongly it seems) Dr. Schendell, the organization's business leader, of corrupt practices.[4] Discontent with Bohner and Schendell at the Ortsgruppe assembly enabled the opposition to push through a number of demands: an end to any kind of tutelage over the Berlin Ortsgruppe by the Main Executive Committee; an end to the SDS Reich leadership's control of the association's organ, Der Schriftsteller; an audit of Schendell's activities as business leader; and common action against Chancellor Brüning's emergency decrees. Furthermore, the Berlin assembly unilaterally upgraded the Berlin Ortsgruppe to a Gau to free it from direct supervision by the Main Executive.[5]

The Main Assembly of the SDS on 29 March revealed that the opposition had made inroads elsewhere in the Reich. Linkskurve had prepared the ground for the assembly in the March issue. In an article entitled "Administrative Corruption in the SDS," the Communist commentator had excoriated the predominance of the Breuer clique, the alleged corruption of Schendell, and the supposed failure of the SDS to guard writers' interests or to combat "terrorist justice and shameful censorship."[6] At the assembly, some provincial representatives joined with the Berlin group in criticizing the business leadership. Three professional sections of the SDS--the lyric poets, the translators, and the press collaborators--revolted. The SDS organizations in Königsberg, Hamburg, Baden and Cologne refused to continue along the course mapped out by the Main Executive Committee.[7]

In April 1931, the Main Executive Committee made a serious tactical error by trying to discipline spokesmen of the opposition. Reacting vigorously, the opposition captured the Berlin Ortsgruppe. Bohner and those allied with him were forced to resign from the Berlin executive committee by a near unanimous vote on 11 May. At the end of June, Jakob Schaffner, a Swiss democrat and a leading member of the opposition, was elected chairman of the Berlin local. In the new executive committee, six members of the opposition confronted one "Breuer man."[8]

During the summer of 1931, the opposition coalesced around a program laid down by its most active element, the Communists. The basis of this program was formulated in an article by Johannes König, "Storm in the SDS," published in the July issue of <u>Die Linkskurve</u>.[9] This article has been aptly described as the first "principled and programmatic opinion expressed by the League of Proletarian-Revolutionary Writers on the occurrences in the SDS."[10] König's program for the SDS was an outgrowth of the policy put forth by Ernst Thälmann at the Central Congress of the KPD in January. Thälmann had then called for stronger efforts to draw the wide middle strata into the revolutionary class front.[11] According to König, activity in the SDS gave the Communists the chance "to approach that part of the middle strata, which indeed does not play a decisive role through its numbers, but which represents a not unimportant factor in the maintenance of the existing social order through its activity for the ruling class."[12]

König demanded of Communist writers a firm adherence to principles and clever tactics that would neither compromise the party line nor alienate the wavering and sympathizing groups. The depression combined with the expansion of censorship provides increasingly favorable conditions for winning over these groups. The true mission of the SDS can be realized only if it is turned into a real writers' union leagued with the class-conscious proletariat. The fight, König insisted, had to be carried on in favor of the free, intellectual worker against the "publishing-house capital," which however was only a part of the larger capitalist system. Therefore, the struggle had to be extended to encompass the ruling social order based on capitalist exploitation. But Breuer, Elösser and Bohner-- these "patented republicans"--have turned the SDS into a pillar of the ruling system. Thus the revolutionary writers' opposition had to lead the way in the war for members' rights and against the "dictatorship" of the Main Executive Committee. Yet, Communist writers must also be sure to educate the rest of the opposition in the political background of the struggle. "The battle against Breuer and consorts," König concluded, "must be expanded into a battle against the entire capitalist system directly through the consistent representation of writers' interests."[13]

Censorship was the explosive issue that gave the proletarian-revolutionary writers the leverage to push their program and leadership of the hitherto amorphous opposition. The Law for the Protection of the Republic, renewed on 25 March 1930, led to the arrest of hundreds of left-oriented writers for literary treason.[14] On 28 March 1931, Brüning's government issued an emergency decree. "It limited freedom of assembly above all, but also empowered the authorities to confiscate printed materials and to forbid newspapers or journals for a period of up to eight months."[15] A second emergency decree, issued on 17 July, gave police officials the authority arbitrarily to confiscate and ban works endangering the public order or security.[16] The SDS officially protested the decree of 17 July without denying that the government did have the right to prevent the spread of false news dangerous to the public in an emergency.[17]

The failure to condemn unequivocally censorship of any kind in any situation provided an easy target for the opposition.[18] The opposition, with Jakob Schaffner's approval, decided to call a demonstration to protest the second emergency decree for 29 July. Schendell, acting for the Main Executive Committee, forbade this demonstration on the grounds that an Ortsgruppe was not entitled to independent political action. At this point, Schaffner shifted ground, agreeing to uphold Schendell's ban. The opposition, however, was determined to carry on with the demonstration. The opposition assembled at the Kammersälen on the 29th only to find the meeting hall possessed by armed police. The Communist press would later blame the SDS leadership for alerting the police. Whatever the truth of this charge, police intervention actually redounded to the benefit of the opposition. Undoubtedly, lukewarm supporters were energized and fence straddlers brought over to the opposition by the affair. The opposition reassembled that very night at another locale and formed a Campaign Committee for the Freedom of Literature (<u>Kampfkomitee für die Freiheit des Schrifttums</u>) to bring its case to the public.[19] This committee issued a "Manifesto for the Freedom of Literature" which, as Albrecht and Klein rightly point out, documented a new stage in the history of the SDS opposition: "It records the first independent and united appearance of the Berlin opposition before the public."[20]

The activated opposition was now thoroughly in the thrall of the League of Proletarian-Revolutionary Writers. Communists dominated the "Kampfkomitee" despite the fact that a few members of the <u>Weltbühne</u> circle fleetingly belonged to it.[21] The overriding Communist influence within the opposition was reflected in the "Program Declaration of the OSDS (Opposition in the Protective Association of German Writers)," which was drawn up in August as the basis for future activity. Indeed, the OSDS program drew heavily from König's article in the July <u>Linkskurve</u>.[22] According to the declaration, the threat posed to literature by censorship and power concentrations in the publishing industry could be met only by transforming the SDS from an organization of luminaries into an aggressive union representative of the "writer masses." A list of concrete reforms to better the lot of writers was put forth. But, the heart of the OSDS program was the insistence on the need for a revolutionary stance by the SDS. Free literature must demand:

(1) The struggle for the lifting of the press emergency decree, the struggle against all emergency decrees and the whole politics of emergency decree; (2) The struggle against fascism and cultural reaction also in their democratic mask in Prussia and in the Reich; (3) The struggle of the united writers against exploitation, in a common front with all the suppressed and exploited.[23]

The fight against censorship and for writers' interests were ideal vehicles to mobilize support for the opposition and thus also indirectly for Communist political aims. On 15 August, a protest demonstration against censorship was staged by the "Kampfkomitee" in the Schubert-Saal in Berlin. Numerous prominent writers reportedly expressed their support. The Berliner Tageblatt, ever vigilant in defense of freedom of expression, gave the affair favorable coverage.[24] In short, König's plan to entice writers into the Communist web through manipulation of writers' grievances seemed to be working exceedingly well.[25] As a matter of fact, these methods were so successful that the Communists planned to extend them to other intellectual fields, perhaps using the SDS opposition as a base. "Our earlier experiences are favorable," Johannes Becher reported in early October. "We came near circles and strata through this movement which we could reach earlier only with difficulty or not at all." The "Kampfkomitee" was expanded into a Working Community for the Freedom of Spiritual Creativity (Arbeits- gemeinschaft für die Freiheit des geistigen Schaffens), designed to encompass "painters, actors, free thinkers, film and radio people and so forth," as well as writers.[26]

The KPD aimed to expand the organized opposition from the provinces to Berlin. The disorderly, occasional opposition in the SDS Gaue and Ortsgruppen had to be developed and unified under the auspices of the "Program Declaration of the OSDS."[27] The Communist writers' fraktion, headed by Johannes Becher, outlined the new mission for its members throughout the Reich:

> We wish to mount the opposition in the SDS (Protective Association of German Writers) throughout the Reich. For this, it is necessary that those of you who are members of the

SDS in your Gau or city kindle such an opposition movement, or if the mood or beginnings for it are already there, [that you] place yourself behind it, unify it and drive it forward along our line. The discontent with the local or Gau executive committee prevailing almost everywhere, like the discontent with the Main Executive Committee, offers from experience the first handhold for this purpose. Possible problems at the beginning--the difficulty of leading and disciplining intellectuals--should not scare you off. The thing will succeed; it has already been tried out.[28]

The fraktion members appear to have been fairly successful in their work. By December 1931, according to the opposition's own estimate of the situation, Hamburg, Rhineland-Westphalia, Königsberg, great portions of Baden, Rhine-Main, Bavaria and Silesia as well as Berlin were aligned against the Main Executive Committee.[29]

The national leadership of the SDS was thus faced with an expanding, totally politicized opposition. The Main Executive Committee moved to suppress the opposition in the provinces.[30] In Berlin, with the help of Jakob Schaffner, the Ortsgruppe was prevented from holding a general assembly between June and November 1931.[31] Schaffner had, at the end of July, allied himself with the Main Executive Committee of the SDS against his original constituents in the opposition. Marxists then as now have blamed Schaffner's switch on "careerist" motives.[32] More likely he belatedly saw that the opposition's unionism was too often a veneer for Communist political goals. By early September, Breuer and Schaffner had decided on a mass expulsion of Communists from the SDS as the only way out of the association's crisis.[33] On 19 October 1931, with the Socialist fraktion in the lead, the Main Executive Committee expelled (or struck from the register) eighteen members of the opposition, including sixteen members of the League of Proletarian-Revolutionary Writers. The expulsions were based on the SDS statutes forbidding activity harmful to the organization. The committee defended its action as essential for the preservation of the association's political and philosophical neutrality.[34]

The purge of the opposition leaders exacerbated rather than ended the SDS crisis. Many of Germany's most respected writers--perhaps as Roda Roda put it, "from a reflex antipathy for tyrannical gestures"--flocked to the oppositional banners.[35] A "Solidarity Declaration for the Opposition in the SDS" was signed by 150 writers, including literary or publicistic giants like Carl von Ossietzky, Kurt Tucholsky, Ludwig Marcuse, Stefan Grossmann, Robert Musil and Ernst Wiechert. The declaration not only condemned the intention of the Main Executive Committee to rid itself of the opposition through mass expulsions. It also maintained that "this opposition, with its criticism and activity, is trying to reinvigorate the SDS and that its goals are appropriate to raise the spiritual and intellectual position of the writer."[36] On Monday, 26 October, some 400 to 500 writers assembled in Berlin to protest the expulsions.[37] A central theme of debate was Walter Bloem's alleged role in the purge. "Very important, indeed decisive," the Berliner Tageblatt reported the next day.

> was the question . . . of how it then stood with the "National Opposition" in the Protective Association. Walter Bloem, the chairman of this recently formed group, is said to be still sitting in the Executive Committee today and to have taken part in the vote against the left opposition. Of course, that would be methods which once again and even more strongly put the Main Executive Committee in the wrong.[38]

What was Walter Bloem's part in the purge of the opposition? Bloem, although he likely sympathized with some opposition demands, was staunchly opposed to politicization of the SDS. And no doubt, he blamed the Communists for introducing party politics into the Protective Association.[39] As a member of the Main Executive Committee, Bloem did attend the meeting of 19 October. There he insisted that stringent measures, even expulsion, should be used in the future to stop activities harmful to the SDS. But, he also vigorously opposed purging members for their past actions.[40] Bloem, along with Monty Jacobs and Alexander Roda Roda, voted against expulsion of any of the opposition.[41] Nor was Bloem the leader of any "National Opposition" within the SDS. He did belong to a literary coterie, called "Die Mannschaft" or The Troops, of nationalist-minded war writers.[42] But the nationalist organization within the SDS was (at this time) a figment of the left opposition's imagination. Bloem himself pointed this out in a declaration to the Berliner Tageblatt, which printed a retraction of its earlier report. The newspaper's commentator observed that the unfounded aspersions cast on Bloem demonstrated "to what end the Protective Association can come and even must come if the members carry party politics into it."[43]

By late November 1931, the SDS was on the brink of dissolution. Jakob Schaffner was forced to call an extraordinary general assembly of the Berlin Ortsgruppe for 23 November. His Berlin executive committee had resigned, necessitating a new election.[44] Both sides viewed the assembly as crucial. The Communist fraktion in the OSDS prepared its members for a united offensive.[45] The Main Executive Committee attended the meeting in toto to represent its own interests. A vote of no-confidence in Schaffner passed despite the fact that the expelled members of the OSDS were not allowed to participate. However, Schaffner refused to resign. As a result, only the other six seats, including the office of deputy chairman, on the Berlin executive committee were at stake. The Main Executive Committee put up a slate headed by Walter Bloem as candidate for deputy chairman. But the opposition swept the election. Heinz Pol, a member of the Weltbühne circle (and a Communist fellow traveler), became the new deputy chairman.[46] When Schaffner refused to cooperate with the new executive committee, it deposed him, making Pol de facto chairman.[47]

The opposition victory on 23 November soon led to a schism in the Berlin SDS. On 11 December, Monty Jacobs, feuilleton leader of the Vossische Zeitung, founded a new Berlin local, the Ortsgruppe Berlin-Brandenburg. Loyal to the Main Executive Committee, the 106 founding members accepted statutes forbidding simultaneous membership in the opposition-dominated Berlin local as well as political activity in the SDS. Max Barthel (the most important SPD novelist) was in the chairman; Theodor Bohner was the deputy chairman.[48] The loyalist Berlin-Brandenburg association managed capture at least 300 members, or about one-third, of the old Berlin SDS by April 1932.[49]

Bloem's run for the deputy chairmanship was the first public step in his rise to leadership within the SDS. His candidacy supplied explosive grist for the opposition's propaganda mills. The opposition's version of its own history, apparently circulated in December 1931, tarred Bloem as a Nazi, charging that the Main Executive Committee had linked its destiny to fascism:

> In the days of its agony the Main Executive allies itself openly with the fascists in the association. In the extraordinary general assembly the Main Executive Committee put up as candidate for deputy chairman Herr Walter Bloem, the leader of the National Socialists in the SDS, who now has emerged for the first time as an outpost of the Third Reich in the Protective Association. . . .Therefore the cause of the opposition is no longer a Berlin affair. The association must, if it does not wish to be smashed or to let itself be made into a nest of fascists, free itself from the hands of the reactionary tyrants.[50]

Both <u>Die rote Fahne</u>, the chief organ of the KPD, and <u>Die Linkskurve</u> played on the Breuer-Bloem alliance as a variant of the hackneyed theme of a "fascist" front, extending from the Social Fascists (the SPD) to the National Fascists (the NSDAP). The Communist publications continued (erroneously) to paint Bloem as the leader of a Nationalist Opposition or "fascist fraktion."[51]

The Social Democratic and liberal circles in the Main Executive Committee had turned to Bloem as the figure best able to de-politicize the SDS. This so-called Breuer-Bohner group wanted to back Bloem for the chairmanship of the Protective Association in the coming January 1932 elections for a new Main Executive.[52] Considerably more study is needed to determine why these circles were willing to support Bloem. Undoubtedly, Bloem's experience in writers' organizations and his defense of both the Jews and the Weimar Republic in books such as <u>Brotherhood</u> played a role in their decision. However, the choice of a nationalist republican seems also to have been tied to their fatal misunderstanding of the totalitarian nature of the NSDAP. According to Bloem's memoirs, the

Main Executive of the SDS, dominated by republicans, viewed him as a kind of life insurance policy for the Protective Association in the event that the Nazis came to power:

> The [Main] Executive Committee, in which the left parties predominated, saw the avalanche-like swelling of Nationalist Socialist votes and felt Hitler's imminent final victory coming ever closer. It feared that the Protective Association would be dissolved as standing all too far to the left if the new party actually got the government in its hands. . . . The Main Executive Committee of the Protective Association hoped, if I stepped to the head of the association, that I would serve as something like a bridge, a connecting link between the old and new. My commitment to restore the political neutrality of the association, to restore the meaning of its establishment--its distinctiveness as a pure representative of corporate interests--now found, at least in the executive committee, unanimous agreement.[53]

Bloem initially refused to run for chairman; he felt that his stance on antisemitism made him unacceptable to the Nazis. In lieu of himself, Bloem proposed his corps brother, Dr. Carl Hänsel, as the man best suited to restore the SDS to its original character.[54]

It soon became clear that Hänsel could not be elected. Those loyal to the old Main Executive Committee and the Berlin-based opposition were locked in a stalemate. Each side had a bastion of organizational power; neither was able to establish its predominance. The vote for a new national executive committee (and thus for a new chairman) promised to be completely splintered--"the future of the association was completely hopeless."[55] Yet neither side wanted complete disintegration of the SDS and at the last minute the situation was retrieved by a compromise.[56] The opposition, at the general assembly of 9-10 January 1932, won several concessions. The expulsion of the eighteen OSDS members was revoked. A proposed change of the SDS statutes to guarantee the association's neutrality was defeated. Three members of the opposition were elected to the Main Executive Committee.[57] On the other hand, the Ortsgruppe

Berlin-Brandenburg remained in existence. Nor did the opposition succeed in its intention of pushing through a vote of no-confidence in the Main Executive.[58] Bloem was elected chairman of the Protective Association as a compromise candidate acceptable to all sides. The overwhelming majority of the opposition voted for him.[59] Even the Communists agreed not to oppose his election. The members of the proletarian writers' league cast blank ballots (since, they reportedly explained, they could not vote for a non-party member in an election for an official office). Furthermore, they promised not to throw any obstacles in the way of Bloem's program to restore the SDS to a body solely concerned with the representation of professional interests.[60]

Bloem agreed to accept the post only with reluctance. He expected--and not without reason--the Communists to resume their agitation within the association. "It was," Bloem reflected, "a form of clumsy, negligent suicide."[61]

How could Bloem, who had been condemned by the KPD press as a Nazi, have won, even for a fleeting moment, the confidence of the whole body of German writers, the opposition included? Bloem owed this trust to the fact that, earlier Communist vituperations notwithstanding, he was regarded by all sides as a mediator.[62] "I appeared to be the appropriate man," he wrote later, "because of the conciliatory nature of my character and demeanor, to work as a mediator, perhaps even as a reconciliator of the antagonisms which pressed the activity of the association from its true goals of the representation of professional interests."[63] His political position was well known: a partyless conservative nationalism, nonetheless loyal to the Weimar Republic and sympathetic to international as well as to class reconciliation.[64] Within the SDS, Bloem, though generally backing the program of the Main Executive Committee, had stood with the opposition against censorship and the expulsion of the eighteen members in October. Moreover, Bloem was already proving his talents as a mediator in the German section of the international PEN-Club.

Bloem had joined the PEN-Club shortly after his resettlement in Berlin. He had found himself somewhat ill at ease in the club. Particularly disturbing was the great role played by Jews. At a congress of the club in

Vienna, Bloem "found it, just as a fighter against antisemitism from principle, regrettable that Jewry played so strongly and predominantly in the foreground."[65] Yet, within two years, Bloem was elected co-president with Theodor Däubler of the German section.[66] Bloem strove to reestablish harmony between ideological opponents in the club. In January 1932, for example, a Congress of the German-speaking (Austrian, Swiss and German) sections of the PEN-Club met in Berlin to found a Working Committee (<u>Arbeitsgemeinschaft</u>). Before the congress, these sections had been troubled by the agitation of a small group of writers for the literature of the countryside (<u>Landschaft</u>) and against that of the city. The controversy was aesthetic and thematic on the surface, but likely political at root. The writers of the landscape were normally national conservative or even radical <u>völkisch</u> in orientation; those of the city, known pejoratively as asphalt literati, were usually slanted to the left. At the congress of the German, Swiss, and Austrian sections, the controversy was defused through discussion "under the wise, mediating leadership of Walter Bloem." The final speech, by Hanns Martin Elster, praised the equality of country irrationality and urban intellectuality. The <u>Berliner Tageblatt</u> reported an atmosphere of sympathetic harmony pervading the congress.[67]

    Bloem's honeymoon at the head of the German writers' organizations was destined to be short-lived. The Communist fraktion in the SDS soon fell out with him. The members of the League of Proletarian-Revolutionary Writers had only suspended out of tactical necessity, not given up their plan to politicize the SDS. The fraktion leadership mobilized its forces to bring about statute changes "in the interest of the opposition" at the 18 January meeting of the Berlin Ortsgruppe.[68] A radio broadcast of Bloem's program for the SDS provided the occasion if not the cause for the Communists' renunciation of the compromise of 9-10 January. Bloem's programmatic declaration for the radio was apparently couched in national conservative terms. He based the projected depoliticization of the SDS on the notion of the writer as representative of the nation rather than of any party or group. The KPD writers charged that Bloem had violated his pledge to lead the Protective Association in an unpolitical fashion, since his program served nationalist goals.[69]

The Communists called a protest assembly which Bloem, accompanied by Roda Roda, attended. Here, Bloem expressed amazement at the Communists' reaction to his declaration. After all, he pointed out with some justice, everyone had known from the start that he was a "National German" bent on furthering the nation's mission to better the future of mankind. Bloem's explanation fell on deaf ears. The tumultuous assembly passed a vote of no-confidence and asked Bloem to resign. This he refused to do; he pointed out that only a general assembly of the SDS could bring him down.[70]

The Communist core of the SDS opposition did not have the votes to fell Bloem. Therefore, it chose to fight its battle on more fertile ground. The opposition's war for the economic interests of writers and against censorship was resumed.[71] The Berlin executive committee called a demonstration on the "Distress of Writers" to meet in Berlin on 12 February. Bloem banned the meeting at the last minute, threatening to expel all those who attended from the Protective Association. The Main Executive Committee apparently viewed the demonstration as an attempt to undercut its own plans for an assembly on the same subject.[72] The oppositional Berlin Ortsgruppe held the demonstration in defiance of Bloem. Keynote speakers hit the bread-and-butter issues nearest and dearest to writers. Heinz Pol, now chairman of the Berlin local, attacked the increasingly arbitrary prohibition of books. The lead-off address, however, by Dr. K. A. Wittfogel, a member of the League of Proletarian-Revolutionary Writers, struck a typically revolutionary note, coupling the struggle against the hardships of authors with a fight against the "system."[73]

Bloem responded to the Berlin local's defiance of his ban with a proposal to expel the Berlin executive committee. This was undoubtedly a poor move tactically. Bloem meant to punish the Berlin executive council for usurping the prerogatives of and refusing to submit to the Main Executive. However, his action gave the appearance of callous indifference to the overwhelming problems then facing writers. And he did this at a time when progressive writers of shadings other than Red were up in arms over censorship.[74]

The worst nightmares of authors seemed realized when, on 15 February 1932, the Third Senate of the Prussian Upper Administrative Court struck down an appeal by the <u>Internationaler Arbeiter-Verlag</u> of the August 1931 prohibition of Hans Marchwitza's <u>Sturm auf Essen</u>. The book, the first Red-One-Mark Novel, had been banned and confiscated throughout Prussia by the Socialist police president of Berlin because it endangered "public security and order." The legal basis for suppressing the book was the emergency decree of 18 July 1931.[75] There can be no doubt that the novel was an incitement to armed rebellion.[76] Yet, the failure of the publisher's appeal seemed ominous even to those without ties to the KPD. The appellate court legitimized the right of local police authorities to ban fictional works without discussion of their literary merit and with no other grounds than alleged threats to order. The <u>Berliner Tageblatt</u> with some justice viewed the case as a watershed.[77] The paper dedicated a whole issue of its Sunday supplement, <u>Die Brücke</u>, to an attack on this kind of censorship.[78] The opposition lost no time in identifying itself with the democratic daily's position and Walter Bloem with negligent defense of writers' vital interests. A "Protest Resolution Against Prohibitions of Books" drove home these points, noting Bloem's attempt to punish the Berlin executive for the demonstration of 12 February.[79]

The month of March marked the final bankruptcy of Bloem's original peace-keeping mission within the SDS. Such a break was inevitable given Bloem's inflexibility and the Berlin local's determination to usurp the functions of the Main Executive Committee. By 9 March, the Ortsgruppe had set up seven commissions as the organizational basis of an activist unionism. These commissions seem to have been designed with more than the local's Berlin constituency in mind.[80] The opposition had failed to capture the SDS; now it was apparently trying to turn the Berlin Ortsgruppe into something akin to an organization of national scope. This attempt was extended from unionism to cultural activity. The Berlin executive scheduled its own Goethe festival for 21 March. The list of speakers for the affair was headed by George Lukás, the Great Communist literary critic.[81]

The Main Executive Committee refused to give permission for the Goethe-Feier, since it was no purely local matter. In a letter of 9 March, Bloem, determined to end the insubordination of the Berlin local, suspended all contact between the Main Executive Committee and the Berlin executive. He informed Heinz Pol that relationships would not be resumed "until the executive committee of the Berlin Ortsgruppe explains to us quite clearly that it subordinates itself once again to the statutes and accordingly recognizes the decisions and resolutions of the Main Executive Committee as binding."[82] Bloem sent a circular to the members of the Berlin Ortsgruppe, informing them that he no longer regarded the Berlin local as part of the SDS. Members should resign from the Ortsgruppe, remaining in the SDS as members at large or joining the loyalist local, Berlin-Brandenburg. The Berlin executive did agree in writing to follow directives of the Main Executive Committee consonant with the SDS statutes.[83] But actions spoke louder than words; the Goethe festival went on as planned (albeit on 23 March).[84]

The opposition, which had no hope of replacing Bloem by itself, was favored in early April by a fortuitous turn of events in the PEN-Club. This development, involving the famous high treason trial of Carl von Ossietzky, soon forced Bloem to step down from his posts atop the SDS and the PEN-Club. The "Ossietzky affair" had begun in March 1929 when an article, "Hot Air in German Aeronautics," by Walter Kreiger (writing under the pen name, Heinz Jäger) appeared in the Weltbühne. Kreiser's article revealed, among other things, that civilian plants, including one known as "Abteilung M.," were testing military airplanes in violation of the Treaty of Versailles. The article also hinted that some of the planes were stationed in the U.S.S.R. Most of the information in Kreiser's essay had already been aired in public in early 1928. But this did not stop the Reichswehr from pushing an indictment of the author and Carl von Ossietzky, responsible editor of the Weltbühne. On 31 March 1930, both men were indicted for "espionage and treason." The Reichsgericht (Supreme Court) found them guilty on 23 November, sentencing them to eighteen months in prison.[85] The severity of the sentence, Istvan Deak writes, "was undoubtedly due to the growing irritation of the Reichswehr Command with the anti-militarist campaign of the Weltbühne." General Gröner, who held both the ministries of defense and of the interior, was probably a sincere, albeit conservative republican. Yet, he would have no truck with pacifism; to combat it he was even willing to prosecute those who were merely pointing out violations of a peace treaty that was also the law of the German Reich.[86]

The German left, with few exceptions, jumped to Ossietzky's defense; the far right celebrated the fall of the "hireling of the Jews."[87] Political lines were so sharply drawn in the electric atmosphere of the late Weimar era that "no force of any consequence from either the conservative camp or from the Center came to Ossietzky's aid."[88] Ossietzky himself was deadset on turning the affair to political account. He wanted to turn the powerful surge of protest in his behalf into, as he put it, "a political campaign against the powerful forces of counterrevolution."[89] Under his guidance, the Weltbühne waged a campaign against the army's usurpation of political power in the republic.[90] In May 1932, all appeals for clemency having failed, the doors of Tegel prison clamped shut on Ossietzky.[91]

Among the organizations determined to support the campaign for the pardon (or for the mitigation of his sentence) of Ossietzky was the German group of the PEN-Club. On 1 February 1932, this organization decided to submit a clemency petition in Ossietzky's behalf. The chairman, Walter Bloem, charged the treasurer, Hanns Martin Elster, with drafting the petition. Martin Beradt, a lawyer as well as a writer, was assigned to help Elster with those aspects of the draft requiring legal expertise. Elster sat on his hands, however, until 22 February.[92] His inactivity, he and Beradt later explained to the Berliner Tageblatt, stemmed from the fact that Beradt was out of Berlin on a winter trip. Further delays in drafting the petition after Beradt's return, they contended, resulted from difficulties in the formulation and in Elster's forced absence to attend a meeting of the Schiller-Stiftung in Weimar.[93] Politics may, however, have played a role in Elster's procrastination; he was a German Nationalist who would shift to the Hitler camp in 1933.[94] At any rate, Elster and Beradt finished their draft of the petition on 8 March, only after being "energetically admonished" by the governing board of the PEN-Club.[95] The petition was submitted to Bloem on 11 March.[96]

However, Bloem did not then sign and immediately circulate the petition. Political considerations clearly played a role in Bloem's failure to sign. Bloem objected to the attacks on the German army being published by the <u>Weltbühne</u>.[97] Neither Bloem's reluctant republicanism nor his distaste for mechanized warfare had precluded a deep, abiding love for the army. Not long before, Bloem had published <u>Front Soldiers</u> (German title: <u>Frontsoldaten</u>), a sort of counter to Remarque's <u>All Quiet on the Western Front</u>.[98] It also seems that Bloem had been personally offended by a recent <u>Weltbühne</u> attack on his leadership within the SDS.[99] Bloem's failure to sign by no means meant suppression of the petition. Bloem, according to Walther von Hollander, secretary of the PEN-Club, made his decision not to sign only after having been assured that the peititon could, without harm to Ossietzky, be sent without him. Bloem was still prepared to sign if no one else could be found to do so in the name of the PEN-Club.[100] Furthermore, Bloem left open the possibility that he might affix his signature in the immediate future. First he wanted to review the documents from the case (which, apparently unbeknownst to him, had been kept secret).[101] Significantly, Bloem, despite his political and personal reservations, did ultimately co-author and sign a protest resolution against Ossietzky's sentence.[102] As for the petition, he dispatched it within a few days after receiving it (on 13 or 14 March) to Theodor Däubler, deputy chairman of the PEN-Club, for an official signature.[103]

Däubler was unfortunately not on hand in Berlin; he lay ill at a sanatorium in Neubabelsberg. Therefore, another large chunk of time was lost. Elster got the petition back from Däubler, who had signed it, only on 22 March. Däubler had, however, not appended any instructions for the further disposition of the petition.[104] The officers of the PEN-Club therefore juggled it around for the next week like a hot potato. Elster sent it to Bloem who passed it on, still without his own signature, to Hollander. Hollander completed the circle on 31 March by returning it to Elster "by reason of competency."[105] That very day, Reich President Hindenburg declined to honor a clemency request from another quarter. The leaders of the PEN-Club had for a variety of reasons, probably at root political, inexcusably procrastinated until it was too late to help Ossietzky.[106]

Bloem's constituents on the governing board of the PEN-Club with good reason regarded his failure to sign and circulate the petition in time as betrayal of a colleague.[107] Bloem had already antagonized certain circles of the PEN-Club at the celebration of the Goethe centennial at Weimar on 22 March. There he had caused a stir by wearing his war decorations and by exchanging pleasantries with a number of uniformed Nazis, including the writer and Hitler confidante Karl Hanfstängel.[108] Now, in the first week of April, the board moved to depose Bloem. The leader of the Fronde against Bloem was Elster; he charged Bloem with holding back the petition out of opposition to Ossietzky. Hollander, Bloem's champion both before the board and in the subsequent press campaign, countered that Bloem had signed the protest declaration in Ossietzky's behalf. Hollander also noted, with some justice, that no member of a left-wing party would have taken a similar stance for a man on the right in Ossietzky's position.[109] The vote against Bloem, however, was lopsided-- eleven to two. Alfred Kerr was elected as the new chairman of the German section of the PEN-Club; Däubler was retained as deputy chairman. The reason given for replacing Bloem (which was leaked to the Berliner Tageblatt) was his leaving a colleague to sit in jail "without stirring a finger" because of "political prejudice" and "personal touchiness."[110]

Bloem's fate astride the SDS was now sealed. Rumors reached him that the opposition was planning to submit a new petition for Ossietzky at the next session of the Main Executive Committee. Bloem, still unable to acquire the documents from the trial, remained unwilling to sign. Instead, he decided to resign his chairmanship of the SDS.[111] Perhaps he saw the handwriting on the wall; Socialist and liberal writers probably would have deserted him on the explosive Ossietzky issue.[112] At any rate, he had definitely concluded that it was impossible to depoliticize the SDS. His autobiography is worth quoting on this point: "I had had enough. I grasped that there was not the slightest hope to restore the Protective Association. It was contaminated politically beyond salvation."[113] It should be noted that Bloem's resignation did not heal the schism in the

SDS. To be sure, the Main Executive Committee did restore relations with the Berlin Ortsgruppe in late May.[114] But after a tumultuous summer, the Main Executive, headed by its new chairman, Theodor Bohner, dissolved the opposition-dominated Berlin local (which refused to recognize the legality of this measure).[115]

The opposition and the press sympathetic to it heaped abuse against Bloem for his supposed betrayal of Ossietzky. The Berliner Tageblatt described the whole affair in the PEN-Club in an article slanted against Bloem.[116] This paper soon afterwards printed the partially conflicting testimony of Elster, Beradt, and Hollander.[117] The editorial staff of the Berliner Tageblatt, at the end of its documentation of the affair, rather cryptically expressed regrets that "an important act of solidarity, one cannot express it otherwise, in the essence of the club has perished."[118] The Communist-affiliated Die Welt am Abend described the episode as "Bloem's Dolchstoss [stab in the back] against Ossietzky."[119] The April Linkskurve accused Bloem--the "male Courths-Mahler, the puppet of Breuer," who had "Hitlered along" at the head of the SDS--with suppressing the Ossietzky petition.[120] On 15 April, the membership assembly of the Ortsgruppe Berlin condemned Bloem for his role in the machinations that had maneuvered [Ossietzky] into jail."[121]

How is one to evaluate Bloem's failure to do his clear duty: to commit the organizations under his stewardship, without delay or reservation, to Ossietzky's defense? There can be no doubt that Bloem, whether by an act of commission or omission, had betrayed the principles for which he had long fought: obedience to law and freedom of expression. It should be noted, however, that Ossietzky and his allies made it very hard indeed for a national conservative like Bloem to make the right decision, for, they had politicized the whole affair, transforming what should have been a battle over principle, over the fundamental rules of the political game, into a fight against the right. The left's actions in the Ossietzky affair in particular were similar to the maneuvers of the SDS opposition in general. Much of the OSDS, especially the Communist core, manipulated the principles of democracy and literary freedom to further short-term political interests. Such manipulation in the long run was bound to discredit the principles among those who did not share the political interests. Small wonder that Bloem and others lost faith in the principle of freedom of expression, which increasingly appeared as a mask for left-wing politics. Small wonder that such men would ultimately cooperate with the cultural dictatorship of the Third Reich.

Bloem took his abrupt plunge from the top of the writers' organizations into infamy hard. He, along with Hollander and Jakob Schaffner, resigned from the PEN-Club.[122] Friedrich Burschell reported that Bloem "exited angrily" from the chairmanship of the SDS.[123] Even time could not defuse Bloem's smoldering bitterness over the Ossietzky debacle. Barely suppressed anger permeates Bloem's account of the affair in his autobiography, written in the ashes of the Third Reich. In his recollections, Bloem noted that the PEN-Club board voted in in April belonged entirely to the parties of the left. Undoubtedly he blamed the republican parties as well as the Communists for his downfall. Bloem seems to have seen the hands of the Jews in his loss of the PEN-Club post. "It should be noted in passing," he observed in his memoirs, "that the collective members of the board were now Jews."[124]

The embittered Bloem soon turned to the anti-republican right. He did stop short of joining the Nazi party; he was apparently uneasy, not without reason, about the prospective fate of the author of <u>Brotherhood</u> in the coming Third Reich.[125] Yet, Bloem had definitely turned against the republic and parliamentarianism. Moreover, he now favored a unified nationalist front, including the Nazis. In October 1932, Bloem, writing for <u>Der Türmer</u> on the occasion of Hindenburg's eighty-fifth birthday, praised the Reich President's break with the democratic system. According to Bloem, Hindenburg had, after his reelection (on 10 April 1932), recognized that the Weimar experiment had failed. The president had come to see that a democracy was unable to cope with the confused present. Parliaments were incapable of moving with sufficient rapidity in an age demanding quick decisions. All Germans, Bloem contended, must stand by Hindenburg, who has taken the lonely road of presidential rule. The titanic work of German renewal can only come out of an unconditionally national spirit.[126] In his <u>Hindenburg the German</u> (German title:

Hindenburg der deutsche; 1932), published by the national-conservative Verlag Reimar Hobbing, Bloem demanded an alliance between the conservatives and the Nazis, "a national German bonding of souls [Seelenverbundenheit]."[127]

Bloem, once he had rejoined the nationalist mainstream, turned his pen with a vengeance against the so-called cultural dictatorship of the "democratic-Marxist Gesinnungskonzern [concern dedicated to implanting democratic-Marxist beliefs]."[128] On 27 September 1932, the Deutsche Allgemeine Zeitung or DAZ (published by Reimar Hobbing) carried Bloem's apoplectic "Open Letter to Heinrich Mann." The letter was occasioned by Mann's declaration of sympathy to an international congress against imperialistic war held in Amsterdam at the end of August.[129] In it, Bloem charged that, during the last decades, writers using the German language, who were nonetheless anti-German in experience and nature, have managed "to form a closed front against the national German literature."[130] Nationalist authors, Bloem sputtered--perhaps reflecting back on the problems with his own Washington trilogy--have been shut off at the Reich borders. Even their names have been stopped from becoming known abroad. Neither true German writers nor the millions of veterans--organized in the Kyffhäuserbund, in the Stahlhelm, and in Hitler's movement--will let anti-war writers speak in their name.[131] Bloem even descended to threatening Mann. He pointed to the swelling anti-republican right and warned: "Whoever dares in the future to scorn and sully our most powerful memories, the proud and unshakable beliefs of the 'militarists' and of the 'nationalists,' he will have to reckon with us."[132]

Bloem, writing during the winter of 1932-33 for the DAZ feuilleton, resurrected the specter of the systematic ruination of the "German drama in tune with the Volk" by the forces of internationalism.[133] Clearly, Bloem now blamed his own dismal stage career entirely on the machinations of a left-wing cultural dictatorship:

> Whoever did not himself live through the madness of the expired epoch of German ensnarement will never understand it: we scarcely had helpers, at least in the sphere of the

German theater. To fight for one's own Volkstum, alone at lost posts, that was the gruesome, bitter destiny of the older of us.[134]

Bloem mustered a pantheon of supposedly suppressed nationalist dramatists; he added quotations from reviews by democratic (and Jewish) critics like Siegfried Jacobsohn and Alfred Kerr who had allegedly assassinated them critically.[135] Bloem welcomed "with a redeemed sigh of relief the standards of the young Germany [i.e., of the Third Reich]--for those creating today."[136]

Both Das Tagebuch and Die Weltbühne--neither of which, sad to say, had found much to say about the republican Bloem--assailed Bloem's version of the myth of left-wing cultural predominance. In a long article in Das Tagebuch (8 October 1932), Werner Hegemann reprinted and criticized the "Open Letter to Heinrich Mann."[137] Bloem, Hegemann noted, had won great trust in republican circles; he had sold a vast quantity of books to republican readers. Hegemann gave a synopsis of Brotherhood, pointing to the novel's condemnation of antisemitism and anti-republicanism.[138] "Bloem's long condemnation of antisemitism," Hegemann wrote, "would do any respectable newspaper honor if similar things had not been said a thousand times before. Only for the corps students are these self-evident arguments new." Hegemann now wondered if Bloem's affirmation of the republic in his novel had not contained a reservatio mentalis (like that of the DVP), whether Bloem had not intended from the beginning to return to barbarism, waiting only for "Michael's Awakening" to give him courage.[139] At any rate, Hegemann added, quoting the close to Brotherhood, an end had been made to the "morning shimmer of a new day for humanity."[140]

On 28 February 1933, Carl von Ossietzky, in his last article for Die Weltbühne, condemned Bloem's tirades against the left-wing domination of the theater. Ossietzky used the mask of a literary dispute with Bloem to lash out at the descending curtain of barbarism that would claim his own life.[141] He denied Bloem any expertise or talent in matters of the theater:

> Herr Bloem belongs as an author of novels to those fortunate ones who use rather than are harmed by their mediocrity. An

industrious, tenacious worker around whose sweat-beaded brow the muse makes an arc. A good fellow, one will say, when one sees how he labors with his handicraft. Nevertheless, one will not be able to concede this uprightness any longer when he [Bloem] falls on a writer of the rank of Heinrich Mann, whose shoelaces he is not fit to untie, in order to attack him as a bad German. Likewise, one will have to reject Herr Bloem's arrogance when he steps up as censor and savior of the German theater.[142]

Ossietzky ridiculed Bloem's pantheon of relics from the Second Reich. He denied that the triumph of a new political order meant the recovery of German drama from an age of ruin. Indeed, the last four decades had been a golden age for the German theater. And nationalism, Ossietzky implied strongly, would never breed anything like cultural magnificence.[143]

When Ossietzky's brilliant pasquinade appeared, Bloem had already made his peace with the new Third Reich. Walter Bloem, whom one democratic critic had called "by far the best of those who live in knights' castles," had come to terms with the mustachioed Mephistopheles and his brood of banal demons.[144]

CHAPTER 9

THE MORAL SUICIDE OF AN HONEST MAN: WALTER BLOEM AS NAZI FELLOW TRAVELER AND PARTY MEMBER

Walter Bloem, after Hitler's seizure of power, dedicated his pen, his oratorical talents, and his expertise in the writers' organizations to the Third Reich. Nevertheless, he remained something of an outsider in the new order. His own relatively moderate völkisch conservatism, albeit refitted with notions of "German blood," continued to deviate from Nazi racist totalitarianism. As the author of Brotherhood, he continued to run afoul of ideological purists like Alfred Rosenberg. Thus Bloem, much to his own despair, remained on the periphery of the official literature of the Third Reich. Except for his part in the self-coordination of the SDS, Bloem, as Ernst Löwy puts it, "played no role worth mentioning the Third Reich."[1]

Hitler's seizure of power undoubtedly left Bloem somewhat uneasy. He correctly perceived that the author of Brotherhood, an apostate until the last minute from the nationalist mainstream, would not be received with open arms by the "Old Fighters." Nor could he, a self-styled "Old Nationalist," a product of the upper-middle class, feel entirely comfortable with what he perceived as the strident, violent scions of the petty bourgeoisie. Besides, Bloem, despite his own contribution to the subjugation of the SDS to the Nazi state, had little use for the control of German culture by party functionaries. Moreover, the motives for Bloem's nationalism differed sharply from those of the Nazis.[2] He never totally gave up his vision of a mankind reconciled under Germany's beneficent tutelage. Even during the Second World War, he retained, according to Zenta Maurina, "a high-sounding dream of mother Germany, who takes all Völker under her wing."[3] True, Bloem tried to blind himself to the vast chasm between his splendid dream and the vicious reality of the Third Reich. He never, however, quite succeeded; occasional but real qualms of conscience seem to have disturbed his confidence in the new order.

Yet, Bloem was unable to resist the sirens of the national renewal. It seemed to him high time to end completely his painful alienation from the Nazi mainstream.[4] Everyone, he told a young Nazi conscience-stricken by Bloem's fictional ode to <u>Brotherhood</u>, must spread an atmosphere of trust in the new regime, committing themselves totally to the Führer.[5] Bloem hailed Hitler's seizure of power almost immediately, regretting most of all that he had contributed nothing to it.[6]

This development [Bloem wrote, on 1 April 1933, of the triumph of the Nazis] was completed almost without the personal collaboration of the German literary world, at least without the older generation. For us, we who have placed our whole life and creativity in the service of our <u>Volk</u>, it is painful to recognize that the standards have slipped from our hands, that a new generation has taken them up and carries them to victory. Nothing else remains to us than to greet with fervor this which has happened, in which we can boast of no intercessory part, and to place ourselves at its service with all the power that remains to us. If one believes that we can be useful, one will know where to find us.[7]

In the next years, Bloem found much in a Nazism triumphant that he had advocated as a reluctant republican. It seemed to him that Hitler's movement had eliminated class differences, reconciling the workers to the state. Hitler, Bloem felt, had solved Germany's economic woes; unemployment had been ended; career opportunities for the gifted had been guaranteed. Moreover, Bloem was enthralled by the resurgence of German power under the Nazis. He especially welcomed the rebuilding of the German army.[8] It appears too that Bloem, who all too often hinged political decisions on personalities and concrete impressions, fell victim to the Führer's spell. He pathetically explained to Maurina: "If you only had heard him [Hitler] speak, even a single time, then you also could not withdraw from his spell. Of that I am convinced. There is something about this man that does not let itself be gripped in words."[9]

Bloem, like many another sailor on the odyssey of the German ship of state, fell victim to the Circe from Linz; Bloem was seduced by Hitlerism into betraying his humane, his moral impulses. True, the Bloem portrayed in Maurina's memoirs never completely succeeded in smothering his own conscience.[10] The moral suicide of an honest man is seldom easy or total. It took heavy doses of self-delusion, tortured rationalization, and nationalism to drug Bloem's ethical impulses. Bloem did overcome his qualms, however; once the poet of political toleration, he now justified the "hardness, gruesomeness, and will to destruction" of the Nazis as the inevitable concomitant of revolution.

> Did not Charles I of England and Louis XVI of France end on the scaffold? Had the guillotine been a child's toy? Was not our idea of humanity and of understanding patience also of those who think otherwise perhaps only the clear proof that we lacked the metal in the blood, which did not fear to create the ruins, from which the new life can bloom?[11]

Bloem, through twisted rationalizations, even managed to convince himself that more courage was needed to take part in the "crisis" of the German Volk than to emigrate.[12]

Bloem, despite numerous attempts to get him to stand up against antisemitism, even accepted without a murmur the Nazis' systematic persecution of the Jews.[13] Whether or not he knew of the holocaust before 1945 is not known. But he was definitely aware of the savage anti-Jewish policies of the Third Reich both inside Germany before 1939 and in Eastern Europe during the Second World War.[14] Not that Bloem ever became a racist in the Nazi mold. But he did delude himself as to the rightness of the cultural-political antisemitism typical of the national conservatives.[15] Bloem justified his refusal to speak out against the official Jewish policy to himself and others by pointing to the supposedly unsatisfactory reception of his philosemitic books and speeches among Jews before 1933 and to his travails in the SDS. These experiences, to Bloem, were proof positive of the cultural-political hegemony of the Jews in the republican era. His defensive reply to a Jew, who demanded that Bloem either declare for or against Brotherhood, is worth quoting at length:

> My novel Brotherhood found in no way in its time the reception which I would have expected. The great Jewish

press so good as killed it completely by silence; the press of the rabbis made it clear to me that I understood nothing of Jewry, for baptized Jews are overall not Jews at all.

I spoke still one more time to Jewry and for Jewry, at the same time under very serious warnings--at the . . . founding day of the Association of Jewish Front Soldiers in Hamburg. My speech appeared under the title <u>German Dissension and Jewry</u> [<u>Deutsche Zwietracht und Judentum</u>] by Grethlein and Company in Leipzig and can be acquired there. The reception was the same. Death by silence in the great Jewish press, sharp rebuttal in the rabbis' press. How justified my warnings were, the further development proves. They have been disregarded. Meanwhile, I had to recognize that I had then [during the years 1918-1930] committed myself for a Jewish type which exists, if at all, only in a very small percentage--the "national German" Jew.

I was later, in my position as chairman of the Protective Association of German Writers, attacked from the Jewish side in an unheard-of fashion. I <u>was</u> an advocate of the national-minded German Jews. This the Jews themselves had weaned me from--long before the victory of antisemitism in Germany had announced itself even as a possibility. Then one believed that such advocates as I, who retained the right to tell Jewry serious truths, were not necessary. One felt oneself so secure that one repulsed the well-meaning friend, because he also dared to criticize. Now everyone comes at once and wants to enlist me for the interests of Jewry. For that it is now too late.[16]

The very stridency of Bloem's tone shows that he was not unaware of his own moral cowardice. Maurina depicts a Bloem hag-ridden by the self-betrayal of his once decent convictions: " 'I must confess to you,' Bloem replied meekly [to Maurina], 'I blushed when I saw my Jewish dentist walking on the Fahrdamm in Berlin with the yellow star, but I said to myself,' and here his voice climbed into the pathetic, 'the Führer knows what he is doing. We can be victorious only through a concessionless stance.'"[17]

In 1933, Bloem put his skill with words at the service of the Third Reich. The first edition of his Hindenburg biography, Hindenburg the German, was unsatisfactory to certain Nazi circles. A new version was ordered (by Goebbels's propaganda ministry?), to be co-written by an anonymous Nazi. Bloem, despite some misgivings, allowed his name to be given as the author of Hindenburg as Reich President (German title: Hindenburg als Reichspräsident), a paeon to the new order, which appeared in 1933.[18] Hindenburg rewarded his biographer with one of the first fifteen Goethe medals awarded in the Third Reich.[19] At the Institute for Newspaper History, Bloem, invited by the famous Professor Dovifat, lectured on Hindenburg and Hitler.[20] In December 1933, Bloem delivered a repulsively adulatory tribute to the Third Reich at the founder's day ceremonies of the Christian-Brandenburg Dining Society (Christlich-Brandenburgische Tischgesellschaft). Bloem, the late Vernunftrepublikaner, described the Weimar era in his poem as the time when "the profiteers and bosses ruled," when "commonness and shabbiness triumphed." After paying respects to Schlageter--"Schlageter be our spiritual father"--Bloem proclaimed that all Germans should be overjoyed

. . . dass Deutschland entstanden ist,
erlöst aus Scham und Schanden ist!
Heil dem Alten und Herzensdank
der Aufrecht stand, als alles versank,
und dreimal Heil dir, herrlicher Recke,
der brachte den alten Drachen zur Strecke,
zu Boden schlug den inneren Feind,
nach zwei Jahrtausenden Deutschland geeint!
Reckt die Arme, die Herzen steil:
unsern drei Helden-Siegheil! Siegheil! Siegheil![21]

Bloem, in the summer of 1933, wrote Immortal Germany (German title: Unvergängliches Deutschland), a book replete with numerous photographs designed, at least in part, to reconcile the so-called "Old Nationalists" to Hitler's brave new world.[22] The book tried to convey, as the prerequisite for German self-consciousness, "a picture of German soil [Scholle], of German blood, of German destiny."[23] The work was divided into three sections. The first examined "the German living space--the immovable foundation of German becoming and essence: the German landscape." In the next section, Bloem discussed "the 'biological material'--the distinctiveness of the German humanity--the German blood." For the first time, racial overtones colored Bloem's definition of the Volk (though he stopped considerably short of the Nazis' savage biological determinism). The book's last section was consecrated to "German destiny," i.e., to Germany's lamentable past, to her glorious present, and to her future mission. According to Bloem, this German destiny resulted from the interaction between "nature-given landscape" and Aryan biological material.[24]

In the closing section of Immortal Germany, Bloem renounced his own recent past and admonished his fellow conservatives to rally around the Nazi banner. He condemned the November revolution, which betrayed Germany's undefeated armies in the field, shattering the spirit of Germanic brotherhood achieved in August 1914 and maintained in the storm of steel. The Weimar constitution was a "Homunculus from the retort," made up "from thoughts about the state foreign to the Volk and from racially foreign political philosophy." The republican era--with the shame of Versailles, the politics of fulfillment, the inflation, the depression--was an age without hope or belief, "in which the German continued only as a vegetable."[25]

At first, those from the old bourgeois upper class who survived the wreck of the Second Reich had only a single point upon which to cling--the titanic, mystical form of Hindenburg, the second Reich President. Only gradually did a second such point emerge--Adolf Hitler. Indeed, "the rise of National Socialism is for our present-day perception absolutely to be equated with the German rebirth."[26] The Nazis rightly saw salvation from the mire of the "democratic-parliamentary-Marxist present" as coming from a true nationalist revolution, not from a return to the "dynastic-constitutional" yesterday.[27] Hitler is the genius who made this possible.

Unlike the "Old Nationalists," he recognized that renewal of the nation must come from the masses up, not from the upper class down.

Bloem admonished the Old Nationalists, among whom he counted himself, not to complain about being pushed aside by the Nazis. Old Nationalists must suppress bitterness over their reduced role. Each must spread an atmosphere of trust, fighting shoulder to shoulder with the Nazis, "if not in a leadership position, then only all the more bravely and in all the more an exemplary fashion in the rank and file."[28] Towards the end of his book, Bloem openly rued his allegiance to Weimar, envying those who adhered to Hitler from the start:

> To whomever it has not turned out so well--to whomsoever the view was muddled through looking back into our great past, through the error of Weimar, through the belief in such distant goals as Pan-Europe or even Pan-Humanity--he must be acquiescent.[29]

Yet Bloem took heart in the fact that even those who had no part in the Nazi victory would be needed in the struggle to defend the German renewal against the hostile great democracies and the enemies within. "Whether a party comrade with a book-number under 100,000, whether a convert just yesterday--none may stand aside."[30]

Germany has a cosmic mission: all young peoples of the earth look to it for "the fulfillment of God's Empire on earth."[31] To accomplish this mission, Germany must become a <u>Volk</u>, knitted together into a "genuine brotherhood. . . ."[32] Hitler is the agent for the great act of unification; if the promise of the Third Reich is fulfilled, "then immortal Germany has become truth in the German present."[33] Bloem had remained true to his guiding notion of a <u>Volk</u> brotherhood. He had, however, purged it of all liberal or true Christian elements, reconstituting it on the basis of blood, soil, and the party.

Bloem served the Nazi state with more than his pen. He also helped to choreograph the death of the SDS as a free institution. Bloem had contributed much to the formation of some of the first organizations for the economic sustenance and legal protection of the free word. Now he participated in the perversion of these associations into instruments of repression. The subjugation of the writers' organizations to the new order began in earnest after the elections of March 1933.[34] In each organization, the fiction of legality was maintained. Coordination was left to nationalist writers (conservatives as well as Nazis) within each organization. To the outside world, it was to appear as if neither the NSDAP nor the state played any part in the coordination. "The impression," Walter writes, "of outer pressure was avoided throughout; instead, it looked as if it was a question, in the matter of the transformation, of a change desired by the members and freely carried out by them."[35] Actually, of course, the "spontaneous" self-coordination was initiated by the Nazi state, at least in the SDS.[36]

Hanns Heinz Ewers, a one-time expressionist turned Nazi novelist, was empowered by Joseph Goebbels, the Reich Minister for Public Enlightenment and Propaganda, "to lead the Protective Association over into the new regime." Ewers, a distant relative of Judith Bloem, turned to her husband, who, as a former chairman of the SDS, seemed just the man to help him in this mission.[37] On 10 March 1933, Ewers and Walter Bloem, at the head of a group of nationalist writers (now definitely organized in a Working Committee of Nationalist Writers), marched into a sitting of the Main Executive Committee of the SDS.[38] Ewers showed his authorization from Goebbels and demanded that the committee regard itself as relieved from office. The committee, still chaired by Theodor Bohner, protested but gave in; eight members resigned at once, being replaced by six of the nationalist authors. Ultimately only four members of the old Main Executive Committee were retained; seventeen were dropped.[39] Ewers tried to get Bloem to take over the chairmanship. "But," Bloem recalled in his memoirs, "I had the right instinct when I declined that. I proposed to him that he report to his master that he had carried out his orders and that he put the association at the disposal of the party."[40]

The new Main Executive began at once to purge the SDS. All Communists were immediately expelled. Commissions were formed to check new members, to review the credentials of old members, and to conduct the necessary "purifications."[41] Bloem, sitting on an admissions board with Hans Richter (a national conservative), Hans Heinz Mantua-

Sadila (a Nazi), and Max Barthel (something akin to the novelist laureate of the SPD during the republic, but a recent convert to the Third Reich), conducted the expulsion of all Communists and left-democratic members, including such prestigious men of letters as Lion Feuchtwanger, Egon Erwin Kisch, and Magnus Hirschfeld.[42] "Each member," Mantua-Sadila reported, "who transgressed against German national feeling, was expelled. Also expelled was everyone of whom it was expected that he would not put himself at the disposal of the new Germany."[43]

Bloem, at the annual main assembly of the SDS, 4 May 1933, became the association's Honorary Chairman. The Nazis thus cleverly sustained the fiction of a widely accepted, free and spontaneous change in the SDS. After all, was not Bloem a conservative who, some scant seventeen months before, had been freely elected association chairman by writers of almost all political directions? Nothing was lost by this maneuver; real power was lodged in totally reliable hands. Götz Otto Stoffregen, a favorite of Goebbels and editor of the cultural-political section of the Völkischer Beobachter, became the actual chairman, and thus the true head of the Protective Association.

New statutes were drawn up at the main assembly for the SDS, requiring commitment to the Third Reich.[44] Now the writers' "Protective" organization was completely distorted into an instrument of political control. Questionnaires were issued to all members. Those designating themselves as Jews had to pay higher membership fees; they received in return special membership numbers. Newspapers and publishers were obligated to demand the SDS numbers of contributors before accepting their manuscripts. Contributions by Jews were regularly refused on the basis of their numbers without their ever learning the reason why.[45] One more example will suffice to underline the metamorphosis of the SDS from an organization defending writers into an organ of the evolving Nazi cultural dictatorship. Erich Mühsam, a cofounder of the SDS, was then incarcerated in a concentration camp; he implored the help of Bloem, the association's honorary chairman, in the name of professional solidarity. Bloem, to his lasting dishonor, disdained even the courtesy of a reply.[46]

The horrible details of Mühsam's death in the concentration camp at Oranienburg in 1934 are too well known to need retelling here.[47]

The Main Executive Committee of the SDS, following Goebbels's orders, brought the Protective Association into the Reich Association of German Writers (<u>Reichverband Deutscher Schriftsteller</u> or RDS) on 31 June 1933. The other writers' organizations were also brought into the Reich Association. Bloem headed a list of ten Honorary Senators of the RDS; the chief of the new association was Reich Führer Stoffregen.[48]

The Nazis were now completely in the driver's seat.[49] The conservative nationalists, who had been so useful in the self-coordination of the SDS, were forced to accept a composition for the RDS executive committee dictated by the National Socialists. Erich Kästner later described the consternation and cowardice of Bloem and his fellow conservatives when at the meeting to elect the RDS executive they were given ten minutes to accept the electoral list drawn up by the Nazis.

> The German Nationals sat silently amazed. The SA-poets laid their watches on the table. Walter Bloem, who sat at a table in my vicinity, blushed right through the dueling scars from his student days.... After expiration of the time limit the list was accepted. The [conservative] opponents submitted to the threat, the extortion, the force and made the astonished eyes of children.[50]

The RDS destroyed the last vestiges of free literature. According to the association's statutes, only Aryans loyal to the Third Reich could join.[51] All publishers had to inform their writers that the Reich Association was the single professional organization of German men of letters.[52] Membership in the RDS was a prerequisite for a literary career; it was compulsory for all authors and just about essential for getting a work published.[53] When a work by an author who did not belong to the RDS appeared, the association's functionaries would send him or her a questionnaire and a membership declaration. "In the summons," Dietrich Strothmann reports, "it said that an author, in the case of a rejection of this duty to report himself, would be permitted no further publications."[54]

The RDS was absorbed intact into the Reich Literature Chamber (Reich Schrifttumskammer or RSK) created by the Reich Culture Chamber Law of 22 September 1933.[55] The Reich Culture Chamber, with the RSK as one of its chief components, opened officially on 15 November 1933.[56] The RDS formed the basis of the RSK, Group Writers, the second of seven departments in the Literature Chamber. At first, the RDS was only appended to the RSK; total dissolution and integration into the Chamber took place only in October 1935.[57] As for Bloem, his honorary senatorship was "wound up."[58] He had proved useful; he was now discarded. National conservative writers, grouped around the Langen-Müller circle and led by the Chamber's first president, Hans Friedrich Blunck, did fight initially for freedom of maneuver and a large measure of self-administration within the RSK. But in October 1935 Blunck was replaced by SS Oberführer and Staatsrat Hanns Johst. From now on the RSK was totally subject to the political guidance of the Reich propaganda ministry. Activity as a writer was impossible if one was not admitted to the RSK. Ongoing censorship of the output of publishers was made unnecessary, since only reliable authors and publishers could work.[59]

Thus Bloem gave not insignificant aid to the Nazi plan for what from the outside was meant to look like the self-adaption of German writers to the new order. His name and expertise helped to cloak in forms of legality what was in fact the murder of free literature in Germany. With Bloem's help, "a political supervision instance for writers was created in the course of various stages from the unionistic interest representation of writers which the SDS once had been."[60] There can be no defense of Bloem's treason toward what had formerly been a significant part of his life's work. It should be noted, however, that he, like many others, misjudged the totalitarian nature of the Third Reich, expecting at least some vestiges of the Rechtsstaat to remain.[61] Ironically, Bloem would complain about the very dictatorship over German culture that he himself had helped to set up.[62] Perhaps with poetic justice, this dictatorship bore down hard on much of his own work.

Bloem, in spite of his services to the coordination of German culture, orchestrated by Goebbels, remained an outsider in the Third Reich, especially before 1938. Bloem's republican past haunted him. Three of his books, including <u>Brotherhood</u>, were confiscated by the political police on the basis of the "Decree of the Reich President for Protection of the <u>Volk</u> and the State," signed by Hindenburg on 28 February 1933. True, only <u>Brotherhood</u> was placed on the later index of Goebbel's propaganda ministry.[63] But in 1936, a board within the Reich Literature Chamber would list <u>Brotherhood, World Conflagration</u>, and <u>Murderess</u> as books with little to recommend them, and thus as works which were unfit for the Factory Libraries (<u>Werkbüchereien</u>).[64] Both Bloem and Grethlein and Company tried to disown <u>Brotherhood</u>. Bloem omitted it from bibliographies of his works.[65] When an expert for the RSK requested a copy of the novel for evaluation, Grethlein noted that the book was sold out and "completely superseded through the relationships of the time."[66]

Bloem's rupture with his philosemitic, republican past may have satisfied Goebbels; it never seems to have mollified Rosenberg or his Reich Office for the Furtherance of German Literature.[67] Rosenberg, unlike Goebbels, insisted on impeccable radical <u>völkisch</u> ideological credentials.[68] This the author of a best-selling philosemitic novel could never provide. Worse still, Bloem made the mistake of poking fun at Rosenberg's Reich Office in a little play put on at the seventy-fifth anniversary of the Association of Berlin Book Traders. Hans Hagemeyer, one of Rosenberg's chief lieutenants, was in the audience. Neither Hagemeyer nor his boss were amused. Bloem claimed in his memoirs (and there is no reason to doubt him) that Rosenberg now singled him out for persecution. Bookstores reportedly were admonished to drop Bloem's books from their stock. Gestapo agents watched him. Rosenberg even tried to get Bloem expelled from the "Mannschaft."[69] Rosenberg may have come up short in the decisive battles for power among Hitler's henchmen. But he was a lethal enemy for intellectuals without staunch backing from some other Nazi satrap. One suspects that only Bloem's services for Goebbels in 1933 saved him from real shipwreck.[70]

In 1938, Goebbels was instrumental in helping Bloem join the NSDAP. Bloem at first doubted whether he could gain admission to the party, although he desperately wanted to end the pressures of his isolation.[71] "The question remained as to whether the party would take in the author of Brotherhood at all--more correctly put, it unquestionably would not."[72] However, the Reich propaganda ministry sent him congratulations for his seventieth birthday (20 June 1938). Encouraged by this rare official manifestation of good will, Bloem wrote directly to Goebbels, asking to be admitted to the Nazi party. Bloem received no immediate answer. But, he was invited for the first time to an affair staged by the party--the first Weimar Poets' Congress. There, Goebbels promised to further his application for membership. On 1 November 1938, Bloem became a Nazi.[73]

In the next years, Bloem received his thirty pieces of silver for the final kiss of death to his own ethical-political independence. Not that party membership seems to have diminished Rosenberg's and Hagemeyer's hostility toward him.[74] But henceforth, Bloem was granted something akin to immunity from persecution. In January 1939, it was announced that all "political attacks" on Bloem were "undesirable."[75] During the Second World War, Bloem received even more tangible rewards from Goebbels for services rendered. Hans W. Hagen delivered a check from the propaganda ministry to Bloem for thirty thousand marks on the occasion of the latter's seventy-fifth birthday, 20 June 1943. Along with a congratulatory telegram from Hitler, Bloem also received the promise of 200 RM monthly from the Schiller Foundation in Weimar.[76]

Bloem welcomed the outbreak of the Second World War. He was convinced that it was a preventive war, a defensive war in the form of attack in no way planned by Hitler but made necessary by Poland, backed as she was by the enemy powers of 1918. Bloem, despite his age, was determined to participate in the war--"I would move heaven and hell in order to observe it up close and to put it as thoroughly as possible before my poetic lens."[77] He used his connections with General Wilhelm Keitel to get himself declared fit for garrison duty.[78]

During the war, Bloem had various assignments, including stints with several high-level staffs: the staff of Army Group C for the invasion of France; the organization of Fritz Todt; Riga, in commission of the Reich propaganda ministry, 1941-42; Germany as a lecturer for "Strength

Through Joy"; the general staff of the Luftwaffe.[79] Usually he was commissioned to write fiction supporting the German war effort. Oddly, the publication of much of it was blocked.[80] A series of four novellas glorifying the Luftwaffe did appear in both the Illustrierte Beobachter and the yearbook of the Hitler Youth. But, for some reason the propaganda ministry would not allow Bloem to publish the series in book form.[81] Bloem also gave speeches to buoy up the war effort, both to troops at the front and to civilians back home.[82]

Bloem during the war either never saw or deceived himself about the monstrous impact of the Third Reich as a whole. Yet, ever one to be affected by concrete impressions, he could still be appalled by its barbarities in particular instances. For example, Bloem spent the winter of 1941-42 at Riga in Latvia, where he was to gather materials for a novel commissioned by the Goebbels ministry with the planned title, Riga, Pioneer of Germany through the Centuries.[83] At Riga, Bloem was genuinely outraged by the inhumane and impolitic policies of the German occupation authorities. His sympathy for the Latvians and his passion for life won over the Latvian woman writer, Zenta Maurina, who heard rumors that Bloem's recall in 1942 stemmed from his friendliness to the natives. "Over the bridge of whispers came the news that the reason for his unexpected transfer was his sympathy for the Latvian people and Latvian art. He himself had strikingly characterized himself when he wrote in my guest book, 'ardour and dash and passion.'"[84]

Whether or not the Latvian rumor mill was correct, Bloem does seem to have been in some disfavor in 1942. There was even an attempt to revoke his right to wear the uniform. He was reassigned to a military organization--the general staff of the Luftwaffe--only in mid-March 1944, after having done something akin to penance by speaking at numerous, small "Strength Through Joy" meetings.[85] It is worth noting that Bloem received no other promotion during the war than a patent of his grade, major of the reserve. He himself thought this was a result of Rosenberg's continued hostility--"a last result of the disfavor in which I was held in the party thanks to my novel Brotherhood, and which was not lifted even through my forced entrance into the party."[86]

Neither distaste for specific Nazi policies nor personal chagrin shook Bloem's faith in the rightness of the Third Reich. He condemned the 20 July 1944 attempt by the German resistance on Hitler's life as treason.[87] Only after Hitler's regime had run into the sands and after the Nuremberg trials had revealed its worst excesses did Bloem have second thoughts. "Yes indeed, I have collaborated in an error," he admitted in his memoirs, while hastening to add, "and if a penance is required for this, so I have performed it with a thousand torments of hell."[88] Bloem even proclaimed that the age of nationalism was over.[89] Yet, he refused to condemn so-called social-minded nationalism. He himself had in Brotherhood propounded the true national socialism. The horrors and failures of the Third Reich stemmed from the perversion of this kind of nationalism by Hitler and a few thousand criminals.[90] Nor did Bloem concede that his refusal to oppose the Nazi state or to emigrate was wrong. He had, to his mind, in contrast to the likes of the brothers Mann, who were literati writing for literati, fulfilled the true mission of the Dichter--to share and articulate the agonies and ecstasies of his Volk--by staying to fight for Germany.[91]

The war had cost Bloem his son and almost his own life as a prisoner of the Russians. He also had to go before a de-Nazification board, which could not understand how the author of Brotherhood could join the NSDAP.[92] Nevertheless, the board released him without penalty.[93] On 8 August 1951, Bloem died at Lübeck. Walter Bloem, once Germany's most popular author and the poet of brotherhood, died a nearly forgotten man, the tatters of his reputation forever tainted by his collaboration with Nazism.

CONCLUSION

THE IMPOTENCY OF WALTER BLOEM'S PHILOSEMITISM

In the wake of World War I, Walter Bloem (like many other writers on the left and right) established what one might term, following Max Weber, a charismatic claim for his fiction. Through his books he tried to create a new German national community transfused with völkisch conservative ideals that for most of the Weimar era embraced philosemitism and republicanism.[1] His quest for political meaning and national integration, while long avoiding the Scylla of völkisch radicalism and the Charbydis of reaction, was hardly profound. His fiction, a hybrid of the entertainment with the thesis novel, evinced at best sincere craftsmanship. Nor were his flaws as political educator of a Brobdingnagian order. Bloem was not one of those evil poetic or theoretic geniuses whom every serious student of society must investigate for their deep penetration and colossal errors alike. Yet both his strengths and weaknesses as a man and thinker repay reflective study since they were widespread in a German middle class that made him "one of the most-read authors of his time."[2] To advance in the understanding of Bloem's odyssey from monarchist to poet of brotherhood to Nazi is to comprehend better the intellectual and moral roots of the German tragedy.

Bloem did not have the spiritual integrity or rigorous commitment to the philosophical pursuit of truth to resist the intellectual relativism or the disregard for principle in political life that became ever more the mark of his time. Without trans-historical standards rooted in religion, moral philosophy, or a principled ideology, Bloem could not steer a permanently moral course or even see the social world clearly. Rather, he confronted his world through sense experience apprehended as pictures. These pictures were not generated by a systematic, reasoned empiricism. Thus, Bloem made the error described by Alexis de Tocqueville of importing the "spirit of literature into politics," of judging by impressions rather than reasons.[3] Bloem's impressions were not random, but selected and interpreted according to his ultimate frames of reference of nation and social elite (the most important segment of which for him was the Bildungsbürgertum or educated burghers). Refraction through the prism of national-conservative ideology unified yet distorted these pictures in his mind's eye. The result was a vision of his times sufficiently askew to merit the term "second reality."[4] His self-comprehension was also deluded. He defined himself in reference to the collective identities of nation and social elite while imagining for himself an absurd great personality as belletristic voice of the Volk. That Bloem's political vision was nonetheless more healthy than that of most of the German right derived from his natural decency, from his readiness to learn from experience, and from the residues in his thought of the principled Judeo-Christian, liberal, and conservative traditions. Yet, while Bloem preferred humane means to sustain the nation and its corollary idol of the traditional social elites, he had no principled foundation for convincing others, or even himself, that vile means were impermissable.

A necessary cause for Bloem's willingness to endorse vile means in 1933 was his sense of isolation after Brotherhood. That Bloem was so dislocated by the animosity engendered by his book has its proximate cause in his interwoven ideological illusions and utopian identities. Hostility from his former constituency called in question his national-conservative collective identities, since he was now rejected by the very groups through which he defined the meaning and direction of his life. Rejection by these groups also rendered his writing problematic; he believed that literature was authentic, that its charismatic claim was legitimate, only when its status as voice of the Volk was affirmed by the applause of those who constituted the nation. Denial of the charismatic claim of his fiction meant also a challenge to his "great personality" as poetic fountainhead of national cohesion and self-consciousness.[5] The ultimate cause of Bloem's extreme reaction to rejection was the very need to be loved, the very vanity that had made him so dependent on his utopian identities, collective and individual, in the first place.

Bloem could have reacted with calm self-confidence to the largely negative reception of his book if he had had a principled comprehension of himself and his world. Such comprehension would have brought insight into the self-deluded nature of those whose thought and action were manifestly inconsistent with public order. Bloem would have seen why those infected with paranoid nationalism and antisemitism inevitably opposed him and often savagely resisted even his limited attempt to expose, to themselves and others, the unreason and inhumanity of their ideas and policy preferences. He would have understood that defense of the right is its own reward, ample compensation for the loss of approval of any individual or group. Integrity is surely so precious a boon to be worth a high price, including the very life that Bloem repeatedly and so willingly risked for arguably lesser goods in the Great War. Surely with an integrity rooted in principle, Bloem would have been better able to resist the continuing temptation, all too likely to become irresistible in time of crisis, to end his painful isolation from the nationalist circles in which he put so much stock by submitting to their dominant political illusions and commitments. Unfortunately, for all his attractive traits, Bloem did not possess even the last measure of character that might have gone far to function as a surrogate for principle. In the 1930s, his moral courage in confronting estrangement from those with whom he identified would prove far less impressive than his wartime physical courage.

Bloem's commitment to Hitler was not, however, merely the last act in a simple historical morality play. He would have needed extraordinary resources of character and intellect to rise above the shaping influences of class, education, Wilhelmine politics, military service, and the theater and literature industries. Even given the intersection of these influences, his own shortcomings, and his painful isolation after <u>Brotherhood</u>, a sequence of extraordinary events was needed to crystallize Bloem the Nazi fellow traveler out of Bloem the nationalistic reform conservative. Some of these events unfolded on a national stage, including the Great Depression (coming as it did after the earlier runaway inflation), the radicalization of German politics, Hindenburg's paradigmatic desertion of parliamentary government, and the thrilling surge of the nationalist parties. Others, perhaps of even greater importance, were events in the literature industry, particularly in the writers' associations, themselves profoundly affected by the destruction of German politics in depression Germany.

Experiences in the literature industry finally impelled Bloem into his unholy allegiance to the Third Reich: his abortive stage career; the unsatisfactory reviews of <u>Brotherhood</u> by republican and Jewish organs; the failure to find publishers abroad; and his conflicts in the SDS and PEN-Club. These failures owed much to Bloem's own inadequacies: his plays were mediocre; his philosemitism and republicanism were weakly rooted; his nationalist novels had little to say to foreigners; and the nationalist tinge to his program to depoliticize the writers' associations made impossible situations worse. Rather than confront the real grounds for these failures, including his own shortcomings, Bloem alighted upon a fictitious explanation, a right-wing myth with antecedents dating back to the genesis of German conservatism in the later 18th century.[6] According to this myth, German literature was in the thrall of a left-wing dictatorship, covert and unofficial, in which the Jews called the tune. This myth may have motivated Bloem's desertion of philosemitic republicanism; at any rate, it helped him rationalize this desertion to others and before the tribunal of his own conscience. By the end of 1932, Bloem was propagating this myth in print while renouncing the republic. Acceptance of this myth goes far to explain Bloem's blackest act, his participation in the Nazi destruction of free literature in Germany. He could see nothing wrong in dismantling a putative cultural dictatorship that had suppressed nationalist authors (keeping, for instance, his plays from succeeding in Berlin or his novels from finding publishers abroad) and in constructing a literature in tune with the deepest longings of the <u>Volk</u> for unity.

Bloem's conversion to Nazism did not mean endorsement of Hitler's programmatic goals as we now know them: a war for <u>Lebensraum</u> or living space in the East (indeed for world domination); removal of the Jews; and establishment of an Aryan millenium.[7] Hitler's control of the Nazi party and after 1933, to a considerable degree, of the German state was based upon what Max Weber called charismatic domination. In a charismatic movement, group cohesion derives from a leader who inspires loyalty through personal magnetism and a messianic mission. A charismatic leader cannot afford to reveal the breadth and depth of his ideology, for that would result in schisms, would necessitate purges, and would culminate in ideas becoming the source of legitimacy. Ideas as radical as Hitler's, moreover, were bound if fully known to estrange both the bulk of the electorate and the ruling elite of army and civil service. On the other hand, Hitler had to reveal some of his ideology to the general public to establish himself as a viable alternative to the system parties, even more to the <u>völkisch</u> minded to win them as party activists, and still more privately to close associates to hammer them into an inner circle of the like minded. Hitler walked the tightrope between showing too much and too little of his ideological cards by mastering the art of selective camouflage and disclosure, revealing only so much of his programmatic goals and their ideological substratum as was needed to influence a particular audience at a particular time. Anyone with sufficient leisure and penetration could have pieced together much of what Hitler believed and portended by examining the whole spectrum of his public statements and deeds. But, Hitler masterfully provided all those who wished to delude themselves as to his intentions the wherewithall to do so, sometimes by masking his real goals, sometimes by lying about them. Bloem was merely one of the more prominent of the millions of Germans who willfully blinded themselves with Hitler's help to the full meaning of the Führer's cleverly but incompletely camouflaged words and actions. The willful (and thus immoral) ignorance that had long lay behind Bloem's misconceptions about himself and his society now bore their most bitter fruit.[8]

The impotency of Bloem's Weimar era republican philosemitism was thus partly intrinsic to his thought and the ego in which it was rooted. A national conservative plea for brotherhood that, because the just impulses behind it were attenuated by intellectual-character faults, lacked sufficient substance to provide even its author with the inner resources to resist extremism during severe crisis could by itself hardly convince the German right as a whole that antisemitism was prima facie evidence of political bankruptcy. Worse still, his writings of the 1920s, led by <u>Brotherhood: A Novel</u>, even reinforced some of the notions that underpinned the radical antisemitism of this time. These included some antisemitic stereotypes, such as the notion that the Jews were invariably proponents of change, and the fundamental <u>völkisch</u> illusions, including the interlocked notions that the Volk was the prime political entity and its unity the chief political task. Bloem merely had accepted the Weimar Republic as suitable grounds for a Volksgemeinschaft (or people's community) and attacked antisemitism as an obstacle to the achievement of this Volk brotherhood. His novel encouraged a readiness to shift allegiance to whatever government form best promised the misty goal of Volk solidarity.

The internal deficiencies of Bloem's philosemitism might have been in no small measure offset if the outer circumstances of its promulgation had been more favorable. In other words, given a better literary and political context Bloem's books of the 1920s might have been a far more potent force in defusing antisemitism and right-wing revolution. After all, Bloem did dare publicly to break, thanks to his war experiences and natural decency, with the accepted ideas and prejudices of his readership when he published Brotherhood in 1922. Rather than try to swim with the tide of antisemitism then flooding the German middle strata (as did other authors of nationalist entertainment fiction like Rudolf Hans Bartsch, Karl Hans Strobl, and Robert Hohlbaum), Bloem tried to stem it.

Bloem's "knight's deed of the spirit," his philosemitic novel, potentially could have influenced the Weimar political struggle in two chief ways. First, it could have furthered the growth of a responsible national conservatism, prepared to operate within the limits of the Weimar Republic. Opposed to revolution, whether from the left or right, this conservatism favored gradual, organic reforms. In short, the triumph of Bloem's viewpoint would have transformed the German right from opponents of the republic into something resembling a loyal opposition. To be sure, this conservatism would have defended the leadership claims of the feudalized upper bourgeoisie, above all of the Bildungsbürgertum. But it would have tolerated and respected the parties and ideologies defending the interests of other social strata. Indeed, Bloem stressed the need to fulfill the socio-economic claims of the working classes.

Second, the substitution of tolerance and reluctant republicanism for ideologies pivoted around racial antisemitism could have helped to heal the chasm between the political thinking of the radical right and the actual social world. This chasm ultimately proved to be almost as harmful to those backing right-wing radicalism as it was to the Jews and to the forces of German democracy. Reality avenges itself on those who confuse illusion with necessity. Racism, with its demand for an anti-Jewish revolution within Germany and Lebensraum without, led inexorably to a Götterdämmerung, not only for Jews, German democrats, and the peoples of Europe, but for the Third Reich and its supporters as well.[9]

For a time, it appeared that the constructive potential of Brotherhood might be actualized. In the short run, the novel was a sparkling success, both as a ware and as a medium of political influence. Ninety-thousand copies went into print within six months, a figure seldom matched in German literary history before 1922. Many of those who bought the novel were undoubtedly linked to parties already hostile to radical racist antisemitism--the Center (and BVP) and the DDP. But there is a good deal of evidence that the book shook the belief of not a few nationalists in antisemitism and anti-republicanism. Indeed, its theoretical weaknesses--its völkisch strains, its residual antisemitic misconceptions, its misplaced faith in the corps and the upper bourgeoisie--were its practical strengths in winning converts from the radical right to a moderate conservative nationalism prepared to operate within the Weimar system. But the history of the novel's working on the public was like a shooting star. Brilliant at first, it was soon extinguished, leaving the night sky of the German right as dark as before. By 1923, the sales and political effectiveness of Brotherhood had evaporated.

The ultimate failure of Brotherhood, which marked a downward turn in Bloem's career, is in itself instructive. The sale, distribution and reading of fiction do not take place in a vacuum. Organizational or publicistic backing of a book with political overtones may be as important to its success as its intrinsic merits--as the beauty of its form or the persuasiveness of its contents. The organizations and press of the right were with few exceptions hostile to Brotherhood. No nationalist group of importance tried to distribute the book. The feuilletons of the right--the organs mediating between the offerings of the book market and the nationalist middle strata--aimed to discourage purchase of the novel or to discredit its message. It was surely no coincidence that the demand for the novel began to plummet just after the nationalist organs cast their brickbats at it. Perhaps, a resolute publisher having substantial economic clout with booksellers could have brought Brotherhood through the storm. Grethlein was not up to this task.

Bloem himself did nothing to rectify the lack of organizational presuppositions for the spread of his brand of national conservatism. He was too deeply imbued with the politically harmful German tradition of the poet unfettered by party ties. According to this tradition, the poet (i.e., creative writer) was the mouthpiece of the whole Volk, not of any of its segments. Thus he could not cast his lot with any party or pressure group. It may well be that Bloem would have been unsuccessful in practical politics. His unorthodox national conservatism may have precluded useful political work in any existing right-wing organization.[10] His stewardship of the writers' associations was hardly a paradigm of flexible political leadership, although there is no evidence that any other German author could have done much better.

Yet Bloem had some of the attributes of an effective politician. He had great personal magnetism, a glittering war record, administrative experience (during the war and in the writers' associations), and proven talent as a writer and orator. One of the greatest defects of Bloem's political vision, his importation of the "spirit of literature into politics," might have been a boon in gathering support in an age of mass politics. Other men carrying the spirit of art into politics--Adolf Hitler, Joseph Goebbels, Arthur Dinter, Baldur von Schirach, Albert Speer--certainly played key roles in paving the way for and running the Third Reich.[11]

Practical political activity by Bloem and those who agreed with him was essential, whatever its prospects for success, because existing right-wing organizations were tainted thoroughly by one type of antisemitism or another. Bloem's travails after 1922 underline the impracticality of philosemitic nationalist fiction unbuttessed by practical politics. Spokesmen for existing right-wing organizations not only resisted philosemitism; they saw it as irrefutable proof of treason to the nationalist cause. A writer (or politician) who publicly opposed antisemitism, however strong his nationalism or conservatism in other respects, had to reckon with the likelihood that he would be henceforth branded as a renegade from the right-wing mainstream. The nationalist aversion to <u>Brotherhood</u> went far to destroy Bloem's popularity and credibility with the majority of his hitherto vast circle of readers. Now Bloem was regarded as a traitor to nationalism; this disturbed his economic well-being and greatly weakened the political power of his pen. Small wonder that no other nationalist author (and there were a number with little sympathy for or even hostile to anti-Jewish bigotry) dared attack anti-semitism in a major work. The failure to combat anti-Jewish propaganda by those most respected by nationalist readers left antisemitism almost uncontested within the German right.[12]

The constructive potential of Bloem's novel (and of his other writings in the same vein) could have been realized and the consequences of its flaws minimized only if Weimar Germany had possessed either a broad-based, principled conservatism or progressivism. The literary agents, especially the critics, of a principled conservatism, would have sustained the distribution of his book, while giving readers the means to separate the wheat from the chaff in his political message. Through constructive criticism they might have helped Bloem to a clearer political vision, thus helping to correct the inner as well as the outer causes of the impotency of his philosemitism. Unfortunately, Germany lacked such a conservatism until the Christian Democratic Union and its Bavarian counterpart, the Christian Social Union, were founded in the western occupation zones after the catastrophe of World War II.

A democratic party embracing a wide spectrum of class interests, confessions, and policy alternatives within a framework of principled commitment to a free, just society might have provided Bloem with a new audience and political home while making him wiser. The Jewish and to a lesser extent, the Catholic response to <u>Brotherhood</u> showed how Bloem could be supported by those who had reservations about his message, how readers could be prepared to assimilate the good and disregard the bad in that message, and how the author could be convinced (if only fleetingly) to improve that message. Unfortunately, neither the Jewish nor Catholic press had access to those most susceptible to radical <u>völkisch</u> propaganda, the Protestant middle classes.

Significantly, no specifically Protestant organ seems to have reviewed <u>Brotherhood</u>. DVP critics did endorse Bloem's message but without improving on it, since these heirs of the national liberal tradition shared his illusions as well as his reluctant republicanism. Besides the People's party had little impact on the masses. Similar was the provincial left liberal press with its small audience and uncritical reception of Bloem's novel. The great democratic liberal newspapers, which had a substantial impact on the book market, ignored the "new Bloem" or damned him with faint praise, since his art was too trivial, his message too problematic.

The Social Democrats, the main pillars of the republic, never freed themselves sufficiently from their self-conception as the Marxist vanguard of the working class to emerge as what they would become in 1959, a non-ideological partisan of a free society with support extending deep into the middle class. At any rate, the literature politics of the SPD was singularly ineffective. Not surprisingly, when Bloem reached out to the Social Democrats and the republic which they had created, they ignored him or responded only in scattered, lukewarm, and belated fashion. As for the Communists, portrayed not only by East German scholars but also by the influential Hans-Albert Walter in accord with their own self-image in the late Weimar era, i.e., as the only conceivable rallying point for anti-fascist literary forces, they never reviewed Bloem the philosemite. Indeed, for the Communists everyone but the democratic writers of the homeless left were fascists, with the actual Nazis the least important of these in the literary sphere. Their literature politics, while aiming to turn the homeless left into fellow travelers, was not designed to create a genuine anti-Nazi front; it was designed, inside and outside the SDS, to destroy the only feasible bulwark against Hitler's barbarism, the republic. In the case of Bloem, the Communists extirpated rather than furthered his faltering impulses towards civilized politics. Of course, Bloem's own attempts in 1933-34 and again after World War II to justify his own adherence to Hitler's Reich by pointing to the republican press's unsympathetic reception of his book should be seen for what they are: shameless rationalizations, renewed flights from his own moral responsibility. Without doubt, however, no little can be learned from the failure of any great political formation on the left to utilize the massive influence of Bloem's pen or to educate him politically.

With Bloem's moral and political suicide, one feels the full impact of the German tragedy. Here was no mental desperado like Arthur Dinter, no true-believing fanatic like Alfred Rosenberg, no crass opportunist like Hanns Heinz Ewers. Here was a man regarded as "honorable" by most of his contemporaries who, like his inferiors, linked his fate to Nazism and either collaborated or acquiesced in detestable acts.[13] The singer of brotherhood ultimately became caught up in a web woven of various strands: the moral relativism of his age; his ideological blinders; his own character weaknesses; the tensions and conflicts within a literature industry beset with economic and political problems. Yet he willfully refused to break free and thus helped the blackest night to eclipse "the morning shimmer of a new day for humanity."

NOTES

INTRODUCTION

1. Ernst Wiechert, "Die Gebärde," in Sämtliche Werke, 10 vols. (Vienna, Munich, and Basel, 1943) 7: 608. See also: Sumner Kirschner "'Even if They Were Guilty': An Unpublished Letter by Ernst Wiechert about the Jews," German Life and Letters: A Quarterly Review 23 (1970): 142-43.

2. Ernst Püschel, Die Juden von Kronburg: Ein Buch von deutschem Volks- und Menschentum. Roman (Neudietendorff, 1924). Quote from Ernst Püschel, "Die wahre völkische Gesinnung," CV-Zeitung 3 (4 Dec. 1924): 769.

3. Judgments about comparative sales statistics must take into account the flawed but useful German Studies in America, vol. 2: Donald Ray Richards, The German Bestseller in the 20th Century: A Complete Bibliography and Analysis, 1915-1940 (Berne: 1968). See also: Ernst Löwy, Literatur unterm Hakenkreuz: Das Dritte Reich und seine Dichtung. Eine Dokumentation (Frankfurt/Main, 1966, 1983), p. 307; Wuppertal, Stadt Bücherei, Nachlass Walter Bloem, [hereafter cited as Nachlass Bloem (Wuppertal)], file 22: Erich Leyens to Bloem, 3 Mar. 1923.

4. Peter de Mendelssohn, S. Fischer und sein Verlag (Frankfurt/Main, 1970), p. 886.

5. The desirability of attempting a definition of philosemitism was pointed out to me by Professor Robert W. Heywood in his perceptive commentary on the preliminary version of this article, delivered as a paper to the Twelfth Annual Great Lakes History Conference, Grand Rapids, Michigan, on 17 Apr. 1986.

6. Paul Johnson argues persuasively that a chief reason for the murderous nature of 20th-century history has been the abandonment, initiated by Lenin, of "the notion of individual guilt, and with it the whole Judeo-Christian ethic of personal responsibility." What Lenin had begun, the assignment of guilt to whole groups which were then targeted for extermination, was continued by the radical antisemites in Germany culminating with Hitler. "The new antisemitism, in short, was part of the sinister drift away from the apportionment of individual responsibility towards the notion of collective guilt--the revival, in modern guise, of one of the most primitive and barbarous, even bestial of instincts." Paul Johnson, Modern Times: The World from the Twenties to the Eighties (New York et al, 1983), pp. 70-71, 118.

7. See Uwe Lohalm, Völkischer Radikalismus: Die Geschichte des Deutschvölkischen Schutz- und Trutz-Bundes 1919-1933 (Hamburg, 1970); George Mosse, The Crisis of German Ideology: Intellectual Origins of the Third Reich (New York, 1964); Klaus Scholder, Die Kirchen und das Dritte Reich: Band I, Vorgeschichte und Zeit der Illusionen 1918-1934 (Frankfurt/Main, Berlin, Vienna, 1977), pp. 93-109.

NOTES

CHAPTER 1

BESTSELLING NOVELIST OF THE WILHELMINE TWILIGHT: THE ROAD FROM MONARCHIST TO RELUCTANT REPUBLICAN

1. Nachlass Bloem (Wuppertal), file 6/29: [Walter Bloem], [Untitled Autobiographical Sketch for the Celebration of Bloem's Fiftieth Birthday; hereafter, Autobiographical Sketch], n.d. [1918], pp. 1-5; Freiburg, Bundesarchiv-Militärarchiv, Nachlass Bloem, [hereafter cited as Nachlass Bloem (Freiburg)], Record Group N31, file 10: Bloem to Georg Engel, 15 Apr. 1915; Hermann A. L. Degener, Wer ist's? (Berlin, 1928), p. 142; Nachlass Bloem (Freiburg), RG N31: Dr. Schmalz, "Findbuch N31, Dr. Walter Bloem [Guide to Bloem Nachlass with Biographical Data]," 19 July 1966; Terrell Carver, Engels (New York, 1981), pp. 3-5; Walter Bloem et al, "Warum werden Ihre Bücher viel gelesen? Das Rätsel des Publikumserfolges," Die literarische Welt 4, no. 19 (1928): 3.

2. Nachlass Bloem (Wuppertal), file 6/29: [Bloem], [Autobiographical Sketch], pp. 4-5; Nachlass Bloem (Freiburg) RG N31: Dr. Schmalz, "Findbuch N31"; Degener, Wer ist's? (1928), p. 142; Bloem, "Warum werden Ihre Bücher viel gelesen?" p. 3.

3. Nachlass Bloem (Wuppertal), file 6/29: [Bloem], [Autobiographical Sketch], pp. 5-11; quote from Nachlass Bloem (Wuppertal), file 6/29: [Bloem] to the Verlag Rheinische Heimat (Dr. Heinrich Öhlers), 10 May 1928; Nachlass Bloem (Wuppertal): Walter Bloem, "Werk und Tat: Zweites Buch erstes bis achtes Kapitel, Seite 180-298" [fragment of Bloem's unpublished autobiography, written shortly after World War II], p. 271; Bloem, "Warum werden Ihre Bücher viel gelesen?," p. 3; Nachlass Bloem (Wuppertal), file 8: Walter Bloem, "Eine Freiburger Theatererinnerung: Dazu allerlei Grundsätzliches," p. 1.

4. Nachlass Bloem (Wuppertal), file 6/29: [Bloem], [Autobiographical Sketch], p. 9; Walter Bloem, Der krasse Fuchs: Roman (Leipzig and Zurich, 1906 [1932]); Werner Hegemann, "Walter Bloem contra Heinrich Mann," Das Tagebuch 13 (1932): 1590-91.

5. Bloem, "Warum werden Ihre Bücher viel gelesen?," p. 3; Nachlass Bloem (Freiburg), RG N31, file 1: Walter Bloem, "Lebenslauf," (copy of a letter from Generalstab des Feldheeres im Auftrage des Herrn Hauptmanns Bloem to Schriftleitung von Dennerts Konversationslexikon, Prof. Dr. Dennert), 19 Apr. 1916; Nachlass Bloem (Wuppertal), file 6/29: [Bloem], [Autobiographical Sketch], pp. 10-11; Nachlass Bloem (Freiburg), RG N31: Dr. Schmalz, "Findbuch N31"; Comp. Bibliographische Abteilung des Börsenvereins der deutschen Buchhändler zu Leipzig, Deutsches Bücherverzeichnis: Eine Zusammenstellung der im deutschen Buchhandel erschienenen Bücher, Zeitschriften und Landkarten mit einem Stich- und Schlagwort-register, 40 vols. published by 1970 (Leipzig, 1916-) 23: 490.

6. Comp. Heinrich Conrad, Christian Gottlob Kaysers vollständiges Bücher-Lexikon: Ein Verzeichnis der seit dem Jahre 1750 im deutschen Buchhandel erschienenen Bücher und Landkarten, vol. 53 (Leipzig, 1911), pp. 292-93; Deutsches Bücherverzeichnis 1: 342; 7: 390; Hegemann, "Bloem contra Mann," Das Tagebuch 13 (1932): 1390.

7. The following Bloem books (almost all novels) came out in first editions of fifty-thousand copies each, Volk wider Volk (1912); Die Schmiede der Zukunft (1913); Das verlorene Vaterland (1914); Vormarsch (?); Gottesferne (1920); Herrin (1921); Brüderlichkeit (1922). Deutsches Bücherverzeichnis 1: 342; 6: 312; 7: 390. See for Bloem popularity: Nachlass Bloem (Wuppertal), file 6/29: [Bloem], [Autobiographical Sketch], p. 12; Bloem, "Warum werden Ihre Bücher viel gelesen?," p. 3; Nachlass Bloem (Wuppertal): Bloem, "Werk und Tat: Zweites Buch," pp. 240-45. Bloem described himself as the best-selling author on the German book market. Ibid., file 22: Bloem to Hermann Hestermann, 26 Apr. 1949.

8. According to Friedrich Albrecht, the belletristic field in the years before the outbreak of World War I was ruled by "apologists for the Empire" like Bloem. Deutsche Schriftsteller in der Entscheidung: Wege zur Arbeiterklasse 1918-1933 (Berlin and Weimar, 1970), p. 22. Kaiser Wilhelm II, on numerous occasions, summoned Bloem to talk over the latter's books. Herbert Eulenberg, "Walter Bloem zum 60. Geburtstag (20. Juni 1928)," CV-Zeitung 17 (22 June 1928): 356. The inside back flaps of later editions of the Franco-Prussian War trilogy contain ecstatic reviews of the novels from the major liberal dailies: Walter Bloem, Das eiserne Jahr: Roman (Leipzig, 1912); Walter Bloem, Die Schmiede der Zukunft (Leipzig, 1913), pp. 513-14. The Vossische Zeitung quotes from: Walter Bloem, Volk wider Volk: Roman (Leipzig, 1912), inside back flaps.

9. Nachlass Bloem (Wuppertal): Bloem, "Werk und Tat: Zweites Buch," pp. 192-94.

10. Nachlass Bloem (Wuppertal): file 65, [Bloem] to Dr. Harald Öldag, 2 Apr. 1925; file 22, Moritz Schauenburg to Herr Dreecken, 30 Jan. 1946.

11. Bloem had entered the army in 1890, being commissioned a Second Lieutenant of the Reserve in 1894. In 1903, he had been promoted to First Lieutenant; in 1911, he rose to Captain. Nachlass Bloem (Freiburg), RG N31: Dr. Schmalz, "Findbuch N31," and file 26, "Stammliste"; Nachlass Bloem (Wuppertal): Bloem, "Werk und Tat: Zweites Buch," pp. 182-83.

12. Quote from Nachlass Bloem (Wuppertal): Bloem, "Werk und Tat: Zweites Buch," p. 182. See also, Nachlass Bloem (Freiburg), RG N31, file 4: Walter Bloem, "Keine Verbitterung! [typescript of war article for unidentified journal]," [1916].

13. Nachlass Bloem (Freiburg), RG N31: file 25, Major [retired] Ludwig Osius to Bloem [for his seventieth birthday], 24 June 1938; file 26, "Stammliste"; Dr. Schmalz, "Findbuch N31." See also, Nachlass Bloem (Wuppertal), "Werk und Tat: Zweites Buch," p. 183.

14. Nachlass Bloem (Freiburg), RG N31: Dr. Schmalz, "Findbuch N31"; Nachlass Bloem (Wuppertal): Bloem, "Werk und Tat: Zweites Buch," p. 184.

15. Gerhard Ritter, The Tragedy of Statesmanship: Bethmann Hollweg as War Chancellor (1914-1917), vol. 3 of The Sword and the Scepter: The Problem of Militarism in Germany, trans. Heinz Norden (Coral Gables, Florida, 1972), pp. 358-72 (quote on 359).

16. Nachlass Bloem (Wuppertal): Bloem, "Werk und Tat: Zweites Buch," p. 184.

17. Ibid., pp. 184-89.

18. Nachlass Bloem (Freiburg), RG N31, file 3: Walter Bloem, "Greülhetze," Kölnische Zeitung (10 Feb. 1915) and [Walter Bloem], draft for a lecture, ultimately published in Die Woche 17 (1 May 1915): 613-19.

19. Nachlass Bloem (Freiburg), RG N31, file 22: article by a Herr Kuhn in the Bayrische Landeszeitung (25 Aug. 1919), attached to and the subject of Bloem to Herr Kuhn, 28 Aug. 1919.

20. Nachlass Bloem (Freiburg), RG N31: Dr. Schmalz, "Findbuch N31."

21. Nachlass Bloem (Wuppertal): Bloem, "Werk und Tat: Zweites Buch," p. 195.

22. Alistair Horne, The Price of Glory: Verdun 1916 (Harmondsworth, Middlesex, England et al, 1962, 1964, 1978), esp. pp. 42-45, 330 (quotes on 13).

23. Nachlass Bloem (Wuppertal): Bloem, "Werk und Tat: Zweites Buch," p. 195.

24. Nachlass Bloem (Freiburg), RG N31: Dr. Schmalz, "Findbuch N31"; file 1, "Lebenslauf"; file 26, "Stammliste"; file 8, Walter Bloem, "Notizen über die Tätigkeit der Feldpressestelle des Generalstabes des Feldheeres, Charlesville, 1916-1918," [n.d.]; Martin Kitchen, The Silent dictatorship: The Politics of the German High Command under Hindenburg and Ludendorff, 1916-1918 (New York, 1976), pp. 45-66 (quote about Section III B on 49); Walter Nicolai, Nachrichtendienst, Presse und Volksstimmung im Weltkrieg (Berlin, 1920), pp. 65-68; Gordon Wright, The Ordeal of Total War, 1939-1945 (New York, Evanston, and London, 1968), p. 69 (footnote 4).

25. Nachlass Bloem (Freiburg) RG N31, file 8: Bloem, "Notizen über die Tätigkeit der Feldpressestelle"; Nachlass Bloem (Wuppertal): Bloem, "Werk und Tat: Zweites Buch," pp. 195-99.

26. Nachlass Bloem (Wuppertal), file 65: Bloem to [Dr. Harald Öldag], 2 Apr. 1925; Dr. Harald Öldag, Bergisch-Märkische Zeitung, Abt. Aussenpolitik, to [Bloem], 23 Mar. 1925.

27. Quote from Nachlass Bloem (Wuppertal): Bloem, "Werk und Tat: Zweites Buch," p. 196 (see also 197-202). Bloem's attack on the Peace Resolution was entitled "From a Front Officer" and appeared in Die Woche. Ibid., p. 202. This was undoubtedly part of the Supreme Command's campaign against the Peace Resolution. For this see Gordon A. Craig, The Politics of the Prussian Army, 1650-1945 (London, Oxford, New York, 1970 [first published by the Clarendon Press, 1955]), pp. 330-31. In his post-World War II autobiography, Bloem described his political conversion with more drama than historical precision. "I can, with mathematical exactness, mark the moment in which I, almost in a jolt, was transformed from a monarchist by education and tradition into an incorrigible

democrat: it was that short admonition--'[his] majesty needs sun'--given to me by the old Plessen after I had explained to His Majesty too much about Verdun, more according to the interpretation of the courtiers than he needed to know." Actually, Bloem's political reorientation was both less abrupt and less absolute. He remained a monarchist of sorts until the November revolution and even retained something of an emotional attachment to the crown long afterwards. Nachlass Bloem (Wuppertal): Bloem, "Werk und Tat: Zweites Buch," p. 196.

28. Nachlass Bloem (Freiburg), RG N31, file 4: Bloem, "Keine Verbitterung!"

29. Nachlass Bloem (Freiburg), RG N31, file 6: Walter Bloem, Wandlungen der Seele im Kriege: Vortrag, gehalten am 20. Januar 1917 im Sieglehaus zu Stuttgart auf Einladung der Vereinigung für Vorträge während des Krieges (Württemberg, n.d. [1917; forward by Bloem dated 27 Jan. 1917]).

30. Nachlass Bloem (Wuppertal): Bloem, "Werk und Tat: Zweites Buch," pp. 205-14, 234. See the following in Nachlass Bloem (Freiburg), RG N31: file 8, Bloem, "Notizen"; file 1, Barmer Zeitung (2 Mar. 1918); Dr. Schmalz, "Findbuch N31"; file 26, "Stammliste"; file 1, Generalstab des Feldheeres, Abteilung IIIb, "Nr. 195431II, geheim," 7 Nov. 1918.

31. The date given in Bloem's autobiography for the lecture is 6 Nov. The date given in Bloem's diary, 4 Nov., is undoubtedly correct. Nachlass Bloem (Wuppertal): Bloem, "Werk und Tat: Zweites Buch," p. 206; Nachlass Bloem (Freiburg), RG N31, file 7: [Walter Bloem], "Maschinenschriftliche Übertragung der stenographischen Tagebuch-Aufzeichnungen des Schriftstellers Walter Bloem über die Ereignisse vom 19. Oktober bis zum 21. November 1918, Kriegspresseamt und Revolution, aus Aktenstück 7 des Bestandes 54 des Bundesarchivs, S. 1-44, dictando-übertragen von Oberregierungsrat a.D. Ludwig Krieger, Bonn [transcription of Bloem's diary from stenographic original]," entry for 4 Nov. 1918, pp. 9-10.

32. Quote from Nachlass Bloem (Wuppertal): Bloem, "Werk und Tat: Zweites Buch," p. 212. It is not clear whether this is a direct quote from or a paraphrase from his speech of 4 Nov. 1918. In this speech, Bloem admitted that the public had not often been told the truth, that he himself had not told it. He had, Bloem went on, been an officer for twenty-eight years--but the time had come when his duty to the fatherland and to the Volk was greater than that to the army. Nachlass Bloem (Freiburg), RG N31, file 11: "Ein eigenartiger Vortrag in der Kolonialgesellschaft," Der Reichsbote (6 Nov. 1918).

33. This sentence and the last three of the preceding paragraph are based on: Nachlass Bloem (Freiburg), RG N31, file 7: [Bloem], "Maschinen- schriftliche Übertragung," entry of 4 Nov. 1918, pp. 9-10; Nachlass Bloem (Wuppertal): Bloem, "Werk und Tat: Zweites Buch," p. 214.

34. Nachlass Bloem (Freiburg), RG N31, file 11: "Ein Eigenartiger Vortrag in der Kolonialgesellschaft," Der Reichsbote (6 Nov. 1918); "Walter Bloems politische Wandlungen," Deutsche Zeitung (5 Nov. 1918).

35. Nachlass Bloem (Wuppertal): Bloem, "Werk und Tat: Zweites Buch," p. 234. Not all those present for the lecture were hostile; the future Reich Chancellor of Germany, Heinrich Brüning, an admirer of Bloem's fiction, was overjoyed by Bloem's stand against

the Pan-Germans. Nachlass Bloem (Wuppertal), file 51: Heinrich Brüning to Bloem, 6 Nov. 1918.

36. Nachlass Bloem (Freiburg), RG N31, file 7: [Bloem], "Maschinenschriftliche Übertragung," entry of 27 Oct. 1918, p. 5.

37. Ibid., entry of 24 Oct. 1918, p. 4.

38. Ibid., entry of 10 Nov. 1918, p. 17.

39. Nachlass Bloem (Wuppertal): Bloem, "Werk und Tat: Zweites Buch," p. 215.

40. Ibid., pp. 215-21.

41. Nachlass Bloem (Freiburg), RG N31, file 7: [Bloem], "Maschinenschriftliche Übertragung," entry of 10 Nov. 1918, p. 17.

42. Ibid., entry of 12 Nov. 1918, p. 19.

43. This was authored by Gerhart Hauptmann. Ibid., entry of 13 Nov. 1918, p. 20. Brüning visited Bloem on this day; Bloem described the visit as "fairly insignificant."

44. Albrecht, Deutsche Schriftsteller, pp. 81, 649 (footnote 7). "Here [affixed to this declaration] one finds, alongside Käthe Kollwitz and Bernhard Kellermann, the notorious reactionary Bloem, who just a few weeks before had summoned the German Volk to hold out...." Ibid., p. 81.

NOTES

CHAPTER 2

THE MIND AND CHARACTER OF WALTER BLOEM: SOME REFLECTIONS

1. For the role of fiction generally and of the entertainment novel in particular in Germany during 1700-1933, see Part I of Rodler F. Morris, "German Nationalist Fiction and the Jewish Question, 1918-1933" (Ph.D. dissertation; University of North Carolina, Chapel Hill, 1979), pp. 8-195. See also, Edgar Herrenbrück, Literaturverständnis im Wilhelminischen Bürgertum (Ph.D. dissertation: Göttingen, 1970); Heide Radeck, Zur Geschichte von Roman und Erzählung in der "Gartenlaube" (1853 bis 1914): Heroismus und Idylle als Instrument nationaler Ideologie (Ph.D. dissertation; Friedrich-Alexander-Universität Erlangen-Nürnberg).

2. Deutsches Bücherverzeichnis 12: 457; 17: 339; 20: 314. One book was published by the Verlag Reimer Hobbing, owner of the Deutsche Allgemeine Zeitung and part of the Hugo Stinnes empire. This was Bloem's book on the war, Der Weltbrand. For the Verlag Reimer Hobbing, see Heinz-Dietrich Fischer, "Deutsche Allgemeine Zeitung," Deutsche Zeitungen des 17. bis 20. Jahrhunderts, ed. Heinz-Dietrich Fischer (Pullach near Munich, 1972), pp. 275-81 and Kurt Koszyk, Deutsche Presse 1914-1945: Geschichte der deutschen Presse, Teil III (Berlin, 1972), pp. 108-9, 135-36, 138-39, 142. For the early history of the publishing concern that became perhaps the main clearing house for nationalist entertainment fiction, see L. Staackmann Verlag, L. Staackmann Leipzig 1869-1919 (Leipzig, 1919). For a discussion of leading authors of nationalist entertainment fare, see Hans Sahl, "Klassiker der Leihbibliothek," Das Tagebuch 7 (1926): 794-98, and 7 (1926): 881-85.

3. For friendship with Rudolf Herzog, Nachlass Bloem (Wuppertal), file 6/29: [Bloem], [Autobio- graphical Sketch], pp. 5-6. See also, "Ein durch und durch Ehrlicher: dichter Bloem 100. Jahre alt," Westdeutsche Rundschau (29 June 1968), which describes Rudolf Herzog as Bloem's "brother in spirit." For Bloem's friendship with Strobl and Hohlbaum, Nachlass Bloem (Wuppertal): Bloem, "Werk und Tat: Zweites Buch," p. 295. Strobl, Hohlbaum, and Herzog all wrote novels dealing with the Jewish question.

4. Sahl, "Klassiker der Leihbibliothek," Das Tagebuch 7 (1926): 794-98 and 7 (1926): 881-85.

5. The first German lending libraries were set up in the late seventeenth and early eighteenth centuries. But, they became common only after 1750. These libraries were private enterprises that lent reading material for a small fee. They were owned and operated in the eighteenth century by bookmen--by binders, printers, booksellers and publishers. Later, all sorts of people, many without experience with books (or things of the mind), entered the lending library business. By 1800, most German towns had a lending library. The stock-in-trade of these libraries was the Unterhaltungsroman. The lending libraries of the 1700s served the less prestigious, educated and wealthy members of the middle class and those who read in the lower classes. Richard Schmidt, "Der Leihbuchhandel," in Der deutsche Buchhandel: Wesen, Gestalt, Aufgabe [hereafter cited

as Buchhandel], eds. Helmut Hiller and Wolfgang Strauss (Gutersloh, 1961), pp. 256-57; Albert Ward, Book Production, Fiction, and the German Reading Public, 1740-1800 (Oxford, 1974), pp. 102-8; Eda Sagarra, Tradition and Revolution: German Literature and Society, 1830-1890 (London, 1971), p. 30. The number of lending libraries continued to expand in the nineteenth century. Indeed, until the advent of television after World War II, the lending libraries did an incredible business. The lending libraries in the Federal Republic of Germany had twenty million volumes in the 1950s. They made 600,000,000 loans per year. In the big cities, these libraries were heavily used by workers. In 1930, one such library in Berlin drew 70 per cent of its patrons from the proletariat (and 30 per cent from the petty bourgeoisie). Schmidt, "Leihbuchhandel, p. 257; Helmut Hiller, Zur Sozialgeschichte von Buch und Buchhandel (Bonn, 1966), p. 111; Fritz Erpenbeck, "Leihbibliothek am Wedding," Die Linkskurve 2, no. 7 (1930): 14. This library loaned out 25-30 books daily, except on Friday and Sunday, when the number reached 80. At times during the winter, as many as 100 books were lent in a day. The fee for borrowing a book was 0.1 marks. See also: Karl Kossow, "Was liest der deutsche Arbeiter," Die Literatur: Monatschrift für Literaturfreunde 29 (1927): 503-5; "Tagebuch der Zeit: Berlin, dritte Aprilwoche," Das Tagebuch 8 (1927): 608. The following articles by Hans Sahl in Das Tagebuch are goldmines for understanding the nature and content of the most demanding lending library novels during the Weimar era: "Klassiker der Leihbibliothek," 7 (1926): 716-20; "Klassiker der Leihbibliothek," 7 (1926): 756-60; "Klassiker der Leihbibliothek: III. Der Scherlstratz," 7 (1926): 794-98; "Klassiker der Leihbibliothek: IV. Skowronnecke und Zobeltitze," 7 (1926): 881-85; "Klassiker der Leihbibliothek: V. Ludwig Wolff," 7 (1926): 1041-45.

6. M. Kay Flavell, "Kitsch and Propaganda: The Blending of Myth and History in Hedwig courts-Mahler's Lissa geht ins Glück (1936)," German Studies Review 8, no. 1 (1985): 65-87 (quotes from 65-66 and 82).

7. Bloem, "Warum werden Ihre Bücher viel gelesen?," p. 3.

8. Nachlass Bloem (Freiburg), RG N31, file 1: Bloem, "Lebenslauf."

9. Bloem, "Warum werden Ihre Bücher viel gelesen?," p. 3. "I have," Bloem wrote in 1925, "dedicated my life and creative activity to the German Volk in its entirety, and will never tire of admonishing it to unity, to reconciliation." Nachlass Bloem (Wuppertal), file 22: Walter Bloem, "Ein Wort zu 'Brüderlichkeit,'" Hamburger Familienblatt (1 Dec. 1925); Walter Bloem, "Offene Antwort zu Rocholl," 16 May 1923.

10. Nachlass Bloem (Freiburg), RG N31, file 1: Kriegspresseamt (War Press Bureau) to Bloem, 7 Nov. 1918. This letter informed Bloem that, according to instructions of the General Staff of the Field Army, Department III, the novel on enemy espionage begun by him was deemed no longer advisable.

11. In 1924, Bloem put his conception of the alternatives facing the contemporary artist in the form of a question to the historian-philosopher Oswald Spengler: "Will the artist strive for pure beauty, or will he acquiesce in producing for the time the great symbols of its necessity in the form of typical representatives?" For Bloem the choice was clear--there was no room for l'art pour l'art; the writer had to face up to his responsibility to the nation. Nachlass Bloem (Wuppertal), file 19: [Walter Bloem], "Gespräch mit Spengler," (in Hamburg), Apr. 1924, p. 3. Spengler answered that he who is not satisfied

"with making entertainment art, therefore art for business purposes, will view himself in the first line as educator of his Volk through the putting up of ideal forms of the national destiny." According to Spengler, the age of the great novel follows that of the great drama. This has not happened in Germany yet. This great novel "will try to form the essential tragic of the life of Völker in symbolic representations of great format." Spengler contended that the Dichter had to paint the tragedy of the Germans in its historical context, to educate the Germans to world historical thinking, to recognition of political reality. Bloem put the greatest stock in Spengler and likely made these views on literature his own. Ibid., pp. 1-4. See also, Bloem, "Warum werden Ihre Bücher viel gelesen?," p. 3. For Bloem's post-World War II condemnation of those whom he perceived to write as literati for the literati, to pursue art for art's sake, see Nachlass Bloem (Wuppertal): [Walter Bloem], "Zweites Buch: Der neue Dreissigjahre Krieg," ["Werk und Tat," vol. 3], n.d. (post-1945), pp. 513-22.

12. Nachlass Bloem (Wuppertal), file 22: Walter Bloem, "Ein Wort zu 'Brüderlichkeit,'" Hamburger Familienblatt (1 Dec. 1925).

13. Nachlass Bloem (Wuppertal), file 22: Walter Bloem, "Offene Antwort zu Rocholl," 16 May 1923.

14. Morris, "German Nationalist Fiction," pp. 8-195.

15. Nachlass Bloem (Freiburg), RG N31, file 11: Bloem to Princess Schönburg, 22 July 1918.

16. Nachlass Bloem (Freiburg), RG N31, file 1: Bloem, "Lebenslauf."

17. Quotes from Flavell, "Kitsch and Propaganda," p. 67.

18. Isaiah Berlin, Russian Thinkers, eds. Henry Hardy and Aileen Kelly (Harmandsworth, Middlesex, England et al, 1979), p. 51.

19. Tolstoy is placed in the "tradition of the older realism" in the influential The Continental Edition of World Masterpieces, eds. Maynard Mack et al (New York, 1962), p. 1436.

20. Quote from Berlin, Russian Thinkers, p. 43.

21. Ibid., p. 22.

22. Ibid., pp. 22-23 (quote on 22).

23. Ibid., pp. 22-81 (especially 24).

24. Quote from Ibid., p. 22.

25. For a discussion of the development of the conception of the exalted role of the writer-poet (Dichter) as it developed in Germany, see Klaus Schröter, "Der Dichter, Der Schriftsteller," Akzente 20 (1973): 168-88, and Helmuth Kiesel and Paul Münch, Gesellschaft und Literatur im 18 Jahrhundert: Voraussetzungen und Enstehung des literarischen Markts in Deutschland (Munich, 1977), pp. 94ff.

26. For "crisis of historicism," in the Europe of circa 1900-33, see Franklin L. Baumer, Modern European Thought: Continuity and Change in Ideas, 1600-1950 (New York and London, 1977), pp. 402-16, 494-513. See also the chapter, "Natural Right and the Historical Approach" in Leo Strauss, Natural Right and History (Chicago and London, 1953), pp. 9-34.

27. Ralf Dahrendorf, Society and Democracy in Germany (Garden City, New York, 1969), pp. 221-36.

28. Ibid., pp. 227

29. Ibid., pp. 221-36 (quote on 221)

30. Ibid., p. 236

31. Ibid., p. 234.

32. Strauss, Natural Right and History, pp. 1-2 (quote on 2).

33. Dahrendorf, Society and Democracy in Germany, pp. 232-36.

34. For the relationship between the decline of neohumanist and legal education and the susceptibility of educated burghers (particularly of the lawyers who nearly monopolized state offices) to illiberal nationalism, see: ibid. and Konrad H. Jarausch, Students, Society, and Politics in Imperial Germany: The Rise of Academic Illiberalism (Princeton, New Jersey, 1982). For Bloem's lack of religious faith, see Nachlass Bloem (Wuppertal): Bloem, "Werk und Tat: Zweites Buch," pp. 223-24.

35. For the breakdown of transhistorical standards in law and morality as the background to 20th-century barbarism, see: Strauss, Natural Right and History; John H. Hallowell, Main Currents in Modern Political Thought (New York, 1950); Eric Voegelin, The New Science of Politics: An Introduction (Chicago and London, 1966); Eric Voegelin, Science, Politics and Gnosticism (Chicago, 1968).

36. Hans Kohn, The Mind of Germany: The Education of a Nation (New York, 1960), p. 159.

37. Quote from "The Declaration of Independence," in George Brown Tindall, America: A Narrative History (New York and London, 1984), p. Al.

38. Nachlass Bloem (Wuppertal): Bloem, "Werk und Tat: Zweites Buch," pp. 276-80; Walter Bloem, Held seines Landes: Roman (Leipzig, 1929).

39. James N. Retallack, "Conservative 'Volks- partei' in the Diaspora: Anti-Semitism and the Conservative Appeal in South-West Germany, 1871-1900," paper presented at the Tenth Annual Conference of the German Studies Association, 26 Sept. 1986.

40. Winfried Baumgart, Deutschland im Zeitalter des Imperialismus (1890-1914): Grundkräfte, Thesen und Strukturen (Frankfurt/Main, Berlin, Vienna, 1972), p. 156.

41. Walter Bagehot, "Intellectual Conservatism," The Portable Conservative Reader, ed. Russell Kirk (Harmandsworth, Middlesex, England et al, 1982), pp. 237-42 (quote on 241).

42. Russell Kirk, "Introduction," Portable Conservative Reader, pp. xv-xix.

43. Beverly Heckart succinctly sums up the German Conservatives' politics of fear, their opposition despite the realities of a new industrial world to "any measures that detracted from their political or economic dominance," in From Bassermann to Bebel: The Grand Bloc's Quest for Reform in the Kaiserreich, 1900-1914 (New Haven and London, 1974), pp. 6-7. See the chapter, "The Conservative Persuasion," in the penetrating Kenneth D. Barkin, The Controversy Over German Industrialization, 1890-1902 (Chicago and London, 1970), pp. 131-85.

44. See James M. Rhodes, The Hitler Movement: A Modern Millenarian Revolution (Stanford, California, 1980).

45. The racial antisemites won the competition for the white-collar workers. Iris Hamel, Völkischer Verband und nationale Gewerkschaft: Der deutschnationale Handlungsgehilfen-Verband 1893-1933 (Frankfurt/M, 1967). See for the typology of conservatism, Klaus Epstein, The Genesis of German Conservatism (Princeton, New Jersey, 1966), pp. 7-22.

46. Epstein, Genesis of German Conservatism, pp. 8-10 (quote on 9).

47. See Klemens von Klemperer, Germany's New Conservatism: Its History and Dilemma in the Twentieth Century, with a foreword by Sigmund Neumann (Princeton, New Jersey, 1968), especially pp. 33-42. Quote from Bagehot, "Intellectual Conservatism," pp. 241-42.

48. Strauss, Natural Right and History, pp. 1-8. Short sketches of the thought of Strauss and Voegelin are provided by Eugene F. Miller, "Leo Strauss: The Recovery of Political Philosophy," pp. 67-99 and Dante Germino, "Eric Voegelin: The In-Between of Human Life," pp. 100-119, both in Contemporary Political Philosophers, eds. Anthony de Crespigny and Kenneth Minogue (New York, 1975). See also, Voegelin, The New Science of Politics.

49. See Leo Strauss, Natural Right and History, pp. 9-34.

50. Ibid., pp. 35-80.

51. Hallowell, Main Currents in Modern Political Thought, pp. 1-2.

52. H. G. Schenk, The Mind of the European Romantics: An Essay in Cultural History (Garden City, New York, 1969), p. 226.

53. The argument in this paragraph is much indebted to Strauss, Natural Right and History, pp. 1-80.

54. Quote from Eric Voegelin, "The German University and the Order of German Society: A Reconsideration of the Nazi Era," The Intercollegiate Review: A Journal of Scholarship and Opinion 20, no. 3 (1985): 15-16 and 25.

55. Quoted in Tindall, America, p. 1012.

56. Rhodes, Hitler Movement, pp. 148-64.

57. Ibid., p. 148.

58. Ibid., pp. 148-50 (quote on 150).

59. Ibid., pp. 150-53 (quote on 150).

60. Ibid., p. 153.

61. Ibid., p. 160.

62. Ibid., p. 153.

63. Ibid., p. 154.

64. Nachlass Bloem (Wuppertal), file 6/29: Bloem to Rheinische Heimat, 10 May 1928. Even after World War II, Bloem continued to view himself as a born dramatist. He took his failure on the stage hard. See Nachlass Bloem (Wuppertal): Walter Bloem, "Werk und Tat: Zweites Buch erstes bis achtes Kapitel, Seite 180-298" (fragment of Bloem's unpublished autobiography, written shortly after World War II), p. 271.

65. The Rhodes theory is discussed at length, criticized and revised in a separate book-length manuscript under preparation by this author, entitled "Adolf Hitler and Arthur Dinter's Christian Nazism."

66. Rhodes, Hitler Movement, pp. 100-133.

67. Ibid., pp. 134-47.

68. Ibid., pp. 148-70.

69. Ibid., pp. 85-90, 125-28, 138-40, 154-56.

70. Ibid., pp. 17-19, 28-38, 54-56, 81-85, 97-99, 128-29, 140-43, 156-57, 198-99.

71. Ibid., pp. 38-42 (quote on 39).

72. Ibid., pp. 42-65 (quote on 44).

73. Ibid., pp. 57-61 (quote on 29).

74. Ibid., pp. 61-71 (quotes on 29-30)

75. Ibid., pp. 71-82.

76. Ibid., p. 77.

77. Ibid., p. 82.

NOTES

CHAPTER 3

THE "KNIGHT'S DEED OF THE SPIRIT":
THE GENESIS, POLITICAL MESSAGE, AND PUBLICATION HISTORY OF
BROTHERHOOD: A NOVEL

1. Nachlass Bloem (Wuppertal): Bloem, "Werk und Tat: Zweites Buch," pp. 234-36 (quote on 234) and Walter Bloem, "Werk und Tat: Exemplar I, Band I, 1 bis 243. Alte Fassung," n.d. [after 1945], pp. 29, 129, 165-66. See also Nachlass Bloem (Wuppertal), file 22: Moritz Schauenburg to Herr Dreecken, 30 Jan. 1946.

2. Nachlass Bloem (Wuppertal): Bloem, "Werk und Tat: Zweites Buch," pp. 237-39; Hans Peter Bleuel and Ernst Klinnert, <u>Deutsche Studenten auf dem Weg ins Dritte Reich: Ideologien-Programme-Aktionen 1918-1935</u> (Gütersloh, 1967), p. 261.

3. Bleuel and Klinnert, <u>Deutsche Studenten</u>, pp. 18-19, 28, 57-58, 84, 144-49; Nachlass Bloem (Wuppertal): Bloem, "Werk und Tat: Zweites Buch," pp. 237ff.

4. Bleuel and Klinnert, <u>Deutsche Studenten</u>, pp. 148-49.

5. Nachlass Bloem (Wuppertal): Bloem, "Werk und Tat: Zweites Buch," p. 237.

6. Quote from ibid., p. 237 [underlines in original]. See also Nachlass Bloem (Wuppertal), file 22: Moritz Schauenberg to Herr Dreecken, 30 Jan. 1946.

7. Nachlass Bloem (Wuppertal): Bloem, "Werk und Tat: Zweites Buch," p. 238.

8. This lecture was not well received. The <u>Deutsche Corpszeitung</u> refused to print a stenogram of the lecture. Nachlass Bloem (Wuppertal), file 22: Bloem, "Offene Antwort zu Rocholl," paragraph 2.

9. Bloem lectured the students at several universities--the university at Göttingen, the Technische Hochschule in Hannover, the Tierärtzliche Hochschule in Dresden. He won agreement from the rectors, only cool respect from the students. Nachlass Bloem (Wuppertal), file 22: Bloem, "Offene Antwort zu Rocholl," paragraph 2.

10. Ibid., paragraph 2: Nachlass Bloem (Wup- pertal): Bloem, "Werk und Tat: Zweites Buch," p. 238.

11. Bleuel and Klinnert, <u>Deutsche Studenten</u>, p. 149.

12. Nachlass Bloem (Wuppertal), file 22: Bloem, "Offene Antwort zu Rocholl," paragraph 3.

13. Nachlass Bloem (Wuppertal): Bloem, "Werk und Tat: Zweites Buch," pp. 238-39.

14. Nachlass Bloem (Wuppertal), file 22: Bloem, "Offene Antwort zu Rocholl," paragraph 3.

15. Quote from Nachlass Bloem (Wuppertal): Bloem, "Werk und Tat: Zweites Buch," pp. 239-40.

16. Ibid., pp. 223-24; Walter Bloem, Gottesferne: Roman, 2 vols. (Leipzig and Zurich, 1920).

17. Jürgen Schwarz, Studenten in der Weimarer Republik: Die deutsche Studentenschaft in der Zeit von 1918 bis 1923 und ihre Stellung zur Politik (Berlin, 1971), pp. 136, 331, 387; Bleuel and Klinnert, Deutsche Studenten, pp. 64-65; Nachlass Bloem (Wuppertal): Bloem, "Werk und Tat: Zweites Buch," p. 239.

18. Nachlass Bloem (Wuppertal), file 22: Moritz Schauenburg to Herr Dreecken, 30 Jan. 1946; Walter Bloem, Brüderlichkeit: Roman (Leipzig and Zurich, 1922), pp. 5-7, 12-13.

19. Bloem, Brüderlichkeit, pp. 7-8 (quote on 15). This is a fictionalized corps; Bloem denied modeling it on his own corps, Teutonia-Marburg. In fact, Bloem claimed that his fictional corps was the "type of the dueling fraternity overall." Nachlass Bloem (Wuppertal), file 22: Bloem, "Offene Antwort zu Rocholl," section 1.

20. Brüderlichkeit, pp. 67-69, 107-8, 141, 144.

21. Ibid., pp. 59-60, 100-102; George L. Mosse, "Die deutsche Rechte," in Entscheidungsjahr 1932: Zur Judenfrage in der Endphase der Weimarer Republik, ein Sammelband, ed. Werner E. Mosse and Arnold Paucker, 2nd rev. ed. (Tübingen, 1966), p. 234.

22. Bloem, Brüderlichkeit, pp. 133-34.

23. Ibid., pp. 21-22, 27, 52.

24. Ibid., pp. 11-19.

25. Ibid., pp. 63, 100-102, 189.

26. Ibid., pp. 64, 69-70, 128-33.

27. Ibid., pp. 108, 125.

28. Ibid., pp. 107-8, 124 (quote on 107-8).

29. Ibid., pp. 124, 145, 159-60.

30. Ibid., pp. 245-49.

31. Ibid., pp. 249-50.

32. Ibid., pp. 246-47 (quote on 246).

33. Ibid., p. 264.

34. Ibid., pp. 160-61.

35. Ibid., pp. 162-63, 202-41.

36. Ibid., pp. 256-58.

37. Ibid., pp. 278-80 (quote on 280).

38. Ibid., pp. 287-319.

39. Ibid., p. 319.

40. Ibid., pp. 319-28 (quote on 328).

41. "In the whole book völkische ideals are indeed extolled, nevertheless their misuse against Jews like the heroes of the novel is condemned." Mosse, "Die deutsche Rechte," p. 234. See for the characteristics of the reform conservative, Epstein, <u>Genesis of German Conservatism</u>, pp. 8-10.

42. Grethlein was based in Leipzig and Zurich. Nachlass Bloem (Wuppertal): file 6/29, [Bloem], [Autobiographical Sketch], pp. 9-11; file 22, "Vertrag [contract between Verlagshandlung Grethlein und Co., G. m.b.H., and Walter Bloem], 16 Oct. 1919; Bloem, "Werk und Tat: Zweites Buch," pp. 249-50, 262.

43. The novel was supposed to appear at the end of April. Nachlass Bloem (Wuppertal), file 22: "Vereinbarungen vom 8. und 9. Januar 1922, paragraph 10," [9 Jan. 1922]. Its appearance was announced in late May and early June as being imminent. See in Nachlass Bloem (Wuppertal), file 61: "Die Brüderlichkeit [Walter Bloem]," <u>Hannoversche Landeszeitung</u> (3 June 1922); "Die Brüderlichkeit [Walter Bloem]," <u>Chemnitzer Tageblatt</u>; "Die Brüderlichkeit [Walter Bloem]," Deutsche Hochschule (May/June 1922). The earliest reviews of the novel after it hit the bookstores appeared in the last week of June 1922 (see below). For official total of first printing, see <u>Deutsches Bücherverzeichnis</u> 7: 390. Actually, 1,100 copies were printed over and above this total, assuming that Bloem's contract was honored. According to this contract, Bloem was to receive 100 free copies for each 100,000 in print; 1,000 more were to be printed for critics and as dedication copies. None of these were to be numbered with the regular editions. Nachlass Bloem (Wuppertal), file 22: "Vertrag," [16 Oct. 1919].

44. According to the title page of Bloem, <u>Die Brüderlichkeit</u>.

45. Josef Setzer, "Die Arbeiterbüchereien," <u>Vorwärts</u> (30 June 1928); Friedrich Schnack, "Billige Bücher, teure Bücher," <u>Die literarische Welt</u> 5, no. 17 (1929): 5. The term bestseller came into currency in Germany during the 1920s. See for example, "Die Best-Seller-Listen," in <u>Die literarische Welt</u> from 14 Oct. 1927 on.

46. A number of critics remarked on the timeliness of the novel's publication just when antisemitism had shown its ugliest face in the murder of Rathenau.

47. Sarah Gordon, Hitler, Germans and the "Jewish Question" (Princeton, New Jersey, 1984), p. 52; Erich Eyck, A History of the Weimar Republic, Volume I: From the Collapse of the Empire to Hindenburg's Election, trans. Harlan P. Hanson and Robert G. L. Waite (New York, 1962, 1970), pp. 213-21; S. William Halperin, Germany Tried Democracy: A Political History of the Reich from 1918 to 1933 (New York, 1946, 1965), pp. 228-40.

48. Various letters from readers collected in Nachlass Bloem (Wuppertal), file 22.

49. Quote from the unpublished historical monograph in Marbach/Neckar, Deutsches Literaturarchiv, Nachlass Langen-Müller: Hans Flörke, "Der Albert Langen Verlag," with marginal notes by Gustav Pezold, n.d., p. 195. See also: Franz Blei, "Verlag, Buchhandel, Autor," Das Tagebuch 4 (1923): 1744; Friedrich Schulze, Der deutsche Buchhandel und die geistige Strömungen der letzten hundert Jahre (Leipzig, 1925), pp. 11, 16, 21-25, 58-59; Mendelssohn, S. Fischer, pp. 873, 937; Kurt Wolff to Hans Mardersteig, 23 Aug. 1923 in Kurt Wolff: Briefwechsel eines Verlegers 1911-1963, Bernhard Zeller and Ellen Otten, eds. (Frankfurt/Main, 1966), p. 399; Hiller, Zur Sozialgeschichte, p. 30; Hans Ferdinand Schulz, Das Schicksal der Bücher und der Buchhandel: System einer Vertriebskunde des Buches, 2nd rev. ed. (Berlin, 1960), p. 11.

50. Mendelssohn, S. Fischer, p. 937.

51. See, among many other accounts, Halperin, Germany Tried Democracy, pp. 241-79.

52. Deutsches Bücherverzeichnis 12: 457.

53. Nachlass Bloem (Wuppertal), file 22: "Verlegerliste über die zum literarischen Nachlass des Schriftstellers Dr. Walter Bloem gehörigen veröffentliche Werke," n.d. [around 1951]. Around 100,000 copies were reportedly sold by October 1932. Hegemann, "Walter Bloem contra Heinrich Mann," p. 1591.

54. For a discussion of this serialization, see below.

55. Nachlass Bloem (Wuppertal), file 22: "Aus dem Roman 'Brüderlichkeit' von Walter Bloem," CV-Zeitung (22 June 1928): 357.

56. Bloem read from Hans Joachim's lecture to the corps on 19 Sept. 1922 at the Gymnasium in Barmen. Nachlass Bloem (Wuppertal), file 22: "Walter Bloem in Barmen," Deutscher Tageblatt (30 Sept. 1922).

57. Nachlass Bloem (Wuppertal): Bloem, "Werk und Tat: Zweites Buch," [pp. 249-50, 262, 506 (quotes on p. 250). Fischer is treated in the classic Mendelssohn, S. Fischer, and Ullstein in Hermann Ullstein, The Rise and Fall of the House of Ullstein (New York, 1943).

58. Nachlass Bloem (Wuppertal): Bloem, "Werk und Tat: Zweites Buch," pp. 457, 506.

NOTES

CHAPTER 4

THE GERMAN RIGHT AND BROTHERHOOD: A NOVEL: POLITICAL IMPACT AND CRITICAL RECEPTION

1. "The great whole of the corps students and furthermore the whole of the dueling students saw in me the renegade, the rebel, the mutineer against the consecrated traditionalism. . . ." Ibid., pp. 240, 244 (quote on 244).

2. Nachlass Bloem (Wuppertal), file 61: Dr. O. F. Scheuer, "Brüderlichkeit [Walter Bloem]," Deutsche Hochschul-Warte (n.d. [1922-1923]).

3. Nachlass Bloem (Wuppertal), file 61: Dr.Karl Konrad, "Brüderlichkeit [Walter Bloem]," Burschenschaftliche Wege (Nov./Dec. 1922).

4. Nachlass Bloem (Wuppertal), file 61: "Brüd- erlichkeit [Walter Bloem]," Burschen heraus (1925).

5. Nachlass Bloem (Wuppertal), file 22: "Brüderlichkeit [Walter Bloem]," Deutsche Corpszeitung: Amtliche Zeitschrift des Kösener S. C. Verbandes 40 (May 1923): 26.

6. Ibid., pp. 26-27.

7. Ibid., pp. 27-28.

8. Nachlass Bloem (Wuppertal), file 61: Dr. Schaffer, "Brüderlichkeit [Walter Bloem]," Die Volkshochschul-Gemeinschaft (26 July 1922).

9. Nachlass Bloem (Wuppertal), file 61: K. "Brüderlichkeit?" Berliner Hochschul-Nachricht no. 2 (1922).

10. Nachlass Bloem (Wuppertal), file 61: "Brüderlichkeit [Walter Bloem]," Akademische Mitteilungen (27 June 1922).

11. Nachlass Bloem (Wuppertal), file 61: Kurt Emig, "Brüderlichkeit [Walter Bloem]," Deutsche Hochschul-Zeitung (15 Apr. 1923).

12. Nachlass Bloem (Wuppertal), file 61: "Brüd- erlichkeit [Walter Bloem]," Hannoversche Landeszeitung (n.d. [1922-1923]).

13. Nachlass Bloem (Wuppertal), file 22: Heinrich Speckert to Bloem (8 Apr. 1923).

14. Nachlass Bloem (Wuppertal), file 22: [name illegible] to Bloem, 15 Nov. 1923. The article in the Pfälzer Corpszeitung was enclosed as a handwritten copy with this letter.

15. Nachlass Bloem (Wuppertal), file 22: Georg Weiss to Bloem, 29 Jan. 1923.

16. Nachlass Bloem (Wuppertal), file 22: Georg Weiss, "Brüderlichkeit: Roman von Walter Bloem," Corpszeitung des Corps Teutonia: Marburg 26 (Dec. 1922): 12-13.

17. Ibid., p. 13. For Fritsch, see Richard S. Levy, The Downfall of the Anti-Semitic Political Parties in Imperial Germany (New Haven and London, 1975), pp. 29, 37-39, 172, 235, 243-44, 260-65 (quote on 37). For Dinter, see Rodler F. Morris, "German Nationalist Fiction," pp. 197-444, and Arthur Dinter, Die Sünde wider das Blut (Leipzig, Hartenstein/Erzgebirge, 1921). Fritsch's essays were undoubtedly a source for Bloem's portrait of Ströbel. Two are contained in Nachlass Bloem (Wuppertal), file 22. Bloem may have been familiar, as Weiss and other critics suspected, with the antisemitic novels of Dinter, whom he knew well from the pre-World War I theater world. Brotherhood may have been consciously constructed as a counter novel to Sin Against the Blood although this cannot be proven.

18. Weiss in Corpszeitung des Corps Teutonia (Dec. 1922): 14.

19. Nachlass Bloem (Wuppertal), file 22: postcard, Georg Weiss to Bloem, 5 Apr. 1923.

20. Nachlass Bloem (Wuppertal), file 22: Land- gerichts-Präsident Dr. Kleinschmidt to Bloem, 22 Feb. 1923.

21. Nachlass Bloem (Wuppertal), file 22: Heinrich Speckert to Bloem, 8 Apr. 1923.

22. Nachlass Bloem (Wuppertal), file 22: Hermann Münzel to Bloem, 25 Mar. 1923.

23. Nachlass Bloem (Wuppertal), file 22: A. H. -Verband, Corps Lusatia, Leipzig, Vertrauens-Kommission (Schriftführer Frey?) to Bloem, 22 Dec. 1922.

24. Nachlass Bloem (Wuppertal): Bloem, "Werk und Tat: Zweites Buch," pp. 243-44; Nachlass Bloem (Wuppertal), file 65: [Walter Bloem], "Meine Vernehmung vor den 'Denazifizierungsausschuss der Hansestadt Lübeck' am 12. Dezember 1947," [12 Dec. 1947], p. 5.

25. The number mentioned in Nachlass Bloem (Wup- pertal), file 22: Otto Grüttefien to Bloem, 16 May 1923.

26. Nachlass Bloem (Wuppertal), file 22: Bloem, "Offene Antwort zu Rocholl."

27. Nachlass Bloem (Wuppertal): Bloem, "Werk und Tat: Zweites Buch," p. 266. See p. 246 for the presence of Walter Julius in Würzburg. It is not clear what relationship the senior Bloem had with the Würzburg corps, although there was clearly some personal contact.

28. Bleuel and Klinnert, Deutsche Studenten, p. 149. It is not known whether this corps is identical with the two Würzburg corps discussed in Bloem's autobiography.

29. Nachlass Bloem (Wuppertal), file 6/29: "Walter Bloem sechzig Jahre Alt," Corpszeitung der Lusatia zu Leipzig (1 Sept. 1928).

30. Nachlass Bloem (Wuppertal): Bloem, "Werk und Tat: Zweites Buch," p. 244.

31. Nachlass Bloem (Wuppertal), file 22: Bloem, "Offene Antwort zu Rocholl," section 3 and Erich Leyens to Bloem, 3 Mar. 1923.

32. Nachlass Bloem (Wuppertal), file 61: M.P., "Die Brüderlichkeit [Walter Bloem]," Montagsblatt (26 Feb. 1923).

33. Nachlass Bloem (Wuppertal), file 22: Wolfgang Winckler to Bloem, 2 Feb. 1934. Enclosed with this letter was Winckler's poem, "Die Nacht zum 30. Januar 1933!"

34. Nachlass Bloem (Wuppertal), file 22: Wolfgang Winckler to Bloem, 9 Feb. 1934.

35. Nachlass Bloem (Wuppertal), file 61: H. L. R., "Die Brüderlichkeit [Walter Bloem]," Rosseger Heimgarten (Aug. 1922). Heimgarten was founded in 1876 by Peter Rosseger. It was völkisch and anti-Jewish. Wilmont Haacke, Feuilletonkunde: Das Feuilleton als literarische und journalistische Gattung, 2 vols. (Leipzig, 1943), 1: 135.

36. Nachlass Bloem (Wuppertal), file 22: Arthur Trebitsch, "Brüderlichkeit [Walter Bloem]," Heimgarten (5 Oct. 1923).

37. Nachlass Bloem (Wuppertal), file 61: Hermann Engelbrecht, "Brüderlichkeit [Walter Bloem]," Deutsche Zeitung (12 Nov. 1922).

38. Nachlass Bloem (Wuppertal), file 61: Hans Joachim, "'Brüderlichkeit,'" Deutsche Zeitung (27 Nov. 1922).

39. [Alfred Rosenberg?], "Walter bloemelt," Der Weltkampf 3 (1926): 91.

40. Nachlass Bloem (Wuppertal): Bloem, "Werk und Tat: Zweites Buch," p. 275.

41. Nachlass Bloem (Wuppertal), file 61: H. W., "Brüderlichkeit [Walter Bloem]," Neue Preussische (Kreuz-) Zeitung (3 Nov. 1922); Kurt Koszyk and Karl Hugo Pruys, Wörterbuch zur Publizistik (Munich, 1969), p. 205; Meinolt Rohleder and Burkhard Trüde, "Neue Preussische (Kreuz-) Zeitung," Deutsche Zeitungen, ed. Fischer, pp. 209-24.

42. Nachlass Bloem (Wuppertal), file 61: "Brüderlichkeit [Walter Bloem], Deutsche Allgemeine Rundschau (15 Nov. 1922).

43. Nachlass Bloem (Wuppertal), file 61: "Brüderlichkeit [Walter Bloem]," Süddeutsche Zeitung (19 Dec. 1922). Kurt Koszyk, Deutsche Presse 1914-1945, pp 215-16, 228.

44. Nachlass Bloem (Wuppertal), file 61: J. St.-g, "Brüderlichkeit [Walter Bloem]," München-Augsburger Abendzeitung (2 Sept. 1922); Kosyzk, Deutsche Presse 1914-1945, p. 185. For quote, see Harold J. Gordon, Jr., Hitler and the Beer Hall Putsch (Princeton, New Jersey, 1972), p. 47. Other nationalist papers panned Brotherhood. Der Tag compared it unfavorably to Erich Wieprecht's Burschen in Not, an orthodox nationalist student novel. Nachlass Bloem (Wuppertal), file 22: Dr. Paul Sysmank, "Studentische Zeitkrisen in Roman," Der Tag: Die grosse nationale Tageszeitung (24 Jan. 1925). The Kreuzburger Nachrichten, apparently a German Nationalist paper, found the book exciting and artistically commendable but criticized the handling of the Jewish question. Bloem

was accused of overlooking the driving spiritual forces behind post-war antisemitism. Nachlass Bloem (Wuppertal), file 61: "Brüderlichkeit [Walter Bloem]," Kreuzburger Nachrichten (23 Aug. 1923). The Dresdner Nachrichten, also seemingly close to the DNVP, denied the book even the least artistic merit. Nachlass Bloem (Wuppertal), file 61: "Ein neuer Bloem," Dresdner Nachrichten (12 July 1922).

45. Nachlass Bloem (Wuppertal), file 61: Stölt- ing, "Brüderlichkeit [Walter Bloem]," Der deutsche Kaufmann im Auslande (20 July 1922).

46. Nachlass Bloem (Wuppertal), file 61: Dr. K., "Brüderlichkeit [Walter Bloem]," Schwäbische Tages- zeitung (7 July 1922); Koszky, Deutsche Presse 1914-1945, p. 165.

47. Nachlass Bloem (Wuppertal), file 61: to., "Brüderlichkeit [Walter Bloem]," Weser-Zeitung (11 July 1922); Koszyk, Deutsche Presse 1914-1945, p. 221.

48. Nachlass Bloem (Wuppertal), file 61: NT., "Brüderlichkeit [Walter Bloem]," Schlesische Zeitung (2 July 1922). Norbert Conrads, "Schlesische Zeitung (1742-1945)," Deutsche Zeitungen, ed. Fischer, pp. 115-30.

49. Nachlass Bloem (Wuppertal): Bloem, "Werk und Tat: Zweites Buch," p. 263.

50. Ibid., pp. 243-44. Before a denazification tribunal after World War II, Bloem claimed that he faced honor tribunals in two officer associations to which he belonged, being acquitted by both. Nachlass Bloem (Wuppertal), file 65: [Bloem], "Meine Vernehmung," p. 5.

51. Nachlass Bloem (Wuppertal): Bloem, "Werk und Tat: Zweites Buch," pp. 240-45; Nachlass Bloem (Wuppertal), file 65: [Bloem], "Meine Vernehmung," p. 5.

52. Chapter 6 of Nachlass Bloem (Wuppertal): Bloem, "Werk und Tat: Zweites Buch," which deals with Brotherhood and its aftermath, is entitled "Die grosse Wendung [The Great Turning Point]," p. 234.

53. First quote on ibid., p. 234, second on 230.

54. Bloem's political avowal in Brotherhood "cost me untold hundreds of thousands in fallen income from my post-war books, whose sales potential now sank from work to work." Ibid., p. 245.

55. Nachlass Bloem (Wuppertal), file 65: [Bloem], "Meine Vernehmung," p. 5; file 22, [Walter Bloem], "Anweissung für meine Erben und Rechtsnachfolger für die Behandlung meines literarischen Nachlasses," n.d. [post 1945], pp. 2-3; Bloem, "Werk und Tat: Zweites Buch," pp. 268-69.

56. Nachlass Bloem (Wuppertal): Bloem, "Werk und Tat: Zweites Buch," p. 244.

57. Nachlass Bloem (Wuppertal), file 22: "Ver- legerliste," p. 2. According to this list, Das Land unserer Liebe (1923), Der Weltbrand (1923), and Mörderin (1924) went into printings of forty thousand copies each. See also Deutsches Bücherverzeichnis 7: 390; 12: 457; 17: 339; 20: 314; 23: 490. The one exception may have been Die grosse Liebe,

which went into sixty-thousand copies in 1941; it is not clear when this novel was first published. Ibid., 23: 490.

58. That is, at any rate, the only figure for the novel given by <u>Deutsches Bücherverzeichnis</u> 12: 457.

59. Nachlass Bloem (Wuppertal): Bloem, "Werk und Tat: Zweites Buch," p. 262.

60. Nachlass Bloem (Wuppertal), file 22: "Ver- legerliste," p. 2.

61. Nachlass Bloem (Wuppertal): Bloem, "Werk und Tat: Zweites Buch," p. 265.

62. Nachlass Bloem (Wuppertal), file 22: Dr. Karl Hans Strobl to Bloem, 25 Feb. 1924.

63. Nachlass Bloem (Wuppertal), file 65: [Bloem] to [Dr. Harald Öldag], <u>Bergische Märkische Zeitung, Abt. Aussenpolitik</u>, 2 Apr. 1925.

64. See especially Nachlass Bloem (Wuppertal): Bloem, "Werk und Tat: Zweites Buch," pp. 240-41.

65. Ibid., p. 268.

66. Ibid., pp. 240-45.

NOTES

CHAPTER 5

**LIBERALS, CATHOLICS, SOCIALISTS, JEWS AND
BROTHERHOOD: A NOVEL:
POLITICAL IMPACT AND CRITICAL RECEPTION**

1. Nachlass Bloem (Wuppertal), file 61: B.E.E., "Brüderlichkeit," Wiesbadener Zeitung (1 Aug. 1922).

2. Ibid.

3. Nachlass Bloem (Wuppertal), file 22: H. Th., "Walter Bloem's 'Brüderlichkeit,'" Magdeburgische Zeitung (15 Dec. 1922); Fritz Faber, "Magdeburgische Zeitung (1664-1945)," Deutsche Zeitungen, ed. Fischer, p. 67.

4. Nachlass Bloem (Wuppertal), file 61: Wa., "Brüderlichkeit [Walter Bloem]," Kattowitzer Zeitung (Jan. 1923); Koszyk, Deutsche Presse, 1914-1945, pp. 72, 78-79.

5. Nachlass Bloem (Wuppertal), file 61: Ws., "Die Judenfrage im Roman," Hildesheimer Allgemeine Zeitung (18 July 1922); Koszyk, Wörterbuch, p. 225. For Nathaniel Jünger, a pseudonym for the Evangelical minister Johann Rump, see: Nathaniel Jünger, Volk in Gefahr: Roman (Wismar, 1922); Rodler F. Morris, "The Jew in the German Novel, 1918-1933," (M.A. thesis; University of North Carolina, Chapel Hill, 1972), pp. 51-55; George L. Mosse, Germans and Jews: The Right, the Left, and the Search for a "Third Force" in Pre-Nazi Germany (New York, 1970), pp. 48-50, 55.

6. Nachlass Bloem (Wuppertal): Bloem, "Werk und Tat: Zweites Buch," p. 228.

7. Nachlass Bloem (Wuppertal), file 61: Theo. Hoffman, "Brüderlichkeit [Walter Bloem]," Leuchtturm (10 Aug. 1923).

8. Ibid.

9. Nachlass Bloem (Wuppertal), file 61: Georg Lutz, "Brüderlichkeit [Walter Bloem]," Bayerischer Kurier (9 Oct. 1922); Gordon, Hitler, pp. 47-48; Karl Aloys Altmeyer, Katholische Presse unter NS-Diktatur: Die katholische Zeitungen und Zeitschriften Deutschlands in den Jahren 1933 bis 1945. Dokumentationen (Berlin, 1962), p. 17.

10. Nachlass Bloem (Wuppertal), file 61: "Brüderlichkeit [Walter Bloem]," Augsburger Postzeitung (6 Dec. 1922); Altmeyer, Katholische Presse, pp. 16, 19, 44-45; Nachlass Bloem (Wuppertal), file 61: "Brüderlichkeit [Walter Bloem]," Bayerische Volkszeitung (21 Dec. 1922); Nachlass Bloem (Wuppertal), file 61: "Brüderlichkeit [Walter Bloem]," Fränkischer Volksblatt (19 Aug. 1922); Koszyk and Pruys, Wörterbuch, p. 401.

11. Nachlass Bloem (Wuppertal), file 61: Dr. Jos. Froberger, "Brüderlichkeit [Walter Bloem]," <u>Kölnische Volkszeitung</u> (10 Feb. 1924); Rudolf Morsey, <u>Die deutsche Zentrumspartei 1917-1923</u>, ed. Kommission für Geschichte des Parlamentarismus und der politischen Parteien (Düsseldorf, 1966), p. 604. While <u>Germania</u> steered a "centralistic-republican course in the sense of Erzberger and Wirth," the <u>Kölnische Volkszeitung</u> pursued a "federalistic and anti-Prussian" line. The Köln (Cologne) organ appeared in editions of 28,000 in 1922. (p. 604). See also, Rolf Kramer, "Kölnische Volkszeitung," <u>Deutsche Zeitungen</u>, ed. Fischer, pp. 257-68.

12. Nachlass Bloem (Wuppertal), file 61: "Brüd- erlichkeit [Walter Bloem]," <u>Deutsche Reichszeitung</u> (29 Dec. 1922). The <u>Deutsche Reichszeitung</u> was one of the most important regional papers of the Center party, with a circulation of 36,000. Morsey, <u>Zentrumspartei</u>, pp. 604-5.

13. Nachlass Bloem (Wuppertal), file 61: Dr. Contzen, "Brüderlichkeit [Walter Bloem]," <u>Münsterischer Anzeiger</u> (14 July 1922); Koszyk, <u>Deutsche Presse 1914-1945</u>, p. 292. This was also one of the most important of the Center's regional organs (circulation, 37,000). Morsey, <u>Zentrumspartei</u>, p. 604.

14. Nachlass Bloem (Wuppertal), file 61: Dr. Gregor, "Brüderlichkeit: Ein neuer Studentroman," <u>Badischer Beobachter</u> (9 Sept. 1922), in part a reprint of "Brüderlichkeit [Walter Bloem]," <u>Berliner Morgenzeitung</u> (23 June 1922). The <u>Badischer Beobachter</u> was a Center regional organ of some importance: its circulation was, however, only ten thousand. Morsey, <u>Zentrumspartei</u>, p. 605. (Circulation figure for the year 1926).

15. Nachlass Bloem (Wuppertal), file 61: Gregor, "Brüderlichkeit," <u>Badischer Beobachter</u> (9 Sept. 1922).

16. Dr. Georg Hayn, "Brüderlichkeit [Walter Bloem]," <u>Der Gral: Monatschrift für Dichtung und Leben</u> 17 (1923): 277-78.

17. "Brüderlichkeit [Walter Bloem]," <u>Stimmen der Zeit</u> (June 1924).

18. There are no clippings from these papers in Bloem's massive collection of reviews now at the Nachlass Bloem (Wuppertal). Bloem believed that he had seen (thus presumably collected) all critiques of the novel. Nachlass Bloem (Wuppertal), file 22: Bloem, "Offene Antwort zu Rocholl," section 5. He was in error, but no doubt had all the major reviews. As will be shown below he bitterly resented being ignored by the great liberal dailies.

19. Nachlass Bloem (Wuppertal), file 61: F. E., "Brüderlichkeit [Walter Bloem]," <u>Berliner Tageblatt</u> (30 July 1922).

20. Karl Würzburger, <u>Vivos Voco: Zeitschrift für neues Deutschtum</u> 3 (1923): 268-69.

21. By 1930, weekday editions of the <u>Berliner Morgen-Zeitung</u> went over 400,000; Sunday editions averaged 630,000. Hans Wallenberg and Arno Scholz, <u>Kleine Geschichte der Zeitungsstadt Berlin</u> (Berlin, 1969), p. 40. Wallenberg and Scholz wrongly attribute ownership of the paper to the Ullstein concern.

22. Mosse founded the Morgen-Zeitung in 1889 as a "liberales Volksblatt im besten Sinne des wortes." Gotthart Schwarz, "Berliner Tageblatt (1872-1939)," Deutsche Zeitungen, ed. Fischer, pp. 320-21.

23. Nachlass Bloem (Wuppertal), file 61: "Brüderlichkeit," Berliner Morgen-Zeitung (23 June 1922).

24. Reviews of "Brüderlichkeit [Walter Bloem], in the following papers were based at least in part on the Berliner Morgen-Zeitung article: Isnabrücker Zeitung (27 June 1922); Schweizerische Freie Volkszeitung (24 June 1922); Eisenacher Zeitung (24 June 1922); Mecklenburg Zeitung (28 Sept. 1923); Bremer Zeitung (n.d.); Kurier für Niederbayern (14 Sept. 1922); Pfälzische Volkszeitung (10 July 1922); Holldauer und Laabertalbote (15 Sept. 1922); Niederrheinische Volkszeitung (Dec. 1927); Bremer Volksblatt (17 July 1922); Dr. Gregor, "Brüderlichkeit," Badischer Beobachter (9 Sept. 1922); Der Nachmittag (1 Feb. 1923); Deutsche Warte (8 July 1922); Pilsner Tagblatt (26 June 1922); Deutscher Landwirt (3 Apr. 1926); Berliner Morgen-Zeitung (23 June 1922); Chemnitzer Allgemeine Zeitung (2 Dec. 1922); Der Büchermarkt des Bahnhofbuchhandels (15 July 1922); General-Anzeiger of Ludwigshafen/Rhein (24 Aug. 1922); Lauterbacher Anzeiger (26 Mar. 1923); General-Anzeiger of Wesel (5 Oct. 1922). Clippings in the Nachlass Bloem (Wuppertal), file 61.

25. Some definitely were, like the Berliner Morgen-Zeitung, and the Pfälzische Volkszeitung. Others may well have been linked to the DDP, but have not yet been definitely classified politically by this author. For the political ties of the Pfälzische Volkszeitung, see Koszyk and Pruys, Wörterbuch, p. 225.

26. For the review in the Badischer Beobachter (9 Sept. 1922), see above. See below for "Brüderlichkeit [Walter Bloem]," Bremer Volksblatt (17 July 1922). For the political affiliation of the Bremer Volksblatt, refer to Kurt Koszyk and Gerhard Eisfeld, Die Presse der deutschen Sozialdemokratie (Hannover, 1966), p. 85.

27. Nachlass Bloem (Wuppertal), file 61: General-Anzeiger of Wesel (5 Oct. 1922); Badischer Beobachter (9 Sept. 1922); Holldauer und Laabertalbote (15 Sept. 1922); Kurier für Niederbayern (14 Sept. 1922); General-Anzeiger of Ludwigshafen/Rhein (24 Aug. 1922); Lauterbacher Anzeiger (26 March 1923); Der Büchermarkt des Bahnhofbuchhandels (15 July 1922); Der Nachmittag (1 Feb. 1923); Deutsche Warte (8 July 1922); Pilsner Tagblatt (Dec. 1927); Schweizerische Freie Volkszeitung (24 June 1922); Niederrheinische Volkszeitung (24 June 1922); Eisenacher Zeitung (24 June 1922); Pfälzische Volkszeitung (10 July 1922); Deutscher Landwirt (3 Apr. 1926).

28. Nachlass Bloem (Wuppertal), file 61: Schwei- zerische Freie Volkszeitung (24 June 1922); Deutscher Landwirt (3 Apr. 1926).

29. Nachlass Bloem (Wuppertal), file 61: Chem- nitzer Allgemeine Zeitung (2 Dec. 1924); Bremer Zeitung (n.d.).

30. Nachlass Bloem (Wuppertal), file 61: Karl Herbert Kuhn, "Brüderlichkeit [Walter Bloem]," Königsberger Hartungsche Zeitung (30 Jan. 1923).

31. Quoted in Kurt Forstreuter, "Königsberger Hartungsche Zeitung, Königsberg (1660-1933)," Deutsche Zeitungen, ed. Fischer, p. 54.

32. Forstreuter, "Königsberger Hartungsche Zei- tung," Deutsche Zeitungen, ed. Fischer, pp. 54-55; Nachlass Bloem (Wuppertal), file 22: Ludwig Goldstein to Bloem, 20 Dec. 1934.

33. Nachlass Bloem (Wuppertal), file 61: M. G., "Brüderlichkeit [Walter Bloem]," Neue badische Landeszeitung (7 July 1922); Koszyk, Deutsche Presse 1914-1945, p. 266.

34. Nachlass Bloem (Wuppertal), file 61: "Wochenplauderei," Karlsruher Tagblatt (2 July 1922).

35. Nachlass Bloem (Wuppertal), file 61: M. R., "Brüderlichkeit [Walter Bloem]," Breslauer Zeitung (2 July 1922).

36. Nachlass Bloem (Wuppertal), file 61: M. P., "Brüderlichkeit [Walter Bloem]," Montagsblatt (26 Feb. 1923).

37. Otto Ernst Hesse, "Roman Ernte," Vorwärts (21 Dec. 1924): 4th supplement.

38. Koszyk and Eisfeld, Die Presse, p. 137; Nachlass Bloem (Wuppertal), file 61: "Brüderlichkeit [Walter Bloem]," Volkstimme of Magdeburg (n.d. [1922 or 1923]).

39. Nachlass Bloem (Wuppertal), file 61: "Brüder- lichkeit," Bremer Volksblatt (17 July 1922); Koszyk and Eisfeld, Die Presse, p. 85.

40. Nachlass Bloem (Wuppertal), file 61: Dr. Herbert Hirschberg, "Brüderlichkeit [Walter Bloem]," Deutsche Republik (20 Oct. 1922).

41. Nachlass Bloem (Wuppertal), file 65: [Bloem], "Meine Vernehmung," p. 5; Nachlass Bloem (Wuppertal): Bloem, "Werk und Tat: Zweites Buch," pp. 244, 268-69; Nachlass Bloem (Wuppertal), file 22: Moritz Schauenburg to Herr Dreecken, 1 Jan. 1946.

42. Nachlass Bloem (Wuppertal), file 61: "Brüd- erlichkeit," Der Büchermarkt des Bahnhofbuchhandels (15 July 1922); Nachlass Bloem (Wuppertal), file 61: "Brüderlichkeit [Walter Bloem]," Literarischer Handweiser (series 11, 1922); Artur Brausewetter, "Brüderlichkeit [Walter Bloem]," Das literarische Echo 25, no. 1 (1922): 50-51; Nachlass Bloem (Wuppertal), file 61: Dr. H. J., "Brüderlichkeit [Walter Bloem]," Deutsche Roman-Zeitung (n.d.); Nachlass Bloem (Wupper- tal), file 22: Tely., "'Brüderlichkeit': Sensationsprozess des Tanzerpaares Janos und Olivia gegen den bekannten Schriftsteller Walter Bloem," Gross-Berliner neueste nachrichten, Wochenschrift: Das Blatt der Berliner Gesellschaft, 6, no 2. (1923). Apparently, the dancers "Janos" and "Olivia," who considered themselves the real-life models for the pair in Brotherhood, sued Bloem. The Gross-Berliner neueste Nach- richten announced that it was the duty of the paper to set up a front against the novel.

43. Quote from Jehuda Reinharz, Fatherland or Promised Land: The Dilemma of the German Jew, 1893-1914 (Ann Arbor, Michigan, 1975), p. vii. Jewish press response did not always take the form of a review. For example, the Monatschrift für Geschichte und Wissenschaft des Judentums (1922 [no month]) recommended the novel in a sentence. "Worth consideration because of its fight against the antisemitic and un-social orientation of the corps." Clipping in Nachlass Bloem (Wuppertal), file 61.

44. Nachlass Bloem (Wuppertal), file 22: Meta Harris (Capetown, South Africa) to Bloem, 9 May 1925. See also, Carl Rheins, "The Verband Nationaldeutscher Juden 1921-1933," Leo Baeck Institute Yearbook 25 (1980): 243-68; Klaus T. Hermann, Das Dritte Reich und die deutsch-jüdischen Organisationen 1933-1934 (Cologne, 1969); Donald L. Niewyk, The Jews in Weimar Germany (Baton Rouge and London, 1980), pp. 165-77.

45. Nachlass Bloem (Wuppertal), file 22: Fried. Kahn to Bloem, 2 May 1926.

46. Nachlass Bloem (Wuppertal), file 22: Erich Leyens to Bloem, 3 Mar. 1923.

47. Nachlass Bloem (Wuppertal), file 22: Gerhard Zuelchaur (?) to Bloem, 29 Nov. 1933. Apparently, the young man, like his father, were (like Ludwig Löwenstein) baptized as Protestants. Both however refused to deny their Jewish blood. Gerhard told Bloem that struggle against the dogma of blood could not be won without help of "Germans in the present-day sense." Apparently, he belonged to the "Reichsverband christlich-deutscher Staatsbürger." Nachlass Bloem (Wuppertal), file 22: Gerhard Zuelchaur (?) to Bloem, n.d. [received 6 Dec. 1933].

48. Nachlass Bloem (Wuppertal), file 22: Ludwig Goldstein to Bloem, 20 Dec. 1934.

49. Bleuel and Klinnert, Deutsche Studenten, pp. 169-71.

50. Reinharz, Fatherland or Promised Land, p. 50

51. Nachlass Bloem (Wuppertal), file 61: F. L., "Brüderlichkeit [Walter Bloem]," K.C. Blätter (Aug. 1922).

52. Ibid.

53. Nachlass Bloem (Wuppertal), file 61: Rabbi Dr. Dienemann, "Brüderlichkeit," Jüdisch-liberale Zeitung (1 Sept. 1922).

54. Nachlass Bloem (Wuppertal), file 22: Alfred Auerbach, "Von Kampf der Künstler um die Judenseele," Liberales Judentum: Monatschrift für die religiöse Erneuerung des Judentums 5, no. 2 (1923), supplement to the Jüdisch-liberale Zeitung: Organ der Vereinigung für das liberale Judentum e.V. Berlin (23 Feb. 1923).

55. Nachlass Bloem (Wuppertal), file 22: Editorial Staff [Schriftleitung] of the Jüdisch-liberale Zeitung to Bloem, 25 Feb. 1924.

56. Nachlass Bloem (Wuppertal), file 61: M., "'Brüderlichkeit,'" Israelitisches Wochenblatt für die Schweiz of Zurich (n.d. [1922 or 1923]).

57. Arnold Paucker, "Der jüdische Abwehrkampf," Entscheidungsjahr 1932: Zur Judenfrage in der Endphase der Weimarer Republik. Ein Sammelband, eds. Werner E. Mosse and Arnold Paucker, 2nd rev. ed. (Tübingen, 1966), p. 432.

58. Nachlass Bloem (Wuppertal), file 61: Dr. Dienemann, "Brüderlichkeit," Israelitisches Familienblatt of Hamburg (19 Oct. 1922).

59. Nachlass Bloem (Wuppertal), file 22: Israelitisches Familienblatt to Grethlein and Co., 24 Oct. 1925.

60. Nachlass Bloem (Wuppertal), file 22: (Bloem) to the Verlag des "Israelitischen Familienblattes," 28 Oct. 1925.

61. Nachlass Bloem (Wuppertal), file 22: Die Redaktion, Israelitisches Familienblatt to Bloem, 5 Nov. 1925.

62. Nachlass Bloem (Wuppertal), file 22: Editorial Staff [Schriftleitung], "An unsere Leser!," Hamburger [Israelitisches] Familienblatt (10 Dec. 1925).

63. Nachlass Bloem (Wuppertal), file 61: Walter Bloem, "Ein Wort zu 'Brüderlichkeit,'" Hamburger Familienblatt (1 Dec. 1925).

64. [Walter Bloem with an introduction by the editors], "Wahre deutsche 'Brüderlichkeit': Walter Bloem über Deutschtum und Judenhass," CV-Zeitung 4 (24 Dec. 1925): 807.

65. [Rosenberg?], "Walter bloemelt," Weltkampf, p. 91.

66. Nachlass Bloem (Wuppertal), file 61: Bloem, "Ein Wort," Hamburger Familienblatt (1 Dec. 1925).

67. Nachlass Bloem (Wuppertal), file 22: Die Redaktion, Israelitisches Familienblatt, [signed Caspar] to Bloem, 1 Apr. 1926; Fried. Kahn to Bloem, 2 May 1926.

68. Nachlass Bloem (Wuppertal), file 22: Die Redaktion [Caspar] to Bloem, 1 Apr. 1926.

69. See in Nachlass Bloem (Wuppertal), file 22: Die Redaktion, Israelitisches Familienblatt [signed Caspar] to Bloem, 21 June 1927; [Bloem] to the Redaktion [of the Israelitisches Familienblatt], 24 June 1927; Die Redaktion, Israelitisches Familienblatt [signed Caspar] to Bloem, 24 June 1927; Bloem to M. Lessman Verlag, Hamburg, 27 June 1927.

70. Justizrat Heinrich Kirschner, "Neuere Romanliteratur: Kyrie Eleison; Das Nackte Leben; Genosse Levi; Brüderlichkeit," CV-Zeitung, 3 (28 Aug. 1924): 525.

71. Nachlass Bloem (Wuppertal), file 22: CV-Zeitung to Bloem, 8 July 1927.

72. Nachlass Bloem (Wuppertal), file 22: Bloem to the Centralverein deutscher Staatsbürger jüdischen Glaubens, 18 July 1927.

73. Nachlass Bloem (Wuppertal), file 22: CV-Zeitung to Bloem, 24 July 1927; Bloem to CV-Zeitung, 27 July 1927; CV-Zeitung to Bloem, 12 Aug. 1927.

74. Nachlass Bloem (Wuppertal), file 6/29: Der Vorsitzende des Central-Vereins deutscher Staatsbürger jüdischen Glaubens E.V. to Bloem, 13 June 1928; [Bloem] to the Herren Vorsitzenden des Zentralvereins deutscher Staatsbürger jüdischen Glaubens E.V., 12 July 1928.

75. Nachlass Bloem (Wuppertal), file 22: Herbert Eulenberg, "Walter Bloem zum 60. Geburtstag (20 June 1928)," CV-Zeitung 17 (22 June 1928): 356-57. Published along with this article was a long excerpt from the brotherhood novel, "Aus dem Roman 'Brüderlichkeit' von Walter Bloem," CV-Zeitung 17 (22 June 1928): 357.

76. Eulenberg, "Walter Bloem zum 60. Geburtstag," pp. 356-57.

77. Nachlass Bloem (Wuppertal), file 22: Fritz Josephtal to Bloem, 2 July 1928.

78. Nachlass Bloem (Wuppertal), file 22: Bloem to Fritz Josephtal, 10 July 1928.

79. Nachlass Bloem (Wuppertal), file 22: CV-Zeitung to Bloem, 24 July 1928.

80. Nachlass Bloem (Wuppertal), file 22: Herbert Eulenberg to [the CV-Zeitung or perhaps to Bloem], n.d. [July 1928].

81. Nachlass Bloem (Wuppertal), file 22: [Bloem] to the Schriftleitung der CV-Zeitung, 27 July 1928.

82. Documentation in Nachlass Bloem (Wuppertal), file 22: "Die Korps: Ein Briefwechsel zwischen Walter Bloem und Herbert Eulenberg," CV-Zeitung, 17 (3 Aug. 1928). Bloem insisted on publication of his letter of 27 July as well as of the earlier letters. [Bloem] to the Schriftleitung der CV-Zeitung, 28 July 1928. The correspondence was almost certainly reprinted in one of Bloem's corps-papers. Bang to Bloem, 27 Aug. 1928, and [Bloem] to Bang, 28 Aug. 1928.

83. The organ of the Central Union wanted an article from Bloem with a title like "Meine Stellung zum Judentum." Nachlass Bloem (Wuppertal), file 22: CV-Zeitung to Bloem, 18 June 1928.

84. Nachlass Bloem (Wuppertal), file 22: [Bloem] to Frau Martha Blumenreich, 12 July 1928; [Bloem] to the Schriftleitung der CV-Zeitung, 23 July 1928; CV-Zeitung to Bloem, 16 Aug. 1928.

85. Nachlass Bloem (Wuppertal), file 22: [Bloem] to CV-Zeitung, 23 July 1928.

86. Nachlass Bloem (Wuppertal), file 22: Walter Bloem, "Das Judentum im Weltbild," n.d. [written June-July 1928]. Bloem received his royalty (200 marks) for the article on 3 Sept. 1928. CV-Zeitung to Bloem.

87. Nachlass Bloem (Wuppertal), file 22: Bloem, "Judentum im Weltbild," recapitulated in Dr. H. W. Placzek, "Neue Festellungen der Nationalitätenkunde: Zugleich eine Antwort an Walter Bloem," CV-Zeitung, 17 (16 Nov. 1928).

88. Placzek, "Neue Festellungen."

89. Nachlass Bloem (Wuppertal), file 22: Bloem, "Offene Antwort zu Rocholl," section 5.

90. Nachlass Bloem (Wuppertal): Bloem, "Werk und Tat: Zweites Buch," pp. 244, 268-69; file 22, [Bloem], "Anweisung für meine Erben"; file 65, [Bloem], "Meine Vernehmung," p. 5; file 22, Moritz Schauenburg to Herr Dreecken, 30 Jan. 1946.

91. Nachlass Bloem (Wuppertal): Bloem, "Werk und Tat: Zweites Buch," pp. 244, 268-69.

92. Nachlass Bloem (Wuppertal), file 22: "Offene Antwort zu Rocholl," section 5. See also Walter Bloem, <u>Deutsche Zwietracht und Judentum: Festrede bei der Feier des Zehnjährigen Bestehens der Ortsgruppe Hamburg des vaterländischen Bundes jüdischer Frontsoldaten an 17 November 1929</u> (Leipzig and Zurich, n.d. [1929], pp. 19-21.

93. Nachlass Bloem (Wuppertal), file 22: [Bloem] to [Gerhardt Zulchaur?], 31 Feb. 1933. See also in ibid.: Bloem to Ludwig Goldstein, 16 Jan. 1935.

94. It was difficult for a republican publisher like S. Fischer to break into Bloem's audience, the nationalist middle strata. Mendelssohn, <u>S. Fischer und sein Verlag</u>, p. 886.

NOTES

CHAPTER 6

THE EROSION OF WALTER BLOEM'S REPUBLICANISM, 1922-1930

1. Nachlass Bloem (Wuppertal): Bloem, "Werk und Tat: Zweites Buch," pp. 222-23.

2. Ibid., p. 230. Margarete or Eta had been born in 1897, Walter Julius in 1898. See Degener, Wer ist's? (1928), p. 142.

3. Nachlass Bloem (Wuppertal): Bloem, "Werk und Tat: Zweites Buch," pp. 231, 275, 280. See also in file 22 the printed engagement announcement: [Walter and Margarethe Bloem], "Walter und Frau Margarethe geb. Kalähne freuen sich, die Verlobung ihrer Tochter Eta mit Dr. Max Rudolf Kaufmann, Chefredaktür der Deutschen Allgemeinen Zeitung, anzuzeigen."

4. Nachlass Bloem (Wuppertal): Bloem, "Werk und Tat: Zweites Buch," p. 231.

5. Ibid., pp. 233, 248, 253, 256. The divorce itself must have been a painful affair. Since sickness of a wife was no grounds for divorce in Germany, pretended adultery had to be manufactured. (p. 256). See also, Degener, Wer ist's? (1928), p. 142.

6. Bloem described the effects of this marriage in his autobiography--"For my humanness [Menschentum], I had found a life harbor [in italics in the original]." Nachlass Bloem (Wuppertal): Bloem, "Werk und Tat: Zweites Buch," p. 256.

7. Ibid., pp. 228-33, 252-58.

8. Ibid., p. 229.

9. Nachlass Bloem (Wuppertal), file 22: "Zusatzvertrag zu den Vertrage vom 16. Oktober 1919," n.d. [January 1922?], paragraph 2.

10. For a full discussion and extensive documentation of the economic and political impact of the inflation on all segments of the literature industry, see Morris, "German Nationalist Fiction," Part I.

11. Nachlass Bloem (Wuppertal): Bloem, "Werk und Tat: Zweites Buch," pp. 229-30.

12. For the date, "around 1930," of Bloem's incipient reconversion to the nationalist mainstream, see the very important letter, West Berlin, Akedamie der Künste [hereafter cited as Akademie der Künste (West Berlin)], Record Group Sektion für Dichtkunst (Senatsgutachten) [hereafter cited as RG Sektion Dichtkunst (Senatsgutachten)], file D-7A: [Bloem] to Herr Marilaun, 1 Apr. 1933.

13. Nachlass Bloem (Wuppertal), file 22: Bloem to [addressee unknown], 25 Oct. 1929.

14. Nachlass Bloem (Wuppertal), file 65: Bloem to Harald Öldag, 23 Mar. 1925.

15. Quoted in Nachlass Bloem (Wuppertal), file 61: W. Th. K., "Ein neuer Walter Bloem," <u>Duisburger Volkszeitung</u> (6 July 1922).

16. Nachlass Bloem (Wuppertal): Bloem, "Werk und Tat: Zweites Buch," p. 260.

17. Ibid., p. 245; Nachlass Bloem (Wuppertal), file 22: Moritz Schauenburg to Herr Dreecken, 30 Jan. 1946.

18. Nachlass Bloem (Wuppertal): Bloem, "Werk und Tat: Zweites Buch," p. 259.

19. Ibid., pp. 259-60.

20. Mosse, <u>Crisis of German Ideology</u>, pp. 228, 345 (footnote 38). The quote is from p. 228. Mahraun did retain an Aryan clause for his organization, p. 345 (footnote 38); Armin Mohler, <u>Die konservative Revolution in Deutschland 1918-1932: Ein Handbuch</u>, 2nd rev. ed. (Darmstadt, 1972), pp. 249, 453-55.

21. Nachlass Bloem (Wuppertal): Bloem, "Werk und Tat: Zweites Buch," pp. 259-60.

22. Ibid., pp. 250-51, 260.

23. For example, see Walter Bloem, <u>Der Weltbrand: Deutschlands Tragödie 1914-1918</u>, drawings by Ludwig Dettmann, 2 vols. (Berlin, 1922), 2: 228-31. Bloem judged Kaiser Wilhelm II to be a man of good intentions with a high sense of responsibility, who was incapable of guiding the ship of state in the Great War and who thus left most major decisions to his advisors. See 1: 201.

24. Ibid., 2: 304-6.

25. Nachlass Bloem (Wuppertal): Bloem, "Werk und Tat: Zweites Buch," p. 251.

26. Bloem, <u>Weltbrand</u>, 2: 306.

27. Ibid.

28. Nachlass Bloem (Wuppertal): Bloem, "Werk und Tat: Zweites Buch," p. 252; file 22: "Verlegerliste."

29. Nachlass Bloem (Wuppertal): Bloem, "Werk und Tat: Zweites Buch," p. 258.

30. Ibid.; Richard Dohse, "Das Land unserer Liebe: Roman [Walter Bloem]," <u>Die Literatur</u>, 27 (Nov. 1924): 114.

31. Otto Ernst Hesse, "Roman Ernte," <u>Vorwärts</u> (21 Dec. 1924): 4th supplement.

32. Ultimately, forty thousand found their way to the bookstores. Nachlass Bloem (Wuppertal), file 22: "Verlegerliste."

33. Nachlass Bloem (Wuppertal): Bloem, "Werk und Tat: Zweites Buch," pp. 269-71.

34. Ibid., pp. 271-75. Bloem began his trip on 26 Apr. 1926. (p. 273).

35. Walter Bloem, Weltgesicht: Ein Buch von heutiger und kommender Menschheit (Leipzig and Zurich, 1928).

36. See especially, Nachlass Bloem (Wuppertal): Bloem, "Werk und Tat: Zweites Buch," pp. 274-75.

37. Quote from Josef Hofmiller, "Bücherschau," Süddeutsche Monatshefte, 26 (Feb. 1929): 401.

38. Bloem, Weltgesicht, pp. 331-33, 353-54 (quote on 333).

39. Ibid., p. 354.

40. Ibid., pp. 347-52 (quote on 348).

41. Ibid., pp. 334-37 (all quotes on 335).

42. Ibid., pp. 1-5, 330-31, 337 (quote on 1).

43. Ibid., pp. 337-41 (quote on 337).

44. Ibid., pp. 340-41.

45. Ibid., pp. 342-44.

46. Ibid., p. 355.

47. Ibid., pp. 356-59 (quote on 358-59).

48. Ibid., pp. 359-60.

49. Both quotes from ibid., p. 361 (see also 359).

50. Nachlass Bloem (Wuppertal): Bloem, "Werk und Tat: Zweites Buch," pp. 276-85; Walter Bloem, Sohn seines Landes: Roman (Leipzig, 1929); Walter Bloem, Held seines Landes: Roman (Leipzig, 1929); Akademie der Künste (West Berlin), RG Sektion Dichtkunst (Senatsgutachten), file D-7A: [Bloem] to Marilaun, 1 Apr. 1933. Bloem never published (and may not have written) the third volume of the trilogy, quite likely because he had no promise of an American market.

51. In his notorious open letter to Heinrich Mann, printed at the end of September 1932 by the Deutsche Allgemeine Zeitung, Bloem accused a "closed front against national German literature [underline italics in the original]" of erecting a barricade along the Reich

border that prevented even the names of nationalist writers from penetrating abroad. Quoted in Hegemann, "Walter Bloem contra Heinrich Mann," Das Tagebuch, 13 (1932): 1588.

    52. Nachlass Bloem (Wuppertal): Bloem, "Werk und Tat: Zweites Buch," p. 283.

    53. Ibid., pp. 285-89 (quote on 287).

    54. Nachlass Bloem (Wuppertal), file 22: Bloem to [addressee unknown], 25 Oct. 1929.

    55. Walter Bloem, Deutsche Zwietracht und Judentum, pp. 4-11.

    56. Ibid., pp. 4-22, 28.

    57. Ibid., pp. 19-21 (quote on 21).

    58. Ibid., p. 32.

    59. Ibid., pp. 24, 29 (quote on 29).

    60. Ibid., p. 32.

    61. Ibid., pp. 29-30.

    62. Ibid., pp. 30-32, 34-37.

    63. Ibid., pp. 37-38 (quote on 38).

    64. Ibid., pp. 39-40 (quote on 39).

    65. Ibid., pp. 40-41 (quote on 41).

    66. Ibid., pp. 42-43 (quote on 43).

    67. Ibid., pp. 43-44 (quote on 44).

    68. Ibid., pp. 44-49 (quote on 45-46).

    69. Letter, Nachlass Bloem (Wuppertal), file 22: [Bloem] to [Gerhard Zülchaur?], 31 Feb. 1933; Wolfgang Winckler to Bloem, 9 Feb. 1934.

NOTES

CHAPTER 7

BACKGROUND TO THE DEATH OF WALTER BLOEM'S REPUBLICANISM: THE OPPOSITION IN THE PROTECTIVE ASSOCIATION OF GERMAN WRITERS (SDS)

1. Nachlass Bloem (Wuppertal): Bloem, "Werk und Tat: Zweites Buch," pp. 288-89.

2. Akademie der Künste (West Berlin), RG Sektion Dichtkunst (Senatsgutachten), file D-7A: [Bloem] to Marilaun, 1 Apr. 1933.

3. Nachlass Bloem (Wuppertal): Bloem, "Werk und Tat: Zweites Buch," pp. 289, 293-95.

4. Roy Pascal, From Naturalism to Expressionism: German Literature and Society, 1880-1918 (New York, 1973), p. 285.

5. Nachlass Bloem (Wuppertal): Walter Bloem, "Werk und Tat: Exemplar I, Band I, 1 bis 243. Alte Fassung," pp. 166-67; Bloem, "Werk und Tat: Zweites Buch," pp. 290-94; and Arthur Dinter, Mein Ausschuss aus dem Verbande Deutscher Bühnenschriftsteller (Munich, 1917).

6. See the introduction, "Die Anfänge der anti- faschistischen Einheitsfront im Schutzverband Deutscher Schriftsteller (SDS) 1931-1933," documentation, and commentary to chapter 4 of Alfred Klein, Friedrich Albrecht, Irmfried Hiebel, and Klaus Kändler, Aktionen, Bekenntnisse, Perspektiven: Berichte und Dokumente von Kampf um die Freiheit des literarischen Schaffens in der Weimarer Republik, ed. Deutsche Akademie der Künste zu Berlin, Sektion Dichtkunst und Sprachpflege, Abt. Geschichte der sozialistischen Literatur (Berlin [East] and Weimar, 1966), pp. 319-465, 602-40.

7. Hans-Albert Walter, Deutsche Exilliteratur 1933-1950, Vol. 1: Bedrohung und Verfolgung bis 1933 (Darmstadt and Neuwied, 1972), pp. 51-53, 177-80. Walter's account is based solely on Klein, Aktionen (see p. 261, footnote 40).

8. The following sketch offers only a modest amount of materials not included or suppressed in Klein, Aktionen. A full account of the politicization of the SDS is planned by this author as a future project.

9. Klein, Aktionen, p. 321; Walter, Bedrohung, pp. 257-58, footnote 17; Pascal, Naturalism to Expressionism, p. 285. Theodor Heuss describes the founding of the SDS in his memoirs. Heuss served as deputy chairman of the SDS from the founding to 1912, then as deputy chairman or chairman from 1920-26. The chairman was supposedly to be always a man generally accepted as a Dichter. Heuss regarded his activity in the SDS as an important constituent of his career: "I was suddenly drawn into the legal and economic problems of the 'free' intellectual profession. . . . This pioneering attempt gives the

foundation of the SDS yet something like a cultural-historical accent." Errinnerungen 1905-1933 (Tübingen, 1963), pp. 95-98 (quote on 97). For a fuller account of the genesis of writers' associations, including the SDS, see Morris, "German Nationalist Fiction," pp. 75-77.

10. [Alexander] Roda Roda [pseudonym for Sandor Friedrich Rosenfeld], "Die Krise im Schutzverband deutscher Schriftsteller," Berliner Tageblatt (24 Oct. 1931).

11. Klein, Aktionen, pp. 321-23.

12. See, for example, Koblenz, Bundesarchiv [hereafter cited as Bundesarchiv (Koblenz)], Record Group Der Reichskunstwart, R32 (fr. Rep. 301), [hereafter cited as RG Reichskunstwart-R32]: file 405, Schutzverband Deutscher Schriftsteller and Reichsverband der Bildenen Künstler to the Schöffengericht Charlottenburg, n.d. [ca. 1929]; file 93, Schutzverband Deutscher Schriftsteller, Gewerkschaft Deutscher Schriftsteller (signed by Arthur Elösser, business-leading director) to the Reichskunstwart, Dr. Redslob, Reichsministerium der Innern, 14 Nov. 1921.

13. Klein, Aktionen, pp. 321-24; Nachlass Bloem (Wuppertal): Bloem, "Werk und Tat: Zweites Buch," p. 290. However, even at the founding of the SDS, Erich Mühsam wanted to represent the writer as the brother of the exploited proletariat. Heuss, Erinnerungen, p. 96.

14. Kurt Tucholsky, "Schriftsteller," Die Weltbühne 16 (1920): 691-96 (quote on 693).

15. Klein, Aktionen, p. 349.

16. Ibid., pp. 336-39. See also Heuss, Erinnerungen, pp. 341-42.

17. Klein, Aktionen, p. 338. Both the KPD and (ultimately) the SPD opposed any indemnification of the princes. Halperin, Germany Tried Democracy, pp. 351-52. For Heuss' account of the demonstration, see his Erinnerungen, pp. 341-42.

18. Even SPD members, who supported expropriation of the princes without compensation, supported the retention of political neutrality. The call by the Ortsgruppe executive for mobilization against those who attempted to terrorize the local into political activity was signed by Robert Breuer and Bruno Schönlank, both prominent Socialists. Bundesarchiv (Koblenz), RG Reichskunstwart-R32, file 120: Bieber, Breuer and others [the Executive Committee of the Berlin Ortsgruppe?] to [the membership of the Berlin Ortsgruppe], 2 Mar. 1926; Der Reichskunstwart [Dr. Edwin Redslob] to the Reichsminister des Innern (concerning: Demonstration on the Distress of the German Writers), 12 Feb. 1926.

19. For a treatment of Heuss' role in the controversy swirling around the Schmutz- und Schundgesetz, see Klein, Aktionen, pp. 339-41; Walter, Bedrohung, pp. 41-42; Theodor Heuss, Erinnerungen, pp. 342-44. For SDS actions against the law, see in Bundesarchiv (Koblenz), RG Reichskunstwart-R32, file 95: the Commission of the United Associations, Walter von Molo (Verband deutscher Erzähler), Robert Breuer (Schutzverband deutscher Schriftsteller and Verband der Kunstkritiker), Fritz Angel(Goethebund and Verband Berliner Theaterkritiker), Paul Nitschmann (Börsen- verein

der deutschen Buchhändler, Vereinigung Schönwissenschaftlicher Verleger, Vereinigung der Kunstverleger), and Curt Baake (Sozialistischer Kulturbund) to [Dr. Edwin Redslob, Der Reichskunstwart], [June?] 1926. Included with this letter was "Gegen den Gesetzenentwurf zur Bewahrung der Jugend vor Schund- und Schmutzschriften." For the 10 Dec. meeting of the Berlin Ortsgruppe, see, besides Walter and Klein, "Der Fall Heuss: Der Schutzverband gegen seiner Vorsitzenden," Vorwärts (12 Dec. 1926). The Socialist organ saw Heuss' role as a great tragedy, since he was one of the best bourgeois politicians. The paper found it a pity that his stance had turned from the DDP many of its best spiritual proponents. The Communist newspaper reporter, Egon Erwin Kisch, tried unsuccessfully, at a meeting of the Berlin Ortsgruppe, 27 Sept. 1926, to get the SDS to join a unified front controlled and led by the KPD. Kisch demanded "that the SDS must take part in the congress of the working people. For one can only fight successfully against the Schund and Schmutz of the German class justice in the rows of the organized working class." Christian Ernst Siegel, Egon Erwin Kisch: Reportage und politischer Journalismus (Bremen, 1973), pp. 99-100.

20. Klein, Aktionen, pp. 337-43.

21. "Until the founding of the League [of Proletarian-Revolutionary Writers in late 1928] the writer-comrades were only fairly loosely organized in the fraktion of the bourgeois SDS (Protective Association of German Writers)." "Bericht über die Tätigkeit des Bundes proletarisch-revolutionärer Schriftsteller im Jahre 1929, 1930," in Zur Tradition der sozialistischen Literatur in Deutschland: Eine Auswahl von Dokumenten, ed. Deutsche Akademie der Künste zu Berlin, Sektion Dichtkunst, Geschichte der sozialistischen Literatur, 2nd rev. ed. (Berlin [East] and Weimar, 1967), p. 164.

22. Bundesarchiv (Koblenz), Record Group Reichskommissar für die Überwachung der öffentlichen Ordnung, Sammelstelle I in RM I, R 134 [hereafter cited as RG Reichskommissar für die Überwachung der öffentlichen Ordnung-R134], document pages 024011-024012.

23. Bundesarchiv (Koblenz), RG Reichskommissar für die Überwachung der öffentlichen Ordnung-R134, document page 035047.

24. Werner T. Angress, "Pegasus and Insurrection: Die Linkskurve and Its Heritage," Central European History 1 (March 1968): 41. The Proletarische Feuilleton-Korrespondenz (PFK) was actually founded on 1 Nov. 1927. Bundesarchiv (Koblenz), RG Reichskommissar für die Überwachung der öffentlichen Ordnung-R134, document page 035038. See also the essay by Klein, "Der Hochverratsprozess gegen Johannes R. Becher und die Herausbildung der proletarisch-revolutionären Literatur," in his Aktionen, p. 60.

25. Angress, "Pegasus," p. 41; Bundesarchiv (Kob- lenz), RG Reichskommissar für die Überwachung der öffentlichen Ordnung-R134, document pages 041078-041080, and 037034-037037. For the formation of the League, see also Gerald Stieg and Bernd Witte, Abriss einer Geschichte der deutschen Arbeiterliteratur (Stuttgart, 1973), pp. 76-85.

26. Klaus Kändler, "Das Thema Literatur und Arbeiterklasse in einigen Umfragen literarischer Zeitschriften zwischen 1928 und 1930," in Klein's Aktionen, p. 131. In 1929-30, 55 per cent of the League belonged to the KPD; 39 percent were Social Democrats or anarchists. The rest belonged to no party. "Bericht," in Zur Tradition, ed. Deutsche Akademie, p. 167.

27. Quoted in Bundesarchiv (Koblenz), RG Reichskommissar für die Überwachung der öffentlichen Ordnung-R132, document page 041079.

28. All quotes from Bundesarchiv (Koblenz), RG Reichskommissar für die Überwachung der öffentlichen Ordnung-R134, document page 040079.

29. Jürgen Rühle, Literature and Revolution: A Critical Study of the Writer and Communism in the Twentieth Century, trans. and ed. Jean Steinberg (New York, Washington, London, 1969), pp. 162-63.

30. P.A.O., "Schriftsteller in Uniform," Berliner Tageblatt (4 Nov. 1931).

31. Angress, "Pegasus," pp. 42-45 (quote on 42).

32. Johannes R. Becher, "Unsere Front," Die Linkskurve 1, no. 1 (1929): 1-2.

33. Johannes R. Becher, "Einen Schritt Weiter!," ibid., 2, no. 1 (1930): 1.

34. Angress, "Pegasus," p. 69, footnote 69. Linkskurve folded with the December 1932 issue because of financial difficulties. (p. 69).

35. Kurt Kläber, "Der proletarische Massenroman," Die Linkskurve 2, no. 5 (1930): 22-25. Die Linkskurve was worried by proletarian reading habits, which included escapist and even nationalist entertainment literature. See besides the Kläber article, Fritz Erpenbeck, "Leihbibliothek am Wedding," ibid., 2, no. 7 (1930): 14-15. Later, Kläber would demand "peasant novels" to help stem the Nazi tide in the countryside. Kurt Kläber, ibid., 3, no. 12 (1931): 20-22.

36. Initially, such prizes were small--a modest 200 marks for a full-length play or novel in January 1930. Ibid., 2, no. 1 (1930): 8. But by March 1931, the Der Neue Deutsche Verlag would offer as much as 4,000 marks for the best "anti-Fascist" novel submitted. Ibid., 3, no. 3 (1931): inside back flap.

37. See ibid., 2, no. 12 (1930): 23-24, for a discussion of the series. Originally, the series was to begin in June 1930, but the first volume appeared sometime in September or October. Kläber's article, "Der proletarische Massenroman," ibid., 2, no. 5 (1930): 22-25, was also meant to prepare the way for this series. Announcements and advertisements made Linkskurve readers aware of the impending appearance of the first volume. Ibid., 2, no. 5 (1930): 19-21; 2, no. 6 (1930): 17; 2, no. 8 (1930); 2, no. 9 (1930): rear flap.

38. Sturm auf Essen was greeted with much applause in Die Linkskurve. See O. Bihä, "Der Soldat und der Kumpel," ibid., 2, no. 11 (1930): 21; "Neue Bücher," ibid., 2, no. 11 (1930): 18; Kurt Kläber, "Marsch auf die Fabriken," ibid., 2, no. 11 (1930): 14-16. The journal announced in December 1930 a sales figure of 15,000; in January 1931, a figure of 14,000 was given. See ibid., 2, no. 12 (1930): 23 and 3, no. 1 (1931): 4.

39. Ibid., 2, no. 5 (1930): 19.

40. Proletarian-revolutionary authors read from their novels at meetings and, beginning in March 1931, engaged in "Mass-Critique Readings," in which writers like Marchwitza interacted with their readers. Ibid., 4, no. 3 (1932): 39-40 and 3, no. 3 (1931): inside rear flap. For dissemination of proletarian literature during the twenties (and thus by extension the thirties), see Jürgen Rühle, Literature and Revolution, p. 161.

41. See the announcement in Die Linkskurve 2, no. 7 (1930).

42. O. Bihä, "Kampfliteratur im Belagerungszustand: Zum Monat des proletarischen Buches," ibid., 3, no. 12 (1931): 2.

43. Johannes R. Becher, "Unsere Wendung: Vom Kampf um die Existenz der proletarisch-revolutionären Literatur zum Kampf um ihre Erweiterung," ibid., 3, no. 10 (1931): 1.

44. Ossip K. Flechtheim, "The Role of the Communist Party," The Path to Dictatorship, 1918-1933: Ten Essays, trans. John Conway with an introduction by Fritz Stern (Garden City, New York, 1966), pp. 108-9. For a full treatment of the KPD during 1929-33, see Ossip K. Flechtheim, Die KPD in der Weimarer Republik, with an introduction by Hermann Weber (Frankfurt/Main, 1969), pp. 248-88.

45. Quote from Istvan Deak, Weimar Germany's Left-Wing Intellectuals: A Political History of the Weltbühne and Its Circle (Berkeley and Los Angeles, 1968), pp. 169-70. See also, Flechtheim, "Role of the Communist Party," pp. 109-10, and Werner T. Angress, "Pegasus," p. 43.

46. Angress, "Pegasus," p. 43; Deak, Weimar Germany's Left-Wing Intellectuals, pp. 174-75.

47. Deak, Weimar Germany's Left-Wing Intellectuals, pp. 170-71. Angress, "Pegasus," pp. 45-46 and Rühle, Literature and Revolution, pp. 163-64, came to similar conclusions.

48. "Die Braunen Hemden," Die Linkskurve 2, no. 7 (1930): 2. In another article, J. Kraus wrote, "Since 1 May 1929 [when Communist workers were killed in a clash with Socialist police in Berlin], millions of workers in Germany and in the whole world know that the expression Social Fascism is no insult but an exact description of the role of Social Democracy in the present period, of its role as supportive organ of the bourgeoisie through the transition to the fascist subjugation of the working masses [and] through the preparation of the crusade of world imperialism against the Soviet Union." "Kampfmai 1930," ibid., 2, no. 5 (1930): 1.

49. Effer, "Kulturfaschismus," Die Linkskurve 3 no. 1 (1931): 3.

50. See O. Bihä, "Der Soldat und der Kumpel," Die Linkskurve 2, no. 11 (1930): 21, and Siefried Nebel, "Der Inflationsroman: Der grosse Betrug," ibid., 3, no. 12 (1931): 29-31.

51. Deak, Germany's Left-Wing Intellectuals, p. 170. Among others, Linkskurve attacked Thomas and Heinrich Mann, Franz Werfel, Erich Maria Remarque, Arnold Zweig, Jakob Wassermann, Gerhart Hauptmann, Alfred Döblin, Erich Kästner, Kurt Hiller, Carl von

Ossietzsky, Joseph Roth, and Artur Landsberger. Even the Bauhaus was targeted as a hidden prop of the ruling class. "Das Bauhaus," Die Linkskurve 2, no. 6 (1930): 29. See also, Angress, "Pegasus," p. 49.

52. Quoted in Rühle, Literature and Revolution, p. 163. Becher insisted that proletarian literature had to separate itself from all "worker's poets," from all poets of religious and pacifist reconciliation, from all sympathizers--all leftist writers who draw the line at joining the KPD are in the final analysis counter-revolutionary. Johannes R. Becher, "Einen Schritt Weiter!," Die Linkskurve 2, no. 1 (1930): 2-3.

53. Quote from "'Berlin Alexanderplatz' [Alfred Döblin]," Die Linkskurve 1, no. 5 (1929): 30-31. Döblin's book, one of the great novels of the twentieth century, aroused the ire of the Communists because it provided the most powerful picture of proletarian life in the capital without endorsing the Communist theory of the "organized class struggle." For other attacks on Döblin and his novel, see Armin Kesser, "Das Labyrinth des Dr. Döblin," ibid., 3, no. 9 (1931): 28-30; ibid., 3, no. 8 (1931): 26; ibid., 2, no. 6 (1930): 22-24; "Herr Döblin wird Gestrichen," ibid., 2, no. 10 (1930): 36.

54. O. Bihä, "Zeitschau der Kulturbarbarei: Chap- lins Odysee," ibid., 3, no. 4 (1931): 1-2.

55. Angress, "Pegasus," pp. 51-52. When the Nazis were discussed, they were often linked with the supposedly graver threat, the SPD. Hans Jäger, in a four-page article entitled "Publizistische Propaganda für den Faschismus in Deutschland," devoted only one paragraph to National Socialism and the radical völk- isch movement. Die Linkskurve 2, no. 5 (1930): 14.

56. Jäger was convinced that the Nazis were literarily "impotent." Hans Jäger, "Das Schrifttum der deutschen Faschisten und ihre literarische Impotenz," Die Linkskurve 3, no. 2 (1931): 15-17.

57. Klein, Aktionen, pp. 343-44.

58. Quote and description of the opposition's demands in "Es ist was faul im Schutzverband Deutscher Schriftsteller," Die Linkskurve 1, no. 4 (1929): 31. See also, Roda Roda, "Die Krise," Berliner Tageblatt (24 Oct. 1931).

59. Quote from "Schutzverband Deutscher Schriftsteller," Die Linkskurve 2, no. 5 (1930): 26-27; Klein, Aktionen, pp. 344-45. Gläser himself had been prosecuted for blasphemous utterances in a play. The trial had been transparently political (the main witness against him being Dr. Roland Freisler, the leader of the Völkische in Cassel). Walter, Bedrohung, p. 42.

60. Quoted word from Roda Roda, "Die Krise," Berliner Tageblatt (24 Oct. 1931). Roda Roda estimated the size of the Communist contingent in the SDS at around sixty in October 1931. The number of forty is probably accurate, since it is given in Fraktionsleitung der OSDS to [the members of the Communist fraktion in the opposition], n.d. [mid-November 1931], in Klein, Aktionen, p. 392.

61. "Verwaltungskorruption im SDS: Von der Generalversammlung des Schutzverbandes Deutscher Schriftsteller," Die Linkskurve 3, no. 3 (1931): 19.

62. Even at the key November 1931 extraordinary general assembly of the Berlin Ortsgruppe, only 219 members out of ca. 900 were present and voting. Der Arbeitsausschuss der Opposition im SDS [Olga Halpern], "Kurzgefasste Geschichte der Oppositionsbewegung im SDS [information material for the Gaue and Ortsgruppen of the SDS]," 4 Dec. 1931, in Klein, Aktionen, p. 400. At one important meeting of the Berlin Ortsgruppe in 1932, reportedly only 19 (out of 500; the Ortsgruppe had split at the end of 1931) members attended. Bundesarchiv (Koblenz), RG Reichskunstwart-R32, files 385/386: Theodor Bohner [chairman of the SDS], "Die Vorgänge im Schutzverband Deutscher Schriftsteller," Die Vossische Zeitung (1932). There are ample examples of Communist efforts to mobilize the maximum number of party members for the various meetings and demonstrations of the Berlin Ortsgruppe in Klein, Aktionen. Roda Roda described the Communists as being "extraordinarily disciplined" in "Die Krise," Berliner Tageblatt (24 Oct. 1931).

63. Friends and foes alike commented on the loudness and turbulence of the Communists. See Roda Roda, "Die Krise," Berliner Tageblatt (24 Oct. 1931); Rudolf Olden, "Oppositioneller im Schutzverband," Berliner Tageblatt (27 Oct. 1931); Nachlass Bloem (Wuppertal): [Bloem], "Zweites Buch," pp. 412-14.

64. Quote from Roda Roda, "Die Krise," Berliner Tageblatt (24 Oct. 1931). See also Bur. [probably Friedrich Burschell], "In Sachen Schutzverband," Berliner Tageblatt (20 Oct. 1931).

65. Deak, Germany's Left-Wing Intellectuals, p. 165.

66. Ibid., p. 170. For the cooperation of left-wing intellectuals, including the luminaries of the Weltbühne circle, see Helmut Gruber, "Willi Münzenberg's German Communist Propaganda Empire, 1921-1933," The Journal of Modern History 38 (Sept. 1966): 278-97. Babette Gross describes Münzenberg as the "patron saint of the fellow travelers." Willi Münzenberg: A Political Biography, trans. Marian Jackson (Lansing, Michigan, 1974), pp. 216-21 (quote on 216).

67. See, for example, Klein, Aktionen, pp. 611, 617-18.

68. Erich Mühsam, "Gewerkschaft der Schriftsteller," [from Die Weltbühne 27 (14 July 1931)]: 58ff, in Klein, Aktionen, pp. 361-66. Mühsam had advocated an alliance between the writer and "the exploited proletarian" even in the discussions that led to the founding of the SDS before World War I. Heuss, Erinnerungen, p. 96. Mühsam was a total revolutionary who had been jailed (up until he was amnestied in 1925) for playing a leading role in the Bavarian Soviet Republic of 1919. "Although he was associated with Münzenberg's Red Aid, his basic creed remained anarchism, and he was often critical of the KPD." Deak, Germany's Left-Wing Intellectuals, pp. 259-60.

69. A whole issue of Die Brücke, the Sunday cultural magazine of the Berliner Tageblatt, was dedicated to the fight against censorship in 1932 under the headline, "Buchverbote--eine Sicherung der öffentlichen Ordnung?," Berliner Tageblatt (28 Feb. 1932). Besides the articles in this supplement, see [P.A.O.], "Romane der Arbeiter: Zu einer Romanreihe des Internationalen Arbeiter-Verlags Berlin," Berliner Tageblatt (11 Oct.

1931); "Polizei Zensur--schon wieder ein Buchverbot," Berliner Tageblatt (11 Feb. 1932); "Buchverbote ohne Ende," Berliner Tageblatt (16 Feb. 1932); "Staatsgefährliche Literatur: 'Sturm auf Essen' vor Gericht," Berliner Tageblatt (19 Feb. 1932).

70. Dr. Lutz Weltmann, "Ein Schritt zum Faschismus," Die Brücke, Sunday supplement of the Berliner Tageblatt (28 Feb. 1932).

71. Dr. Apfel, "Die Technik der Verbote," in ibid. Apfel was a member of the Weltbühne circle as well as a successful criminal and political lawyer. Deak, Germany's Left-Wing Intellectuals, p. 232.

72. Olden was foreign policy editor of the Ber- liner Tageblatt. He defended Carl von Ossietzsky in the famed Weltbühne trial and was himself an important figure in the Weltbühne circle. His Hitler biography caused quite a stir when it was published in 1936. Klein, Aktionen, p. 635; Deak, Germany's Left-Wing Intellectuals, pp. 260-61. See also, Kurt Hiller, Köpfe und Tröpfe: Profile aus einem Vierteljahrhundert (Hamburg, Stuttgart, 1950), pp. 353-57.

73. Rudolf Olden, "Oppositioneller im Schutzverband," Berliner Tageblatt (27 Oct. 1931).

74. Quote from Friedrich Burschell, "Die Schriftsteller," Die Brücke (17 Apr. 1932). This whole issue was dedicated to the question, "Geistesarbeiter ohne Gewerkschaften!" For what are almost certainly Burschell's views, see Bur., "Im Sachen Schutzverband," Berliner Tageblatt (20 Oct. 1931). Burschell ultimately became a leader of the opposition. See the various documents and commentaries in Klein, Aktionen, pp. 384, 404, 411, 413, 442, 547, 625.

75. Klein, Aktionen, p. 610.

76. This is a constant theme in Klein, Aktionen.

77. Walter, Bedrohung, p. 51.

78. Ibid., p. 53. This contention needs more study. The powerful Bavarian Gau of the SDS was heavily influenced by Thomas Mann who, in 1932 at least, was the Gau chairman. Bavaria usually stood by the Main Executive Committee against the opposition. For Mann's chairmanship, see "Internationale Protestaktion gegen den Ausschluss des Berliner Vorstandes," Aug. 1932, in Klein, Aktionen, p. 451.

79. Deak, Germany's Left-Wing Intellectuals, p. 236.

80. Breuer became Deputy Press Chief of the Reich Chancellery in 1918. "Later, he edited Die Glocke, the journal of the controversial Social Democratic millionaire, Dr. Helphand-Parvus." Ibid., p. 234. Breuer and Elösser had long been active in SDS affairs. Heuss, Erinnerungen, pp. 97, 340. Elösser's predecessor as SDS chairman was Arnold Zweig, then a pacifist and a Zionist closer to the SPD than the KPD. Zweig, who later became a sort of novelist laureate of the German Democratic Republic, himself condemned attempts to politicize the SDS in 1930.

81. Bohner was also Oberschulrat for Berlin-Brandenburg. Klein, Aktionen, pp. 606-7.

82. Nachlass Bloem (Wuppertal): Bloem, "Werk und Tat: Zweites Buch," pp. 289-95.

83. "Ein Nationalverband," Berliner Tageblatt (14 Oct. 1931).

84. Quote from Ein Oppositioneller, "Gewerk- schaftsprogramm des SDS," Die Linkskurve 3, no. 12 (1931): 35-36. See also, Klein, Aktionen, pp. 350-51, for Breuer's program. For Bohner's defense of the taking of subventions by the SDS from the state, see Bundesarchiv (Koblenz), RG Reichskunstwart-R32, file 385/386: Bohner, "Die Vorgänge im Schutzverband," Vossische Zeitung (1932).

85. Olden, "Oppositioneller," Berliner Tageblatt (27 Oct. 1931).

86. Bundesarchiv (Koblenz), RG Reichskunstwart-R32, file 120: Bieber, Breuer and others to [the Berlin Ortsgruppe], 12 Mar. 1926.

87. Bundesarchiv (Koblenz), RG Reichskunstwart-R32, file 385/386: Bohner, "Die Vorgänge im Schutzverband," Vossische Zeitung (1932). The Berlin Ortsgruppe did hold an assembly on the occasion of Breuer's arrest. Wieland Herzfelde, the Communist publisher, claimed that Breuer had fallen victim to the same powers that he had called forth. Herzfelde, reflecting the political myopia of the Communist elements in the opposition, saw no difference between Hitler and Breuer other than a certain "Tempos" (speed or pace). See "Schriftsteller in der Anti- faschistischen Front," Die Welt am Abend (30 July 1932) in Klein, Aktionen, p. 420.

88. Roda Roda, "Die Krise," Berliner Tageblatt (24 Oct. 1931).

89. Nachlass Bloem (Wuppertal): Bloem, "Zweites Buch: Der neue Dreissigjahre Krieg," p. 408.

90. Bundesarchiv (Koblenz), RG Reichskunstwart-R32, file 385/386. Bohner, "Die Vorgänge im Schutzverband," Vossische Zeitung (1932).

NOTES

CHAPTER 8

THE DEATH OF WALTER BLOEM'S REPUBLICANISM: THE BATTLE WITHIN THE SDS

1. Bundesarchiv (Koblenz), RG Reichskunstwart-R32, file 385/386: Bohner, "Die Vorgänge im Schutzverband," Vossische Zeitung (1932); Klein, Aktionen, pp. 346-47; "Was Geht im SDS Vor...?," Die Linkskurve 2, no. 7 (1930):27.

2. Olden, "Oppositioneller," Berliner Tageblatt (27 Oct. 1931).

3. Klein, Aktionen, p. 347.

4. Fluhme's charges against Werner Schendell (and the SDS chairman Elösser) are contained in Bundesarchiv (Koblenz), RG Reichskunstwart-R32, file 385/386: Dr. Ernst Fluhme to the Mitglieder des SDS [July 1931?]. See also: Roda Roda, "Die Krise," Berliner Tageblatt (24 Oct. 1931); "Verwaltungskor- ruption im SDS: Von der Generalversammlung des Schutzverbandes Deutscher Schriftsteller," Die Linkskurve 3 no. 3, (1931): 18-19; Mühsam, "Gewerk- schaft der Schriftsteller," in Klein, Aktionen, pp. 361-66.

5. Klein, Aktionen, p. 347. See also Mühsam, "Gewerkschaft der Schriftsteller," in ibid., p. 362.

6. "Verwaltungskorruption," Linkskurve 3, no. 3 (1931): 18-19.

7. Der Arbeitsausschuss, "Kurzgefasste Gesch- ichte," in Klein, Aktionen, p. 398.

8. Ibid., p. 399 (see also the commentary on 606-9).

9. Johannes Karl König, "Sturm im SDS," Die Linkskurve 3, no. 7 (1931): 25-26.

10. Klein, Aktionen, p. 604.

11. Ibid.

12. König, "Sturm," Linkskurve 3, no. 7 (1931): 25.

13. Ibid., pp. 25-26.

14. Der Arbeitsausschuss of the Kampfkomitee für die Freiheit des Schrifttums, "Aufruf für die Freiheit des Schrifttums," in Klein, Aktionen, p. 366; Walter, Bedrohung, p. 56.

15. Walter, Bedrohung, p. 58.

16. Ibid., p. 59.

17. Klein, Aktionen, p. 611.

18. Kurt Tucholsky was infuriated by what he saw as an equivocal stand by the SDS; he announced his resignation from the Protective Association in Die Weltbühne. Kurt Tucholsky, "Erklärung [from Die Weltbühne 27 (18 Aug. 1931): p. 276]," in Gesammelte Werke: Band III 1929-1932, ed. Mary Gerold-Tucholsky and Fritz J. Raddatz (Reinbek bei Hamburg, 1960), p. 919.

19. Klein, Aktionen, pp. 611-12; "Der SDS für Faschismus und die Folgen," Die Linkskurve 3, no. 9 (1931): 9-10.

20. Kampfkomitee für die Freiheit des Schrifttums, "Aufruf für die Freiheit des Schrifttums," in Klein, Aktionen, pp. 366-68. For Albrecht and Klein's estimation of this document's importance, see the commentary on p. 610.

21. Kurt Hiller, Walther Karsch, and Erich Kästner resigned from the "Kampfkomitee" in Aug. 1931. Ibid., p. 612.

22. Ibid., pp. 612-13.

23. Die Opposition im Schutzverband Deutscher Schriftsteller, "Programmerklärung der OSDS (Opposition im Schutzverband Deutscher Schriftsteller)," Die Linkskurve 3, no. 9 (1931): 20-21. The OSDS program was intended to provide a positive program for an opposition hitherto more concerned with criticism of the Main Executive. Der Arbeitsausschuss der Opposition im SDS, "Begleitsschreiben zur Programmerklärung, Opposition im SDS, Ortsgruppe Berlin," Sept. 1931, in Klein, Aktionen, pp. 374-75.

24. P.A.O., "Die Freiheit des Schrifttums: Ein Kundgebung im Schubert-Saal," Berliner Tageblatt (15 Aug. 1931).

25. According to the Arbeitsausschuss, "Begleits- schreiben," in Klein, Aktionen, p. 374, the OSDS program had won over the active cooperation as well as the acceptance of the "best and most progressive heads of literature and publicism" in Berlin.

26. Fraktionsleitung der kommunistischen Schrift- steller (Johannes Becher) to the fraktion members, 3 Oct. 1931, in Klein, Aktionen, pp. 376-77. The Communist fraktion included KPD members of the League of Proletarian-Revolutionary writers and of the SDS. Becher was the fraktion leader. Ibid., p. 616.

27. "Entwurf zu einem Aktionsprogramm der SDS-Fraktion," n.d. [Aug.-Sept. 1931], in ibid., p. 615.

28. Fraktionsleitung (Becher) to fraktion members, in ibid., p. 376.

29. Vorstand der Ortsgruppe Berlin to the Gaue, 1 Dec. 1931, in ibid., p. 613.

30. Ibid., pp. 613-14.

31. Arbeitsausschuss, "Kurzgefasste Geschichte," in ibid., p. 399.

32. "Der SDS für Faschismus," Linkskurve 3, no. 9 (1931): 9; Klein, Aktionen, pp. 608-9.

33. Klein, Aktionen, pp. 616-17.

34. Arbeitsausschuss, "Kurzgefasste Geschichte," in ibid., pp. 399-400; Der Arbeitsausschuss der Opposition im SDS to the members of the Opposition im SDS Ortsgruppe Berlin, Oct. 1931, in ibid., pp. 377-81; Berhard von Brentano, Heinz Pol, Georg Lukacs, Anna Seghers (commissioned by the Arbeitsausschuss der Opposition im SDS) to [fellow writers], 13 Oct. 1931, in ibid., [pp. 381-82; Arbeitsausschuss der Opposition im SDS, "Bericht über die grosse Ausschlusssitzung des Hauptvorstandes am 19. Oktober 1931," [October 1931], in ibid., pp. 385-89; Bur., "Im Sachen Schutzverband," Berliner Tageblatt (20 Oct. 1931); Roda Roda, "Die Krise," Berliner Tageblatt (24 Oct. 1931); "Der grosse Krach im SDS," Die Linkskurve 3, no. 11 (1931): 30.

35. Roda Roda, "Die Krise," Berliner Tageblatt (24 Oct. 1931).

36. Bundesarchiv (Koblenz), RG Reichskunstwart-R32, file 385/386: "Solidaritätserklärung für die Opposition im SDS."

37. "Schriftsteller stossen vor: Breuer schickt Segall-Einmütiger Kampf," Die Rote Fahne (28 Oct. 1931), in Klein, Aktionen, pp. 390-91; "Die Opposition der Schriftsteller," Berliner Tageblatt (27 Oct. 1931).

38. "Opposition der Schriftsteller," Berliner Tageblatt (27 Oct. 1931).

39. Nachlass Bloem (Wuppertal): Bloem, "Werk und Tat: Zweites Buch," p. 290.

40. Bloem's explanation of his role in the meeting of 19 Oct. 1931 was carried verbatim in "Irrungen," Berliner Tageblatt (28 Oct. 1931).

41. Ibid., and Arbeitsausschuss, "Bericht über die grosse Ausschlusssitzung," in Klein, Aktionen, pp. 386-87.

42. Nachlass Bloem (Wuppertal): [Bloem], "Zwe- ites Buch: Der neue Dreissigjahre Krieg," p. 419.

43. "Irrungen," Berliner Tageblatt (28 Oct. 1931).

44. Arbeitsausschuss, "Kurzgefasste Geschichte," in Klein, Aktionen, p. 400.

45. Members of the KPD in the SDS were required to attend the Communist writers' fraktion meeting on 17 Nov. and the OSDS meeting on 19 Nov. to prepare for the extraordinary general assembly on 23 Nov. "It is party duty to come to the fraktion sitting, to the opposition conference, and to the extraordinary general assembly. These three evenings are to be held free." [Communist] Fraktionsleitung der OSDS to [members of the fraktion], n.d. [early Nov. 1931], in ibid., pp. 392-93.

46. For this description of the extraordinary general assembly, see Arbeitsausschuss der Opposition im SDS, "Voller Sieg der Opposition im Gau Berlin," in ibid., pp. 393-95; Arbeitsausschuss, "Kurzgefasste Geschichte," in ibid., pp. 400-401. Heinz Pol was an

assistant editor of the Vossische Zeitung from 1923 until 1931, when he left because of censorship of his articles. "Between 1931 and 1933, he was editor of the Neue Montagszeitung and assistant editor of the Welt am Abend, both published by Willi Münzenberg. Although sympathetic to Communism, he criticized the KPD in his pseudonymous Weltbühne articles from a Trotskyist point of view." Deak, Germany's Left-Wing Intellectuals, p. 263. Münzenberg, the great Communist publisher, made Pol promise not to join the KPD when he hired him. Gruber, "Münzenberg's German Communist Propaganda Empire, 1921-1933," p. 290. Pol's election helped mask the Communist predominance in the Berlin executive committee elected on 23 Nov. For Münzenberg and Welt am Abend, see Gross, Münzenberg, pp. 160-62.

47. Dr. Georg Lukacs and Heinz Pol, "Protokoll der Konstituierenden Sitzung des Vorstandes der Berliner Ortsgruppe des SDS am 27. November 1931," 27 Nov. 1931, in Klein, Aktionen, pp. 396-97. Pol headed the Berlin Ortsgruppe--at first as de facto and then as de jure chairman--until the local's dissolution in the summer of 1932. See the commentary in ibid., p. 624.

48. For accounts of the formation of the Ortsgruppe Berlin-Brandenburg, see Arbeitsausschuss, "Kurzgefasste Geschichte," in ibid p. 401 and the commentary in ibid., pp. 624-25. The Berlin executive committee (controlled by the opposition) declared Jacob's action a violation of the SDS statutes and harmful to the association and, thus, moved to expel him. Lukacs and Pol, "Protokoll," in ibid., p. 397.

49. Burschell, "Die Schriftsteller," Die Brücke (17 Apr. 1932). Theodor Bohner asserted in mid-1932 that half of the Berlin membership joined the new Ortsgruppe Berlin-Brandenburg, which offered them "ein Weg ins Freie." Bundesarchiv (Koblenz), RG Reichskunstwart-R32, file 385/386: "Die Vorgänge im Schutzverband."

50. Arbeitsausschuss, "Kurzgefasste Geschich- te," in Klein, Aktionen, p. 401.

51. "Ohrfeigen für den Reformismus: Von Gewerkschaftskampf der Schriftsteller," Die rote Fahne (26 Nov. 1931), in Klein, Aktionen, p. 623. Ein Oppositioneller, "Gewerksschaftsprogramm des SDS," Linkskurve 3, no. 12 (1931): 36.

52. Nachlass Bloem (Wuppertal): [Bloem], "Zwei- tes Buch: Der neue Dreissigjahre Krieg," p. 407.

53. Ibid., pp. 407-8.

54. Ibid., pp. 408-9.

55. Ibid., pp. 409-10.

56. Neither Klein, Aktionen, nor Walter, Bedrohung, recognize the outcome of the general assembly of 9-10 Jan. 1932 as a compromise. However, the outcome of the assembly is inexplicable with any other interpretation of the event.

57. "Erfolge im Schutzverband: Der Verlauf der Generalversammlung; Ausschlüsse zurückgenommen," Die Welt am Abend (Jan. 1932), a Communist-affiliated newspaper, saw the meeting as an opposition victory, although the majority of the new Main Executive was not from the OSDS ranks.

58. Dissolution of the loyalist Berlin-Brandenburg Ortsgruppe had been a major demand of the opposition. Klein, <u>Aktionen</u>, pp. 626-27.

59. "Walter Bloems Hemmungen," <u>Berliner Tageblatt</u> (12 Apr. 1932).

60. Nachlass Bloem (Wuppertal): [Bloem], "Zwei- tes Buch: Der neue Dreissigjahre Krieg," pp. 410-11. Klein reports wrongly that Bloem was elected with the votes of the SPD against those of the opposition. Indeed, Klein's documentation and commentary on Bloem's election and on his chairmanship is very thin. Just enough materials are presented to make Bloem's election look like the product of an alliance between the Social Fascists (the SPD) and the National Fascists. Klein, <u>Aktionen</u>, pp. 626-27. Walter, <u>Bedrohung</u>, p. 52, uncritically takes over Klein's information and interpretation. According to Walter, Bloem's election with Breuer's help proved that Breuer constantly took sides in the SDS struggles with "the Conservatives and Nationalists."

61. Nachlass Bloem (Wuppertal): [Bloem], "Zwei- tes Buch: Der neue Dreissigjahre Krieg," pp. 410-11.

62. According to "Hemmungen," <u>Berliner Tageblatt</u> (12 Apr. 1932), "Bloem's reconciliatory stance" had won him the votes for chairman of the overwhelming majority of the opposition.

63. Nachlass Bloem (Wuppertal): Bloem, "Werk und Tat: Zweites Buch," p. 292.

64. Ibid., pp. 290-92.

65. Ibid., pp. 294-95.

66. Nachlass Bloem (Wuppertal): [Bloem], "Zwei- tes Buch: Der neue Dreissigjahre Krieg," pp. 405-6.

67. Peter Flamm, "'Stadt und Land': Der Kongress der deutschsprachigen P.E.N.-Klubs," <u>Berliner Tageblatt</u> (19 Jan. 1932).

68. Die Fraktionsleitung to all members in the KPD who are members of the SDS, 15 Jan. 1932, in Klein, <u>Aktionen</u>, p. 406.

69. Nachlass Bloem (Wuppertal): [Bloem], "Zwei- tes Buch: Der neue Dreissigjahre Krieg," pp. 411-13.

70. Ibid., pp. 411-14.

71. Ibid., p. 414; Klein, <u>Aktionen</u>, p. 627.

72. "Die Not der Schriftsteller: Kundgebung in den Johann Georg-Sälen," <u>Die Welt am Abend</u> (15 Feb. 1932), in Klein, <u>Aktionen</u>, p. 405; Der Ortsvorstand Berlin (Heinz Pol, Dr. Georg Lukacs, Meta Kraus-Fessel, David Luschnat, Dr. Andor Gabor, F. C. Weiskopf) to [all members of the Berlin Ortsgruppe], mid-March 1932, in ibid., pp. 410-11; Burschell, "Die Schriftsteller," <u>Die Brücke</u> (17 Apr. 1932).

73. "Die Not der Schriftsteller," in Klein, Aktionen, p. 405.

74. Klein, Aktionen, p. 628.

75. [Notice of the ban and confiscation of Hans Marchwitza, Sturm auf Essen], Die Linkskurve 3, no. 9 (1931): 18; Peter Waldschmidt, "Verordnungs-Guillotine," Die Linkskurve 4, no. 3 (1932): 7-9; "Schriftsteller, Journalisten, Künstler!," Die Linkskurve 3, no. 10 (1931): 18; P.A.O., "Romane der Arbeiter," Berliner Tageblatt (11 Oct. 1931); "Buchverbote ohne Ende," Berliner Tageblatt (16 Feb. 1932); Klein, Aktionen, pp. 628-29; Walter, Bedrohung, pp. 59-60; Dr. Apfel, "Die Technik der Verbote," Die Brücke (28 Feb. 1932).

76. Rühle, Literature and Revolution, pp. 161-62.

77. "The police censorship, armed with the full- est powers, has been removed from public control. . . . The freedom of literature has been in danger for months, and since two days ago in the highest of all dangers." "Staatsgefährliche Literatur," Berliner Tageblatt (19 Feb. 1932).

78. The lead article by Dr. Apfel, the lawyer for the Internationaler Arbeiter-Verlag in the Sturm auf Essen case, focused on the implications of the failure of the appeal. See "Die Technik der Verbote," Die Brücke (28 Feb. 1932). Lion Feuchtwanger, "Motive, die nicht zu ergründen sind," Alfred Kurella, "Zensur auf Nebenwegen," and Dr. Lutz Weltmann, "Ein Schritt zum Faschismus," also contributed articles to Die Brücke, supplement to the Sunday, Berliner Tageblatt, 28 Feb. 1932. See for Apfel's defense of the Internationaler Arbeiter-Verlag, Walter, Bedrohung, pp. 59-60.

79. "Protestentschliessung gegen Buchverbote," 29 Feb. 1932, in Klein, Aktionen, pp. 406-7.

80. Der Ortsvorstand Berlin to [all members of the Ortsgruppe], in ibid., pp. 412-13; SDS Ortsgruppe Berlin, Vorstand, to the [chairmen and executive committee members of the Gau and Orts groups of the SDS], mid-August 1932, in ibid., p. 630.

81. This was for the centennial of Goethe's death. "Goethe und der offizielle SDS: Ein Kulturdokument," n.d. (mid-March 1932), in ibid., pp. 408-9.

82. Ibid., pp. 408-9; quote from Der Ortsvorstand Berlin to [all members of the Ortsgruppe], in ibid., p. 411.

83. Der Ortsvorstand Berlin to [all members of the Ortsgruppe], in ibid., pp. 410-12; "Massregelung der Ortsgruppe Berlin des SDS," mid-March 1932, in ibid., p. 414.

84. "Was ist uns heute Goethe? Der Diskussionsabend der Berliner Ortsgruppe des Schutzverbandes," Die Welt am Abend (24 Mar. 1932), in ibid., p. 629. The Ortsgruppe passed a resolution in mid-March declaring the Main Executive Committee's actions contrary to SDS regulations and vowing "to continue its activity in the sense of a fruitful union work undisturbed and at the same time to wage in strengthened measure the fight for its rights as the greatest Ortsgruppe of the SDS." "Massregelung," in ibid., pp. 414-15.

85. This account is drawn from Deak, Germany's Left-Wing Intellectuals, pp. 189-92. Rudolf Olden and Alfred Apfel, collaborators on both Die Weltbühne and the Berliner Tageblatt and members of the OSDS, were two of Ossietzky's defenders. (p. 191). See also the chapter, "Der 'Weltbühne'-Prozess," in Kurt R. Grossmann, Ossietzky: Ein deutscher Patriot (Munich, 1963), pp. 261-94; Bruno Frei, Carl von Ossietzky: Ritter ohne Furcht und Tadel (Berlin and Weimar, 1966), pp. 151-76; Walter, Bedrohung, pp. 61-62.

86. Deak, Germany's Left-Wing Intellectuals p. 192.

87. Quoted in ibid., pp. 192-93.

88. Ibid., pp. 193-94.

89. Quoted in ibid., p. 194. See also Ossietzky's various essays on the affair in the chapter, "Über sich Selbst," Carl von Ossietzky, Schriften II, eds. Bruno Frei and Hans Leonard (Berlin and Weimar, 1966), pp. 201-39.

90. Deak, German's Left-Wing Intellectuals, pp. 194-97.

91. Frei, Ossietzky, pp. 186-87.

92. Walther von Hollander [secretary of the German group of the PEN-Club], "Bloem und Ossietzky," Berliner Tageblatt (12 Apr. 1932).

93. Hanns Martin Elster and Martin Beradt, "Nochmals: Bloem und Ossietzky," Berliner Tageblatt (13 Apr. 1932).

94. Walter, Bedrohung, p. 188. According to Bloem, Elster attacked him during the Third Reich for supporting Ossietzky. Nachlass Bloem (Wuppertal): [Bloem], "Zweites Buch: Der neue Dreissigjahre Krieg," note on back of p. 419.

95. Hollander, "Bloem und Ossietzky," Berliner Tageblatt (12 Apr. 1932).

96. Ibid., and Elster and Beradt, "Nochmals: Bloem und Ossietzky," Berliner Tageblatt (13 Apr. 1932).

97. Hollander, "Bloem und Ossietzky," Berliner Tageblatt (12 Apr. 1932); "Walter Bloems Hemmungen," Berliner Tageblatt (12 Apr. 1932); Walter, Bedrohung, p. 264, footnote 61.

98. Nachlass Bloem (Wuppertal): Bloem, "Werk und Tat: Zweites Buch," p. 288.

99. "Walter Bloems Hemmungen," Berliner Tageblatt (12 Apr. 1932); Hollander, "Bloem und Ossietzky" (12 Apr. 1932); P. F., "Skandal in Schutzverband der Schriftsteller: Bloems Dolchstoss gegen Ossietzky," Die Welt am Abend (11 Apr. 1932), in Klein, Aktionen, pp. 630-31.

100. Hollander, "Bloem und Ossietzky," Berliner Tageblatt (12 Apr. 1932).

101. Nachlass Bloem (Wuppertal): Bloem, "Zweites Buch: Der neue Dreissigjahre Krieg," pp. 415-415A. Bloem told a board meeting of the PEN-Club that Ossietzky's political position was in direct opposition to his own. Yet, he declared that, as a matter of principle in a state with constitutionally guaranteed freedom of the press, it was wrong for an author to be sentenced by a court for a public declaration of convictions. But, Bloem concluded, before he could sign the petition for clemency, he would have to read the Weltbühne article and the trial proceedings. (pp. 415-415A).

102. Ibid., p. 415A; Hollander, "Bloem und Ossietzky," Berliner Tageblatt (12 Apr. 1932).

103. Hollander, "Bloem und Ossietzky," Berliner Tageblatt (12 Apr. 1932).

104. Elster and Beradt, "Nochmals: Bloem und Ossietzky," Berliner Tageblatt (13 Apr. 1932).

105. Quote from ibid., and "Walter Bloems Hemmungen," Berliner Tageblatt (12 Apr. 1932). See also P. F., "Skandal im Schuzverband der Schriftsteller," in Klein, Aktionen, pp. 630-31.

106. "Walter Bloems Hemmungen," Berliner Tageblatt (12 Apr. 1932).

107. Ibid.

108. [Bloem], "Zweites Buch: Der neue Dreissigjahre Krieg," p. 406A.

109. Ibid., pp. 415b-16.

110. The new board of the PEN-Club was made up entirely of men close to republican parties. Ibid., p. 416. For the election results and the quoted justification of Bloem's replacement, see "Walter Bloems Hemmungen," Berliner Tageblatt (12 Apr. 1932).

111. [Bloem], "Zweites Buch: Der neue Dreissigjahre Krieg," p. 406A.

112. According to "Walter Bloems Hemmungen," Ber- liner Tageblatt (12 Apr. 1932): "Rather the incidents in the PEN-Club have manifestly sharpened the already abundantly present tensions within the not-oppositional group to the point of an open break." Burschell, "Die Schriftsteller," Die Brücke (17 Apr. 1932), also hinted at a break between Bloem and the rest of the Main Executive.

113. Nachlass Bloem (Wuppertal): Bloem, "Zweites Buch: Der neue Dreissigjahre Krieg," pp. 417-18. See also, "Walter Bloems Hemmungen," Berliner Tageblatt (12 Apr. 1932).

114. Klein, Aktionen, p. 630.

115. "Verlauf der 'Auflösung' der Ortsgruppe Berlin," late Sept. 1932, in ibid., pp. 437-46; Bundesarchiv (Koblenz), RG Reichskunstwart-R32, file 385/386: Bohner, "Die Vorgänge im Schutzverband," Vossische Zeitung (1932).

116. "Walter Bloems Hemmungen," Berliner Tageblatt (12 Apr. 1932).

117. Elster and Beradt, "Nochmals: Bloem und Ossietzky," Berliner Tageblatt (13 Apr. 1932); Hollander, "Bloem und Ossietzky," Berliner Tageblatt (12 Apr. 1932).

118. "Nachschrift der Schriftleitung," appended to Hanns Martin Elster and Martin Beradt, "Nochmals Bloem und Ossietzky," Berliner Tageblatt (13 Apr. 1932).

119. P. F., "Skandal im Schutzverband," in Klein, Aktionen, p. 631.

120. "Der skandallose SDS," Die Linkskurve 4, no. 4 (1932): 37-38.

121. "Zwei Entschliessungen der Ortsgruppe Ber- lin: 1. Zum Fall Ossietzky-Bloem," n.d. [mid-April 1932], in Klein, Aktionen, pp. 415-16.

122. Nachlass Bloem (Wuppertal): g [Bloem], "Zweites Buch: Der neue Dreissigjahre Krief," p. 416.

123. Burschell, "Die Schriftsteller," Die Brücke (17 Apr. 1932).

124. Nachlass Bloem (Wuppertal): [Bloem], "Zwe- ites Buch: Der neue Dreissigjahre Krieg," p. 416.

125. Ibid., p. 425.

126. Nachlass Bloem (Wuppertal), file 60: Walter Bloem, "Hindenburg, dem Deutschen! (Zum 85. Geburtstag am 2 Oktober)," Der Türmer (Oct. 1932): 8-9.

127. Quoted in Mosse, "Die deutsche Rechte," p. 234.

128. Quoted in Carl von Ossietzky, "Herr Walter Bloem [from Die Weltbühne (28 Feb. 1933)]," in Carl von Ossietzky, Schriften II, eds. Frei and Leonard, p. 140.

129. Walter, Bedrohung, p. 55.

130. In italics in the original. Quoted in Hegemann, "Bloem contra Mann," Das Tagebuch 13 (1932): 1588.

131. Ibid.

132. Quoted in ibid., p. 1592; "Offener Brief an Heinrich Mann," Deutsche Allgemeine Zeitung (27 Sept. 1932), in Klein, Aktionen, p. 631; Walter, Bedrohung, p. 55.

133. Quoted in Ossietzky, "Bloem," p. 136.

134. Quoted in ibid., pp. 136-37.

135. Ibid., pp. 137-39.

136. Quoted in ibid., p. 142.

137. Hegemann, "Bloem contra Mann," Das Tagebuch 13 (1932): 1588-93.

138. Ibid., pp. 1588-92. Actually, the majority of the copies of the war novels cited by Hegemann were bought before 1918.

139. Ibid., p. 1592.

140. Ibid., p. 1593.

141. Frei, <u>Ossietzky</u>, p. 202.

142. Ossietzky, "Bloem," p. 136.

143. Ibid., pp. 137-42.

144. Robert Neumann, "Historische Romane," <u>Die Literatur</u> 31 (1929): 707.

NOTES

CHAPTER 9

THE MORAL SUICIDE OF AN HONEST MAN: WALTER BLOEM AS NAZI FELLOW TRAVELER AND PARTY MEMBER

1. Ernst Löwy, Literatur unterm Hakenkreuz: Das Dritte Reich und seine Dichtung: Eine Dokumentation, with a forward by Hans-Jochen Gamm (Frankfurt/Main, 1966), p. 339.

2. Nachlass Bloem (Wuppertal): [Bloem], "Zweit- es Buch: Der neue Dreissigjahre Krieg," pp. 425-44 (especially 425, 434-35, 442).

3. Zenta Maurina, Die eisernen Riegel Zerbrechen: Geschichte eines Lebens (Memmingen and Allga, 1957), p. 191.

4. Nachlass Bloem (Wuppertal), file 65: Bloem, "Meine Vernehmung vor den Denazifizierungsausschuss."

5. Nachlass Bloem (Wuppertal), file 22: Winckler to Bloem, 9 Feb. 1934. In this letter, Winckler recounted what Bloem had told him in a personal conversation.

6. In Oct. 1933, Bloem, along with eighty-seven other writers, declared his loyalty to Hitler. From the Schleswig-Holsteinische Zeitung (26 Oct. 1933), in Joseph Wulf, Literatur und Dichtung im Dritten Reich: Eine Dokumentation (Gütersloh, 1963), p. 96.

7. Akademie der Künste (West Berlin), RG Sektion für Dichtkunst (Senatsgutachten), file D-7A: Bloem to Marilaun, 1 Apr. 1933.

8. Nachlass Bloem (Wuppertal): Bloem, "Zweites Buch: Der neue Dreissigjahre Krieg," pp. 429, 442.

9. Maurina, Die eisernen Riegel, p. 188.

10. See ibid., pp. 182-91.

11. Nachlass Bloem (Wuppertal): Bloem, "Zweites Buch: Der neue Dreissigjahre Krieg," pp. 447-48.

12. Nachlass Bloem (Wuppertal), file 65: Bloem, "Meine Vernehmung vor den Denazifizierungsausschuss."

13. For attempts to get Bloem's opinion on Nazi antisemitism, see Nachlass Bloem (Wuppertal), file 22: Winckler to Bloem, 9 Feb. 1932; [Zuelchaur?] to Bloem, 29 Nov. 1933; Bloem to [Zuelchaur?], 31 Nov. 1933.

14. Maurina, Die eisernen Riegel, pp. 187-88; Nachlass Bloem (Wuppertal), file 65: Bloem, "Meine Vernehmung vor den Denazifizierungsausschuss," p. 8.

15. There will still, Bloem admitted in private to a certain Dr. Winckler, "German-thinking and acting Jews." But these had to share the fate of their racial companions and it was not for him to complain about it. Nachlass Bloem (Wuppertal), file 22: Winckler to Bloem, 9 Feb. 1934.

16. Nachlass Bloem (Wuppertal), file 22: Bloem to [Zuelchaur?], 31 Nov. 1933. See also, in ibid., Bloem to [Goldstein], 16 Jan. 1935.

17. Maurina, Die eisernen Riegel, pp. 187-88.

18. Nachlass Bloem (Wuppertal): Bloem, "Werk und Tat: Zweites Buch," pp. 180-81; Walter Bloem, Hindenburg als Reichspräsident (Berlin, 1934).

19. Nachlass Bloem (Wuppertal): [Bloem], "Zweit- es Buch: Der neue Dreissigjahre Krieg," p. 431.

20. Ibid., p. 440.

21. All Germans should be overjoyed ". . . that Germany has arisen,//has been saved from shame and disgrace!//Hail to the Old One [Hindenburg] and thanks from the heart//to those who stood upright when everything sank,//and three times hail to you, magnificent warrior [Hitler],//who bagged the old dragons,//struck down to the ground the inner enemy,//united Germany after two thousand years!//Stretch the arms in a Hitler salute, the hearts uplifted: to our three heroes [Schlageter, Hindenburg, Hitler]--Siegheil! Siegheil! Siegheil!" Nachlass Bloem (Wuppertal), file 58: Walter Bloem, "Der Christlichbrandenburgischen Tischgesellschaft zum ersten Stiftungsfest im Dritten Reich," 16 Dec. 1933. For another such poem see, in ibid., Walter Bloem, "Zur Weihe der Schlageter-Flamme," n.d. [1933?]. Albert Schlageter was a Free Corps officer shot by the French for sabotage during the occupation of the Ruhr, 1923. He became a hero to both the Nationalists and the Communists. Bracher, The German Dictatorship: The Origins, Structure, and Effects of National Socialism, trans. Jean Steinberg (New York, Washington, 1970), p. 104.

22. For the approximate date of writing, see Walter Bloem, Unvergängliches Deutschland: Ein Buch von Volk und Heimat, with 150 original photographs by J. B. Malina (Berlin, 1933), p. 126.

23. Ibid., p. 8.

24. Ibid., p. 82.

25. Ibid., pp. 110-14 (quotes on p. 114).

26. Ibid., pp. 114-15.

27. Ibid., pp. 115-16.

28. Ibid., pp. 119-20.

29. Ibid., pp. 122-23.

30. Ibid., p. 123.

31. Ibid., p. 124.

32. Ibid., p. 127.

33. Ibid., p. 128.

34. Walter, Bedrohung, p. 177. Coordination of the Sektion Dichtkunst of the Prussian academy began on 16 Feb., when Heinrich Mann was forced to resign as chairman. Dietrich Strothmann, Nationalsozialistische Literaturpolitik: Ein Beitrag zur Publizistik im Dritten Reich (Bonn, 1960), p. 67.

35. Walter, Bedrohung, p. 177.

36. National conservatives grouped around the Albert Langen-Georg-Müller Verlag tried to deny that those coordinating the SDS were acting in Goebbel's charge. This Langen-Müller circle [discussed in Morris, "German Nationalist Fiction," pp. 446-826, and Gary D. Stark, Entrepreneurs of Ideology: Neoconservative Publishers in Germany, 1890-1933 (Chapel Hill, 1981)] hoped to gain decisive influence over these organizations and thus to lead them in a national conservative sense. However, the coordination of the Sektion Dichtkunst of the Prussian Academy was initiated by the Nazi Reich Commissar Bernhard Rust; that of the SDS was initiated by Goebbels and conducted by his proteges, as Bloem's memoirs prove. For the contentions of the Langen-Müller circle see Will Vesper, "Das grosse Reinemachen," Die Neue Literatur (May 1933), in Wulf, Literatur und Dichtung, pp. 134-35. Vesper attacked Hanns Heinz Ewers and Bloem, initially the two leaders of the Goebbels-induced coordnation of the SDS. "Also such as Herr Walter Bloem must always be there when the wind turns the weathervanes--those whose flexibility stems from spiritual loutishness and who one will ultimately put in mothballs." (p. 135). For the coordination of the Sektion Dichtkunst, see Inge Jens, Dichter Zwischen rechts und links: Die Geschichte der Sektion für Dichtkunst der Preussischen Akademie der Künste dargestellt nach den Dokumenten (Munich, 1971), pp. 181-218. For Goebbels's initiation of the self-coordination of the SDS, see Nachlass Bloem (Wuppertal): [Bloem], "Zweites Buch: Der neue Dreissigjahre Krieg," p. 433; Strothmann, Nationalsozialistische Literaturpolitik, p. 68.

37. This is Bloem's description of Ewer's mission. Nachlass Bloem (Wuppertal): [Bloem], "Zweites Buch: Der neue Dreissigjahre Krieg," p. 433.

38. Ibid.; Walter, Bedrohung, p. 178; Strothmann, Nationalsozialistische Literaturpolitik, p. 68.

39. Nachlass Bloem (Wuppertal): [Bloem], "Zweit- es Buch: Der neue Dreissigjahre Krieg," p. 433; Strothmann, Nationalsozialistische Literaturpolitik, p. 68; Klein, Aktionen, p. 331.

40. Nachlass Bloem (Wuppertal): [Bloem], "Zweit- es Buch: Der neue Dreissigjahre Krieg," pp. 433-44.

41. Klein, Aktionen, pp. 330-31.

42. Saüberung im Schutzverband deutscher Schriftsteller," Deutsches Schrifttum: Unabhängige kritische Monatschrift 23 (May 1933): 4. This journal was edited by Adolf Bartels, the extraordinarily energetic and influential radical völkisch literary critic.

43. Quoted in Klein, Aktionen, pp. 330-31.

44. For the 4 May 1933 main SDS assembly, see ibid., pp. 331-32; Walter, Bedrohung, p. 179; Strothmann, Nationalsozialistische Literaturpolitik, p. 68.

45. Walter, Bedrohung, p. 279.

46. Mühsam, Bruno Frei writes, "hoped in his loneliness that the professional colleague [Bloem] will make his influence felt in favor of the imprisoned writer, 'guaranteeing human help despite all objective opposition.'" Frei, Carl von Ossietzsky, p. 218.

47. Mühsam's death was officially reported as and made to look like suicide by hanging. Thus the tender consciences of collaborators like Bloem were spared. See Hiller, Köpfe und Tröpfe, pp. 309-18.

48. The formal dissolution of the SDS into the RDS took place in December 1933. Walter, Bedrohung, p. 179. See also: Nachlass Bloem (Wuppertal): [Bloem], "Zweites Buch: Der neue Dreissighsahre Krieg," p. 434; Strothmann, Nationalsozialistische Literaturpolitik, p. 68, footnote 20.

49. Stoffregen and his deputy Richter controlled the organizational and "cultural-political" work of the new organization. Klein, Aktionen, p. 332. A representative of the propaganda ministry, Dr. Heinz Wismann, was a member of the Reich leadership. "Deutsches Schrifttum geeinigt," Berliner Lokal-Anzeiger (29 July 1933), in Wulf, Literatur und Dichtung, p. 166.

50. Erich Kästner, "Sogenannte deutsche Dichter preisen die Sklaverei (1946/1959)," in Kästner für Erwachsene, ed. Rudolf Walter Leonhardt (Frankfurt/ Main, 1966), pp. 440-44 (quote on 442).

51. "Deutsches Schrifttum geeinigt," in Wulf, Literatur und Dichtung, p. 165; Walter, Bedrohung, p. 179.

52. See Mendelssohn S. Fischer, pp. 1274-75.

53. Hans Richter, deputy Reichsführer of the RDS, proclaimed on 28 July 1933, to quote the paraphrase of the Berliner Lokal-Anzeiger, that "the purpose of the association is to lead German literature into a closed association and to build this association into a compulsory organization, in which membership would be decisive in the future for whether a literary work can be published in Germany or not. Beside this association there will be no other professional organizations of its kind. Only writers of German blood, free of political reproach, become members." "Deutsches Schrifttum geeinigt," in Wulf, Literatur und Dichtung, p. 165. According to Strothmann, "the RDS initiated the 'compulsory

registration' of German authors and thereby performed the most important preliminary work for the steering activity of the RSK [Reich Literature Chamber]." Nationalsozialistische Literaturpolitik, pp. 31, 68 (quote on 31).

54. Strothmann, Nationalsozialistische Literaturpolitik, pp. 68-69.

55. Bundesarchiv (Koblenz): Dr. Werner, "Rechtliche Grundlagen und organisatorische Entwicklung," Reichsschrifttumskammer R56V [Findbuch or locator-book of the Bundesarchiv Koblenz], (released for use on 23 Sept. 1974), p. 2.

56. Strothmann, Nationalsozialistische Literaturpolitik, p. 27.

57. Bundesarchiv (Koblenz): Werner, "Rechtliche Grundlagen," Reichsschrifttumskammer R56V, p. 3-4. See also, Handbuch der Reichskulturkammer, eds. Hans Hinkel and Günther Gentz (Berlin, 1937).

58. Bloem's own description in Nachlass Nloem (Wuppertal): "Zweites Buch: Der neue Dreissigjahre Krieg," p. 434.

59. Bundesarchiv (Koblenz): Werner, "Rechtliche Grundlagen," Reichsschrifttumskammer R56V, p. 2.

60. Walter, Bedrohung, p. 180.

61. See Nachlass Bloem (Wuppertal): [Bloem], "Zweites Buch: Der neue Dreissigjahre Krieg," p. 408.

62. Ibid.

63. Strothmann, Nationalsozialistische Literaturpolitik, pp. 227-31 (especially 228, 231).

64. Bundesarchiv (Koblenz), Record Group Reichsschrifttumskammer R56V, file 72: Reichsarbeitsgemeinschaft deutscher Werkbüchereien in der Reichsschrifttumskammer to Dr. Heinl, Reichsschrifttumskammer, 20 May 1936.

65. Mosse, "Die deutsche Rechte," p. 234.

66. Nachlass Bloem (Wuppertal), file 22: President of the Reich Literature Chamber (signed Hampt) to the Verlag Grethlein and Co., Leipzig, 14 June 1934; [Grethlein] to Bloem, 15 June 1934.

67. Rosenberg was named by Hitler "Beauftragte des Führers für die Überwachung der gesamten geistigen und weltanschaulichen Schulung und Erziehung der NSDAP." His Reich Office (Reichstelle zur Förderung des deutschen Schrifttums) developed out of the Kampfbund für deutsche Kultur, founded in the Weimar Republic. The Reich Office was later renamed the Amt Schrifttumspflege and finally the Hauptamt Schrifttum. It was popularly known as the Amt Rosenberg. See Strothmann, Nationalsozialistische Literaturpolitik, pp. 36-42; "Amt Rosenberg," in Wulf, Literatur und Dichtung, pp. 203-6; Bundesarchiv (Koblenz): Werner, "Rechtliche Grundlagen," Reichsschrifttumskammer R56V, pp. 5-6.

68. Goebbels was willing to use authors with philosemitic, republican and/or expressionist backgrounds, like Bloem, Hanns Heinz Ewers, and Arnolt Bronnen. Rosenberg had especial distaste for Ewers and Bronnen. Rosenberg had little use for Goebbels's ministry, condemning its "combination of political propaganda and art." Rosenberg claimed that Goebbels "had not one original or creative word to say about art"; Goebbels, furthermore, was a "scribbler" not a writer. Alfred Rosenberg, Memoirs of Alfred Rosenberg, eds. Serge Land and Ernst von Schenck, trans. Eric Posselt (Chicago, New York, 1949), pp. 159-68 (quotes on 167).

69. In the play, "Revolte in der Mottenkiste," known authors and publishers played themselves. At the end, Bloem and Rudolf Presber, both of whom were being honored by the book traders, were led off to a concentration camp. The episode, it is worth noting, demonstrates Bloem's midjudgment of the totalitarian nature of the Third Reich and his light-headed political irresponsibility, which could find "harmless" humor in allusions to concentration camps. The executive committee of the Mannschaft did resist the attempt to have Bloem expelled; but Rosenberg made it clear that Bloem should stay away from meetings. Nachlass Bloem (Wuppertal): [Bloem], "Zweites Buch: Der neue Dreissigjahre Krieg," pp. 435-39. For Rosenberg's hostility to Bloem, see also ibid., file 65: Bloem, "Meine Vernehmung," p. 4, and ibid., file 22: [Walter Bloem], "Anweisung für meine Erben und Rechtsnachfolger für die Behandlung meiner literarischen Nachlasses." In this "Anweisung," Bloem claimed that he narrowly missed being hauled off to a concentration camp.

70. Bloem himself was acutely aware of the competency struggles between the agencies of the Third Reich claiming a right to supervise German culture. Backing from the propaganda ministry kept afloat other authors, such as Hans Heinrich Ewers and Arnolt Bronnen, heartily detested by Rosenberg. For Bloem's awareness, see Nachlass Bloem (Wuppertal): [Bloem], "Zweites Buch: Der neue Dreissigjahre Krieg," p. 435.

71. Bloem gave three reasons for joining the NSDAP to a de-Nazification board in 1947: (1) to end his isolation; (2) to gain a chance to observe Nazism at first hand, since the duty of the poetic writer (Dichter) was to grasp his time; (3) to get an opportunity to take part in the nest war, which he saw as imminent. Bloem himself gave the most weight to reason number three. Nachlass Bloem (Wuppertal), file 65: Bloem, "Meine Vernehmung," pp. 3-7.

72. Nachlass Bloem (Wuppertal): [Bloem], "Zwei- tes Buch: Der neue Dreissigjahre Krieg," p. 451.

73. Ibid., pp. 456-59.

74. Ibid., p. 459.

75. Strothmann, Nationalsozialistische Literaturpolitik, p. 281 (footnote 87).

76. Nachlass Bloem (Wuppertal): [Bloem], "Zwei- tes Buch: Der neue Dreissigjahre Krieg," pp. 497-500.

77. Ibid., p. 463.

78. Ibid., pp. 464-65.

79. Ibid., pp. 465-509; Nachlass Bloem (Wupper- tal), file 22: [Bloem] to Heinrich Wendt, 3 Aug. 1949.

80. Included among the novels planned or written by Bloem were a novel on the activity of a high staff (based on his experiences with Army Group C), a novel dedicated to Todt dealing with the auxiliary troops building the West Wall, a novel on Riga as a pioneer of Germandom in Latvia, a novel about fighter pilots. Nachlass Bloem (Wuppertal): [Bloem], "Zweites Buch: Der neue Dreissigjahre Krieg," pp. 465-66, 470-72, 524-26; file 22: [Bloem] to Wendt, 3 Aug. 1949.

81. Nachlass Bloem (Wuppertal): [Bloem], "Zwei- tes Buch: Der neue Dreissigjahre Krieg," pp. 465-66. See, for example, Walter Bloem, "Gegen den Befehl: Eine Flieger Novelle," Illustrierte Beobachter 15 (15 Aug. 1940).

82. From Sept. to Oct. 1941, Bloem gave a lecture tour through the General Government of Poland for the Auslandsabteilung des Oberkommandos der Wehrmacht. In 1942-1943(?), he gave a series of lectures for Strength through Joy within Germany. Nachlass Bloem (Wuppertal): [Bloem], "Zweites Buch: Der neue Dreissigjahre Krieg," pp. 472-73, 484.

83. Ibid., p. 472; Nachlass Bloem (Wuppertal), file 22: [Bloem] to Wendt, 3 Aug. 1949.

84. Maurina, Die Eisernen Riegel, pp. 188-91 (quote on 191). Bloem did not mention being recalled for pro-Latvian sympathies in his memoirs, although he did report leaving Riga on friendly terms with the Latvians. Nachlass Bloem (Wuppertal): [Bloem], "Zweites Buch: Der neue Dreissigjahre Krieg," p. 481.

85. Nachlass Bloem (Wuppertal): [Bloem], "Zweit- es Buch: Der neue Dreissigjahre Krieg," pp. 482-509f.

86. Nachlass Bloem (Wuppertal), file 22: [Bloem] to Wendt, 3 Aug. 1949.

87. Nachlass Bloem (Wuppertal): [Bloem], "Zweit- es Buch: Der neue Dreissigjahre Krieg," p. 522.

88. Ibid., p. 515.

89. Ibid., p. 541.

90. Ibid., p. 515; Nachlass Bloem (Wuppertal): Bloem, "Werk und Tat: Zweites Buch," pp. 240-46.

91. Nachlass Bloem (Wuppertal): [Bloem], "Zwei-

tes Buch: Der neue Dreissigjahre Krieg," pp. 513-22.

92. Nachlass Bloem (Wuppertal), file 65: Bloem, "Meine Vernehmung vor den Denazifizierungsausschuss," pp. 2-3, 11.

93. Nachlass Bloem (Wuppertal), file 60: Denazifizierungsausschuss der Hansestadt Lübeck to Bloem, 22 Dec. 1947.

NOTES

CONCLUSION

THE IMPOTENCY OF WALTER BLOEM'S PHILOSEMITISM

1. See for charisma and fiction in 20th-century Germany, Russell A. Berman, The Rise of the Modern German Novel: Crisis and Charisma (Cambridge, Massachusetts and London, England, 1986).

2. Löwy, Literatur unterm Hakenkreuz (1966), pp. 338-39.

3. See the excerpt from Alexis de Tocqueville, Recollections, trans. Alexander Teixeira de Mattos (New York, 1896), in The Western Tradition: From the Enlightenment to the Present, ed. Eugen Weber, 3rd ed. (Lexington, Massachusetts et al, 1972), p. 691.

4. Voegelin, "The German University," pp. 15-16.

5. Rhodes, Hitler Movement, pp. 148-54.

6. Epstein, Genesis of German Conservatism, pp. 503-46.

7. See Eberhard Jäckel Hitlers Weltanschauung: Entwurf einer Herrschaft, rev. ed. (Stuttgart, 1981).

8. See Joseph Nyomarkay, Charisma and Factionalism in the Nazi Party (Minneapolis, 1967). I discuss the interrelationship between charismatic domination, ideology, and layered disclosure in a work in preparation, "Adolf Hitler and Arthur Dinter's 'Christian' Nazism."

9. I owe the genesis of these ideas, although not their precise formulation or application, to the late Professor John L. Snell.

10. Philosemitism may have doomed any political efforts by Bloem in advance. The minority in the DNVP opposed to antisemitism declined in influence during the Weimar period. Mosse, "Die deutsche Rechte," p. 233.

11. See Peter Viereck, Metapolitics: The Roots of the Nazi Mind, rev. ed. (New York, 1965), pp. 156-57.

12. It was difficult, if not impossible, for a high-quality republican publisher, like S. Fischer, to break into the nationalist middle strata. Moritz Heimann, famous publisher's reader for the S. Fischer house, wrote that there were ideological barriers barring entry into opposing circles of the public. Heimann found no easy answer on how Fischer's authors were to break into the massive readership of the "'national' success-author Walter Bloem." Mendelsohn, S. Fischer und sein Verlag, p. 886.

13. "Ein durch und durch Ehrlicher: Dichter Bloem 100 Jahre alt," <u>Westdeutsche Rundschau</u> (29 June 1968).

BIBLIOGRAPHY

I. PRIMARY SOURCES

A. Archival Sources

Freiburg, Bundesarchiv-Militärarchiv Nachlass Bloem, Record Group N31

Koblenz, Bundesarchiv:
Record Group der Reichskunstwart, R32
Record Group Reichskommissar für die Überwachung der öffentlichen Ordnung, Sammelstelle I in RMI, R 134
Record Group Reichsschrifttumskammer R56V

Marbach am Neckar, Deutsches Literaturarchiv
Nachlass Langen-Müller

West Berlin, Akademie der Künste
Record Group Sektion für Dichtkunst (Senatsgutachten)

Wuppertal, Stadt Bücherei
Nachlass Walter Bloem

B. Periodicals

Abwehrblätter, Mitteilungen aus dem Verein zur Abwehr des Antisemitismus, 1930 and February 1931

Die Aktion, January 1914

Archiv für Rassen- und Gesellschaftsbiologie Einschliesslich Rassen- und Gesellschafthygiene: Eine Deszendenztheoretische Zeitschrift für die Erforschung des Wesens von Rasse und Gesellschaft und ihres gegenseitigen Verhältnisses, für die biologischen Bedingungen ihrer Erhaltung und Entwicklung, sowie für die grundlegenden Probleme der Entwicklungslehre, 1921

Die Aufbau, 1947

Berliner Tageblatt, 1929-32

Die Bücherstube: Blätter für Freunde des Buches und der zeichnenden Künste, 1920

Der Bücherwurm: Monatschrift für Bücherfreunde, selected numbers from 1919, 1926-31

Bühne und Welt: Monatschrift für das deutsche Kunst und Geistesleben, 1914-16

CV-Zeitung: Blätter für Deutschtum und Judentum: Organ des Central-Vereins deutscher Staatsbürger jüdischen Glaubens, 1922-25

Das deutsche Drama, 1919

Deutsche Rundschau, selected numbers from 1926-32

Deutsches Schriftum: Unabhängige kritische Monat- schrift, January-August 1930, 1931, and selected numbers from 1932 and 1933

Deutsches Volkstum: Monatschrift für das Kunst- und Geistesleben, 1917-27

Deutschlands Erneuerung: Monatschrift für das deutsche Volk, 1917-18, 1921-24, 1926, 1930-31

Eckart: Blätter für evangelische Geisteskultus, 1924-31

Eckart Ratgeber: Ein Führer duch das Schriftum der Gegenwart, 1926-32

Die Flöte: Monatschrift für neue Dichtung, selected numbers from 1919

Die Gesellschaft: Halbmonatschrift für Literatur, Kunst und Sozialpolitik, 1898

Der Gral: Monatschrift für Dichtung und Leben, 1920-33

Die Hilfe: Wochenschrift für Politik, Literatur und Kunst, selected numbers from 1907

Hochland: Monatschrift für alle Gebiete des Wissens, der Literatur und Kunst, 1919-33

Das Inselschiff: Eine Zweimonatschrift für die Freunde des Insel Verlages, 1921

Der Jude: Eine Monatschrift, 1916-24

K.C. -Blätter: Monatschrift der im Kartell-Convent vereinigten Korporationen, selected numbers from 1919

Der Kreis: Zeitschrift für Kunstlerische Kultur, selected numbers from 1925, 1927, 1931

Die Linkskurve, 1929-32

Das literarische Echo: Halbmonatschrift für Literaturfreunde, 1909, 1917-23

Die literarische Welt, 1925-32

Die Literatur: Monatschrift für Literaturfreunde, 1923-33

Der Morgen, 1925-32

Die neue Bücherschau, selected numbers from 1919, 1928, 1931

Die neue Literatur, 1925, 1928, 1930-31

Der neue Merkur: Monatshefte, February, 1925

Neue Revue, 1930

Die neue Rundschau, selected numbers from 1919, 1928-32

Orplid: Literarische Monatschrift in Sonderheften, selected numbers from 1926-29

Der Querschnitt, 1930, 1932

Reichswart, 1920-32

Die Rettung: Blätter zur Erkenntnis der Zeit, 1919

Die Schaubühne, selected numbers from 1906, 1908

Stimmen der Zeit: Katholische Monatschrift für das Geistesleben der Gegenwart, 1921

Süddeutsche Monatshefte, 1919-32

Das Tagebuch, 1920-March 1933

Die Tat: Monatschrift für die Zukunft deutscher Kultur, selected numbers from 1917, 1923

Vivos Voco: Zeitschrift für neues Deutschtum, selected numbers from 1922-23

Vorwärts, 1 January 1919-26 January 1931

Die Weltbühne, selected numbers from 1920-32

Der Weltkampf: Monatschrift für die Judenfrage aller Länder, 1924-32

Welt und Wort: Literarische Monatschrift, 1950

Zeitwende: Monatschrift, 1925-26

C. Books

Altmeyer, Karl Aloys. Katholische Presse unter NS-Diktatur: Die katholische Zeitungen und Zeit- schriften Deutschlands in den Jahren 1933 bis 1945. Dokumentationen. Berlin, 1962.

Bloem, Walter. Brüderlichkeit: Roman. Leipzig and Zurich, 1922.

Bloem, Walter. Das eiserne Jahr: Roman. Leip- zig, 1912.

Bloem, Walter. Der krasse Fuchs: Roman. Leipzig and Zurich, 1906 [1932].

Bloem, Walter. Der Weltbrand: Deutschlands Tragödie 1914-1918. Drawings by Ludwig Dettmann. 2 vols. Berlin, 1922.

Bloem, Walter. Deutsche Zwietracht und Judentum: Festrede bei der Feier des Zehnjährigen Bestehens der Ortsgruppe Hamburg des vaterländischen Bundes jüdischer Frontsoldaten an 17 November 1929. Leipzig and Zurich, n.d. [1929].

Bloem, Walter. Die Schmiede der Zukunft. Leip- zig, 1913.

Bloem, Walter. Gottesferne: Roman. 2 vols. Leipzig and Zurich, 1920.

Bloem, Walter. Held seines Landes: Roman. Leip- zig, 1929.

Bloem, Walter. Hindenburg als Reichspräsident. Berlin, 1934.

Bloem, Walter. Sohn seines Landes: Roman. Leipzig, 1929.

Bloem, Walter. Unvergängliches Deutschland: Ein Buch von Volk und Heimat. With 150 original photographs by J. B. Malina. Berlin, 1933.

Bloem, Walter. Volk wider Volk: Roman. Leipzig, 1912.

Bloem, Walter. Wandlungen der Seele im Kriege: Vortrag, gehalten am 20. Januar 1917 im Sieglehaus zu Stuttgart auf Einladung der Vereinigung für Vorträge während des Krieges. Württemberg, n.d. [1917; forward by Bloem dated 27 January. 1917].

Bloem, Walter, et al. "Warum werden Ihre Bücher viel gelesen? Das Rätsel des Publikumserfolges," Die literarische Welt 4, no. 19 (1928): 3-6.

Bloem, Walter. Weltgesicht: Ein Buch von heutiger und kommender Menschheit. Leipzig and Zurich, 1928.

Deutsche Akademie der Künste zu Berlin, Sektion Dichtkunst, Geschichte der sozialistischen Literatur, ed. Zur Tradition der sozialistischen Literatur in Deutschland: Eine Auswahl von Dokumenten. 2nd rev. ed. Berlin [East] and Weimar, 1967.

Dinter, Arthur. Die Sünde wider das Blut. Leipzig, Hartenstein/Erzgebirge, 1921.

Dinter, Arthur. Mein Ausschuss aus dem Verbande Deutscher Bühnenschriftsteller. Munich, 1917.

Heuss, Theodor. Erinnerungen 1905-1933. Tübingen, 1963.

II. Secondary Sources

Albrecht, Friedrich. Deutsche Schriftsteller in der Entscheidung: Wege zur Arbeiterklasse 1918-1933. Berlin and Weimar, 1970.

Angress, Werner T. "Pegasus and Insurrection: Die Linkskurve and Its Heritage," Central European History 1 (March 1968): 35-55.

Barkin, Kenneth D. The Controversy Over German Industrialization, 1890-1902. Chicago and London, 1970.

Baumer, Franklin L. Modern European Thought: Continuity and Change in Ideas, 1600-1950. New York and London, 1977.

Baumgart, Winfried. Deutschland im Zeitalter des Imperialismus (1890-1914): Grundkräfte, Thesen und Strukturen. Frankfurt/Main, Berlin, Vienna, 1972.

Berlin, Isaiah. Russian Thinkers. Eds. Henry Hardy and Aileen Kelley. Harmandsworth, Middlesex, England et al, 1979.

Berman, Russell A. The Rise of the Modern German Novel: Crisis and Charisma. Cambridge, Massachusetts and London, England, 1986.

Bibliographische Abteilung des Börsenvereins der deutschen Buchhändler zu Leipzig, comp. Deutsches Bücherverzeichnis: Eine Zusammenstellung der im deutschen Buchhandel erschienenen Bücher, Zeitschriften und Landkarten mit einem Stich- und Schlagwort-Register. Leipzig, 1916- .

Bleuel, Hans Peter, and Klinnert, Ernst. Deutsche Studenten auf dem Weg ins Dritte Reich: Ideologien-Programme-Aktionen 1918-1935. Gütersloh, 1967.

Bracher, Karl Dietrich. The German Dictatorship: The Origins, Structure, and Effects of National Socialism. Trans. Jean Steinberg, New York, Washington, 1970.

Carver, Terrell. Engels. New York, 1981.

Conrad, Heinrich, comp. Christian Gottlob Kaysers vollständiges Bücher-Lexikon: Ein Verzeichnis der seit dem Jahre 1750 im deutschen Buchhandel erschienenen Bücher und Landkarten. Vol. 53. Leipzig, 1911.

Craig, Gordon A. The Politics of the Prussian Army, 1650-1945. London, Oxford, New York, 1970.

Crespigny, Anthony de, and Minogue, Kenneth, eds. Contemporary Political Philosophers. New York, 1975.

Dahrendorf, Ralf. Society and Democracy in Germany. Garden City, New York, 1969.

Hiller, Kurt. <u>Köpfe und Tröpfe: Profile aus einem Vierteljahrhundert</u>. Hamburg, Stuttgart, 1950.

Kästner, Erich. <u>Kästner für Erwachsene</u>. Ed. Rudolf Walter Leonhardt. Frankfurt/Main, 1966.

Klein, Alfred; Albrecht, Friedrich; Hiebel, Irmfried; and Kändler, Klaus. <u>Aktionen, Bekenntnisse, Perspektiven: Berichte und Dokumente von Kampf um die Freiheit des literarischen Schaffens in der Weimarer Republik</u>. Ed. Deutsche Akademie der Künste zu Berlin, Sektion Dichtkunst und Sprachpflege, Abt. Geschichte der sozialistischen Literatur. Berlin [East] and Weimar, 1966.

Löwy, Ernst. <u>Literatur unterm Hakenkreuz: Das Dritte Reich und seine Dichtung: Eine Dokumentation</u>. Forward by Hans-Jochen Gamm. Frankfurt/Main, 1966.

Löwy, Ernst. <u>Literatur unterm Hakenkreuz: Das Dritte Reich und seine Dichtung. Eine Dokumentation</u>. Frankfurt/Main, 1983.

Maurina, Zenta. <u>Die eisernen Riegel Zerbrechen: Geschichte eines Lebens</u>. Memmingen and Allga, 1957.

Nicolai, W. <u>Nachrichtendienst, Presse und Volksstimmung im Weltkrieg</u>. Berlin, 1920.

Ossietzky, Carl von. <u>Schriften II</u>. Eds. Bruno Frei and Hans Leonard. Berlin and Weimar, 1966.

Püschel, Ernst. <u>Die Juden von Kronburg: Ein Buch von deutschem Volks- und Menschentum. Roman</u>. Neudiet- endorff, 1924.

Püschel, Ernst. "Die wahre völkische Gesinnung," <u>CV-Zeitung</u> 3 (4 December. 1924): 769.

Rosenberg, Alfred. <u>Memoirs of Alfred Rosenberg</u>. Eds. Serge Land and Ernst von Schenck; trans. Eric Posselt. Chicago, New York, 1949.

Tucholsky, Kurt. <u>Gesammelte Werke: Band III 1929-1932</u>. Eds. Mary Gerold-Tucholsky and Fritz J. Raddatz. Reinbek bei Hamburg, 1960.

Ullstein, Hermann. <u>The Rise and Fall of the House of Ullstein</u>. New York, 1943.

Weber, Eugen, ed. <u>The Western Tradition: From the Enlightenment to the Present</u>. 3rd ed. Lexington, Massachusetts et al., 1972.

Wiechert, Ernst. <u>Sämtliche Werke</u>. 10 vols. Vienna, Munich, and Basel, 1943.

Wolff, Kurt. <u>Kurt Wolff: Briefwechsel eines Verlegers 1911-1963</u>. Eds. Bernhard Zeller and Ellen Otten. Frankfurt/Main, 1966.

Wulf, Joseph. <u>Literatur und Dichtung im Dritten Reich: Eine Dokumentation</u>. Gütersloh, 1963.

Deak, Istvan. Weimar Germany's Left-Wing Intellectuals: A Political History of the Weltbühne and Its Circle. Berkeley and Los Angeles, 1968.

Degener, Hermann A. L. Wer ist's? Berlin, 1928.

"Ein durch und durch Ehrlicher: Dichter Bloem 100. Jahre alt," Westdeutsche Rundschau (29 June 1968).

Epstein, Klaus. The Genesis of German Conservatism. Princeton, New Jersey, 1966.

Eyck, Erich. A History of the Weimar Republic, Volume I: From the Collapse of the Empire to Hindenburg's Election. Trans. Harlan P. Hanson and Robert G. L. Waite. New York, 1962, 1970.

Fischer, Heinz-Dietrich, ed. Deutsche Zeitungen des 17. bis 20. Jahrhunderts. Pullach near Munich, 1972.

Flavell, M. Kay. "Kitsch and Propaganda: The Blending of Myth and History in Hedwig Courths-Mahler's Lissa geht ins Glück (1936)," German Studies Review 8, no. 1 (1985): 65-87.

Flechtheim, Ossip K. Die KPD in der Weimarer Republik. Introduction by Hermann Weber. Frankfurt/ Main, 1969.

Flechtheim, Ossip K. "The Role of the Communist Party." The Path to Dictatorship, 1918-1933: Ten Essays. Trans. John Conway with an introduction by Fritz Stern. Garden City, New York, 1966.

Frei, Bruno. Carl von Ossietzky: Ritter ohne Furcht und Tadel. Berlin and Weimar, 1966.

Gordon, Harold J., Jr. Hitler and the Beer Hall Putsch. Princeton, New Jersey, 1972.

Gordon, Sarah. Hitler, Germans and the "Jewish Question." Princeton, New Jersey, 1984.

Gross, Babette. Willi Münzenberg: A Political Biography. Trans. Marian Jackson. Lansing, Michigan, 1974.

Grossmann, Kurt R. Ossietzky: Ein deutscher Patriot. Munich, 1963.

Gruber, Helmut. "Willi Münzenberg's German Communist Propaganda Empire, 1921-1933." The Journal of Modern History 38 (September 1966): 278-97.

Haacke, Wilmont. Feuilletonkunde: Das Feuilleton als literarische und journalistische Gattung. 2 vols. Leipzig, 1943.

Hallowell, John H. Main Currents in Modern Political Thought. New York, 1950.

Halperin, S. William. Germany Tried Democracy: A Political History of the Reich from 1918 to 1933. New York, 1946, 1965.

Hamel, Iris. Völkischer Verband und nationale Gewerkschaft: Der deutschnationale Handlungsgehilfen-Verband 1893-1933. Frankfurt/Main, 1967.

Heckart, Beverly. From Bassermann to Bebel: The Grand Bloc's Quest for Reform in the Kaiserreich, 1900-1914. New Haven and London, 1974.

Hermann, Klaus T. Das Dritte Reich und die deutsch-jüdischen Organisationen 1933-1934. Cologne, 1969.

Herrenbrück, Edgar. Literaturverständnis im Wilhelminischen Bürgertum. Ph.D. diss., Göttingen, 1970.

Hiller, Helmut. Zur Sozialgeschichte von Buch und Buchhandel. Bonn, 1966.

Hiller, Helmut and Strauss, Wolfgang, eds. Der deutsche Buchhandel: Wesen, Gestalt, Aufgabe. Gütersloh, 1961.

Hinkel, Hans, and Gentz, Günther. Handbuch der Reichskulturkammer. Berlin, 1937.

Horne, Alistair. The Price of Glory: Verdun 1916. Harmondsworth, Middlesex, England et al., 1962, 1964, 1978.

Jäckel, Eberhard. Hitlers Weltanschauung: Entwurf einer Herrschaft. Rev. ed. Stuttgart, 1981.

Jarausch, Konrad H. Students, Society, and Politics in Imperial Germany: The Rise of Academic Illiberalism. Princeton, New Jersey, 1982.

Jens, Inge. Dichter zwischen rechts und links: Die Geschichte der Sektion für Dichtkunst der Preussischen Akademie der Künste dargestellt nach den Dokumenten. Munich, 1971.

Johnson, Paul. Modern Times: The World from the Twenties to the Eighties. New York et al., 1983.

Kiesel, Helmuth, and Münch, Paul. Gesellschaft und Literatur im 18 Jahrhundert: Voraussetzungen und Entstehung des literarischen Markts in Deutschland. Munich, 1977.

Kirk, Russell, ed. The Portable Conservative Reader. Harmondsworth, Middlesex, England et al, 1982.

Kirschner, Summner. "'Even if They Were Guilty': An Unpublished Letter by Ernst Wiechert About the Jews." German Life and Letters: A Quarterly Review 23 (1970): 142-43.

Kitchen, Martin. The Silent Dictatorship: The Politics of the German High Command under Hindenburg and Ludendorff, 1916-1918. New York, 1976.

Klemperer, Klemens von. Germany's New Conservatism: Its History and Dilemma in the Twentieth Century. Forward by Sigmund Neumann. Princeton, New Jersey, 1968.

Kohn, Hans. The Mind of Germany: The Education of a Nation. New York, 1960.

Koszyk, Kurt. Deutsche Presse 1914-1945: Geschichte der deutschen Presse, Teil III. Berlin, 1972.

Koszyk, Kurt, and Eisfeld, Gerhard. Die Presse der deutschen Sozialdemokratie. Hannover, 1966.

Koszyk, Kurt, and Pruys, Karl Hugo. Wörterbuch zur Publizistik. Munich, 1969.

Levy, Richard S. The Downfall of the Anti-Semitic Political Parties in Imperial Germany. New Haven and London, 1975.

Lohalm, Uwe. Völkischer Radikalismus: Die Geschichte des Deutschvölkischen Schutz- und Trutz- Bundes 1919-1933. Hamburg, 1970.

Mack, Maynard et al., eds. The Continental Edition of World Masterpieces. New York, 1962.

Mendelssohn, Peter de. S. Fischer und sein Verlag. Frankfurt/Main, 1970.

Mohler, Armin. Die Konservative Revolution in Deutschland 1918-1932: Ein Handbuch. 2nd rev. ed. Darmstadt, 1972.

Morris, Rodler F. "German Nationalist Fiction and the Jewish Question, 1918-1933." Ph.D. diss., University of North Carolina, Chapel Hill, 1979.

Morris, Rodler F. "The Jew in the German Novel, 1918-1933." M.A. thesis, University of North Carolina, Chapel Hill, 1972.

Morsey, Rudolf. Die deutsche Zentrumspartei 1917-1923. Ed. Kommission für Geschichte des Parlamentarismus und der politischen Parteien. Düsseldorf, 1966.

Mosse, George L. Germans and Jews: The Right, the Left, and the Search for a "Third Force" in Pre-Nazi Germany. New York, 1970.

Mosse, George L. The Crisis of German Ideology: Intellectual Origins of the Third Reich. New York, 1964.

Mosse, Werner, and Paucker, Arnold, eds. Entscheidungsjahr 1932: Zur Judenfrage in der Endphase der Weimarer Republik, ein Sammelband. 2nd rev. ed. Tübingen, 1966.

Niewyk, Donald L. The Jews in Weimar Germany. Baton Rouge and London, 1980.

Nyomarkay, Joseph. Charisma and Factionalism in the Nazi Party. Minneapolis, 1967.

Pascal, Roy. From Naturalism to Expressionism: German Literature and Society, 1880-1918. New York, 1973.

Radeck, Heide. Zur Geschichte von Roman und Erzählung in der "Gartenlaube" (1853 bis 1914): Heroismus und Idylle als Instrument nationaler Ideologie. Ph.D. diss., Friedrich-Alexander-Universität Erlangen-Nürnberg.

Reinharz, Jehuda. Fatherland or Promised Land: The Dilemma of the German Jew, 1893-1914. Ann Arbor, Michigan, 1975.

Retallack, James N. "Conservative 'Volkspartei' in the Diaspora: Anti-Semitism and the Conservative Appeal in South-West Germany, 1871-1900." Paper presented at the Tenth Annual Conference of the German Studies Association, 26 Sept. 1986.

Rheins, Carl. "The Verband Nationaldeutscher Juden 1921-1933." Leo Baeck Institute Yearbook 25 (1980): 243-68.

Rhodes, James M. The Hitler Movement: A Modern Millenarian Revolution. Stanford, California, 1980.

Richards, Donald Ray. The German Bestseller in the 20th Century: A Complete Bibliography and Analysis, 1915-1940. Berne, 1968.

Ritter, Gerhard. The Tragedy of Statemanship: Bethmann Hollweg as War Chancellor (1914-1917). Vol. 3 of The Sword and the Scepter: The Problem of Militarism in Germany. Trans. Heinz Norden. Coral Gables, Florida, 1972.

Rühle, Jurgen. Literature and Revolution: A Critical Study of the Writer and Communism in the Twentieth Century. Trans. and ed. Jean Steinberg. New York, Washington, London, 1969.

Sagarra, Eda. Tradition and Revolution: German Literature and Society, 1830-1890. London, 1971.

Schenk, H. G. The Mind of the European Romantics: An Essay in Cultural History. Garden City, New York, 1969.

Scholder, Klaus. Die Kirchen und das Dritte Reich: Band I, Vorgeschichte und Zeit der Illusionen 1918-1934. Frankfurt/Main, Berlin, Vienna, 1977.

Schröter, Klaus. "Der Dichter, Der Schriftsteller," Akzente 20 (1973): 168-88.

Schulz, Hans Ferdinand. Das Schicksal der Bücher und der Buchhandel: System einer Vertriebskunde des Buches. 2nd rev. ed. Berlin, 1960.

Schulze, Friedrich. Der deutsche Buchhandel und die geistige Strömungen der letzten hundert Jahre. Leipzig, 1925.

Schwarz, Jürgen. Studenten in der Weimarer Republic: Die deutsche Studentenschaft in der Zeit von 1918 bis 1923 und ihre Stellung zur Politik. Berlin, 1971.

Siegel, Christian Ernst. Egon Erwin Kisch: Reportage und politischer Journalismus. Bremen, 1973.

Staackmann Verlag, L. L. Staackmann Leipzig 1869-1919. Leipzig, 1919.

Stark, Gary D. Entrepreneurs of Ideology: Neoconservative Publishers in Germany, 1890-1933. Chapel Hill, 1981.

Stieg, Gerald, and Witte, Bernd. Abriss einer Geschichte der deutschen Arbeiterliteratur. Stuttgart, 1973.

Strauss, Leo. Natural Right and History. Chicago and London, 1953.

Strothmann, Dietrich. Nationalsozialistische Literaturpolitik: Ein Beitrag zur Publizistik im Dritten Reich. Bonn, 1960.

Tindall, George Brown. America: A Narrative History. New York and London, 1984.

Viereck, Peter. Metapolitics: The Roots of the Nazi Mind. Rev. ed. New York, 1965.

Voegelin, Eric. Science, Politics and Gnosticism. Chicago, 1968.

Voegelin, Eric. "The German University and the Order of German Society: A Reconstruction of the Nazi Era." The Intercollegiate Review: A Journal of Scholarship and Opinion 20, no. 3 (1985): 7-27.

Voegelin, Eric. The New Science of Politics: An Introduction. Chicago and London, 1966.

Wallenberg, Hans, and Scholz, Arno. Kleine Geschichte der Zeitungsstadt Berlin. Berlin, 1969.

Walter, Hans-Albert. Deutsche Exilliteratur 1933-1950. Vol. 1: Bedrohung und Verfolgung bis 1933. Darmstadt and Neuwied, 1972.

Ward, Albert. Book Production, Fiction, and the German Reading Public, 1740-1800. Oxford, 1974.

Wright, Gordon. The Ordeal of Total War, 1939-1945. New York, Evanston, and London, 1968.

INDEX

"Abteilung M.," 129
Action Council of Proletarian-Revolutionary Writers, 103
Agis Verlag, 105
Agrarian League (Bund der Landwirte), 23, 56
Akademische Mitteilungen, 50
Aktionen, Bekenntnisse, Perspektiven (eds. Klein et al), 98
Albrecht, Friedrich, 98, 118
All Quiet on the Western Front (Remarque), 59, 131
Amsterdam, 135
Angress, Werner, 104
antisemitism: deeply rooted in German right, 58; fueled by inflation, 46; genesis of German, 28; and notion of collective guilt, 167; opposition to, 1, 5; portrayed in Brotherhood, 42-45; radical Völkisch (racial) variety of, 5-6, 25, 40, 177; rising tide of after World War I, 4; in student corps, 39-44; within the Conservative party, 22-25
Apfel, Dr., 111, 208, 215-16
Archilochus, 18
Aristotle, 28
Army Group C, 151, 226
artisans, 24
Aryan Paragraph (of the KSC), 40-41, 44
Association of Berlin Book Traders, 150
Association of German Novelists, 98
Association of German Playwrights, 98
Association of Old Corps Students, 40
Auerbach, Alfred, 73
Augsburger Postzeitung, 63
Austria, 21
avante-garde, political irresponsibility in, 71

Baden, 23
Badische Beobachter, 64, 67
Bagehot, Walter, 24, 26
Barmen, 7
Barrikaden auf Wedding (Neukrantz), 107
Bartels, Adolf, 108, 223
Barthel, Max, 122, 147
Bartsch, Rudolf Hans, 160
Bauhaus, 206
Baumgarten, Hermann, 22
Bavaria, 23, 56
Bavarian Soviet Republic, 207
Bayerischer Kurier, 63
Bayerischer Volkszeitung, 63
Becher, Johannes, 103-07, 119, 206, 211

Beer Hall Putsch, 84
Belgium, 9-10
Beradt, Martin, 130, 133
Bergisch-Märkische Zeitung, 59
Berlin, 97, 106, 108-09, 119-20, 125, 128
Berlin Alexanderplatz (Döblin), 107, 206
Berlin Artists and Writers, Declaration of, 13
Berlin, Isaiah, 18-19
Berlin Lokal-Anzeiger, 223
Berlin Ortsgruppe (SDS): 99, 101-02, 108-10, 115-16, 120, 122, 126-29, 133, 202-03, 209, 213, 215; and demonstration of 29 July 1931, 117-18; extraordinary general assembly of 23 November 1931, 122, 212-13
Berliner Hoschschul-Nachricht, 50
Berliner Morgen-Zeitung, 64, 66-67, 70, 190-91
Berliner Tageblatt: 65, 120-21, 130, 132-33, 216; and censorship, 110-11, 119, 128, 207-08, 215; on SDS internal conflict, 121; and SDS opposition, 110-11
Bildungsbürgertum (educated burghers), 4, 7, 19, 20-22, 32-33, 156, 176. See also Bloem, Walter: and the Bildungsbürgertum
Bismarck-Schönhausen, Otto von, 21-23, 25-26, 32
Bissing, Colonel General von (Chief of the General Government of occupied Belgium), 9
Bleuel, Hans Peter, 53
Bloem, Judith (second wife), 81, 97, 146, 197
Bloem, Julius (father), 7, 39
Bloem, Margarete (daughter), 7, 81, 197
Bloem, Margarethe (first wife; née Kalähne), 7, 81
Bloem, Walter (1868-1951), 3, 7; acquiesces in Nazi anti-Jewish policy, 141-43; admired by Wilhelm II, 8; antirepublicanism, birth of his, 2, 58-59, 79, 97-98, 134-36; antirepublicanism, expression of his, 143-44; antisemitic misconceptions of, 42, 45, 86, 91-95, 159-60; his antisemitic interpretation of struggle in the writers' associations, 125-26, 134, 142, 158; antisemitism criticized by, 40-45, 76, 91-92, 97; antisemitism excused by, 94-95; antisemitism in students corps fought by, 40-45; attitudes closely resemble position of DVP, 61; and the August days (1914), 12, 31, 36, 92, 144; autobiography of, 52, 55, 58, 60, 70, 87, 111, 132, 170, 185, 222; and Belgium (W.W.I.), 9-10, 16; as bestselling novelist, 8, 45-46, 58, 153, 169, 227; and the Bildungsbürgertum (educated burghers), 4, 7, 19, 20, 156; "brotherhood" and national unity, 90; and his castle on the Sinn (Franconia), 9, 81-82, 90-91; Catholic church, his admiration of, 41; character of, 3-4, 30-37, 139-41, 152, 155-57; charismatic leader, attracted to, 84; as charismatic novelist (i.e., as mirror and educator of the Volk), 15-16, 19-20, 31-33, 153, 155; his collective identities (national and conservative), 31-34, 156; Colonial Society Speech, 12; defines nationhood, 79, 88-89; and de-Nazification trial of, 3, 153, 187; and disillusionment with Imperial leadership, 11-13, 85; and his distorted vision of his times, 19, 30, 34, 36; early fiction of, 8-9; evaluated as writer, 18, 30, 155; Face of the World (German title: Weltgesicht; 1928), 87-90; fictional themes of, 16; false idols of, 19-20, 26, 29-30; financial troubles of, 7-8, 58-59, 82-83, 90-91; as fox, 19, 36; The Freshman (German title: Der krasse Fuchs; 1906), 8; Front Soldiers (German title: Frontsoldaten), 131; German Dissension and Jewry (German title: Deutsche Zwietracht und Judentum; 1929), 90-95, 142; and the German resistance, 2, 153; Gottesferne, 62; Die grosse Liebe, 187-88; as hedgehog, 19, 26; Hero of His Land (German title: Held seines Landes, 1929), 90; Heroes of Yesterday, 59; Herrin, 62; and higher education of, 7, 21-22, 32; and Hindenburg, 134-35, 143-44, 157;

Hindenburg as Reich President (German title: Hindenburg als Reichspräsident; 1933), 143; Hindenburg the German (German title: Hindenburg der Deutsche; 1932); 134-35, 143; and Hitler, Adolf, 2, 14, 84, 143-45, 158-59, 220; and the Idealist tradition, 19, 89-90; his ignorance of the new social sciences, 29; Immortal Germany (German title: Unvergängliches Deutschland; 1933), 143-45; "Influences of Jewry upon German Culture," 77; and internationalism, 88-90, 97; "Das Judentum im Weltbild," 78-79; Der Kürfürst (1924), 87; The Land of Our Love (German title: Das Land unserer Liebe; 1924), 69, 199; as lawyer, 7, 20-21, 32, 40; and millenarianism, 36; and the military, 2, 9-13, 16, 32, 39, 42-43, 57, 60, 85-86, 97, 131, 151-52, 187; moral suicide of, 2-3, 139-41; 151, 165; Murderess, 150; and myth of Jewish (or left-wing) cultural hegemony, 90-91, 93, 95, 134-37, 141, 158, 199-200; as national conservative, 5, 19-20, 29-30, 36, 88-89, 91-92, 97, 155-56; and national Jews, 39, 92-95, 221; and National Liberalism, 22; as Nazi apologist, 2, 141-45, 158-59; and Nazi conservative alliance, 135; and Nazi destruction of literary freedom, 2, 134, 139, 145-49, 158, 222-23; Nazi convert, causes of his becoming a, 3-4, 157-58, 163-64; Nazi emnity towards, 2, 55, 139, 150-52; and Nazi party membership, 2, 150-51, 225; and Nazi rewards to, 143, 147, 151; and Nazis in the Weimar era, 42-43, 55, 84; as novelist laureate of the Second Reich, 1, 8; and the Old Nationalists, 2, 139, 144-45; and the "Open Letter to Heinrich Mann," 135-37; as outsider in Third Reich, 2, 149-50; and the PEN-Club, 2, 125-26, 129-34, 217; personal woes of, 82-83; as philosemite, 1, 3-6, 34, 37-45, 86, 92, 97, 150-60, 227; and pictorial mode of ordering and communicating reality, 17-18, 155; political isolation of, 3, 17, 47, 84, 87, 98, 162-63; political opportunism of, 19-20, 33; his political vision, relative health of, 34, 36-37, 45, 156; politicization of his writing, 13, 16-17; and the Protective Association of German Writers (SDS), 98-99, 111-30, 132-34, 142, 145-49, 158, 162, 164, 212, 214, 217, 222; racist misconceptions of, 144; and reconciliation with the proletariat, 41, 43, 86-87; reform conservatism of, 6, 26, 42-45, 47; rejection as source of distorted self-images, 32, 156-58; religious views of, 21, 26, 41; as representative author, 1, 3, 4, 8, 13, 15; as republican, 9, 13, 34, 36-37, 39-45, 83-84, 87-91, 170-71; Riga, Pioneer of Germany through the Centuries, 152; right-wing treats as renegade, 1, 2, 12-13, 39, 57-60, 139, 156-57, 184; and Romanticist tradition, 18-19; sales of his books, 45-47, 58-59, 86-87, 155, 161; sales of his books, collapse of, 49, 83, 163; and "second reality" (i.e., his world picture), 30, 32, 156; and self-delusion of, 30-36, 139-41, 152, 156-57, 159; seventieth birthday of (20 June 1938), 151; sixtieth birthday of (20 June 1928), 77-78, 90; Son of His Land (German title: Sohn seines Landes; 1928), 90; standards (transhistorical), his lack of, 26, 29-30, 32, 37, 80; standards (transhistorical), residues in, 36; student corps, his faith in the, 41, 43-45, 53, 78; The Teutons (German title: Teutonen; 1926), 59; theater career of, 7-8, 32, 39, 135-36, 158, 178; and the thesis novel (Tendenzroman), 17; trip around the world of, 77, 87-90, 199; his utopian psychological identity (distorted self-image), 30-34, 36, 156; as völkisch, 6, 19, 45, 47, 53, 79, 144-45, 159-60, 182; War Novel Trilogy of 1870-71, 8, 45, 169, 219; and Washington novels of, 22, 59, 90, 135, 199; wealth produced by his fiction, 58, 82; his works removed from libraries, 70; The World Conflagration (German title: Der Weltbrand), 85-86, 150, 173; and World War I, 9-13, 16, 85-86, 88; and World War II, 2, 151-52. See also Brotherhood

Bloem, Walter Julius (son; pseudonym Killian Koll), 7, 13, 53, 153, 185, 187
Blunck, Hans Friedrich, 149
Bohemia (German), 69
Bohner, Theodor, 112-15, 117, 122-23, 132, 146, 208-09, 213
Brausewetter, Artur, 70

Bremer Volksblatt, 67, 69-70
Breslauer Zeitung, 68
Breuer, Robert, 112-13, 115-17, 120, 123, 133, 202, 208-09, 214
Bronnen, Arnolt, 225
Brotherhood (German title: Die Brüderlichkeit; 1922) 1, 134, 140, 150; alienates German nationalists, 49, 58-60, 156; antisemitic misconceptions in, 42, 45, 159-60; antisemitism assailed in, 39, 43-45; and Bildungsbürgertum 43, 45; and the Catholic social movement, 41, 44-45, 62; as cause of Bloem's conversion to Hitlerism, 80; as cause of Bloem's declining marketability, 1, 2, 49, 58-59, 163, 187; as cause of Bloem's political isolation, 2, 49, 52, 57-60, 79-80, 139, 152, 162-63, 184, 187; as cause of Bloem's psychological stress, 59-60, 156-57; as cause of Bloem's rise in writers' associations, 2, 123; circulation of, 1, 45-47, 161-62; confiscation of, 150; and courts of honor, Bloem's officer associations, 57, 187; and courts of honor, Teutonia and Lusatia, 52, 57; and de-Nazification board, 153; disowned by Bloem and Grethlein, 150; excerpted in CV-Zeitung, 46, 195; genesis of, 39-41; impact on corps students, 52-53, 57; impact on German nationalists, 49, 57, 160-61; impact on "national Jews," 71; impact on völkisch radicals, 53-54, 69; people's edition (1927), 46, 76; plot of, 42-45; political message of, 1, 42-45, 80, 153, 159-61; political message of, Bloem's continued adherence to the, 78, 83-91, 150; political message of, renounced by Bloem, 79, 141-42; reception by corps students, 184; reception by Jews, 1, 2, 46, 71-72; reception by liberals, 1; reception by nationalists, 1, 57-58; reception by socialists, 1; reviews of, Bavarian People's party (BVP), 61, 63-64, 163; reviews of, Catholic, 61-65, 67, 163; reviews of, Center party, 61, 64-65, 163; reviews of, collected by Bloem, 190; reviews of, corps students, 49-53; reviews of, German National People's party (DNVP), 55-57; reviews of, German People's party (DVP), 61-62, 164; reviews of, Jewish, 61, 72-74, 77, 79-80, 141-42, 163, 191-92; reviews of, liberal democratic, 65-69, 79-80, 136, 164; reviews of, literature industry (non-aligned) periodicals, 70-71; reviews of, nationalist, 46, 57-58, 161-63, 186-87; reviews of, republican, 79-80; reviews of, Social Democratic party (SPD), 69-70, 79, 164; reviews of, völkisch radical, 54-55; and Rocholl, 52-53; serialized in Israelitisches Familienblatt, 46, 71,74-76; as singular event in Weimar Republic, 1; as turning point in Bloem's life, 58, 161-62, 187; and World Conflagration, 86, 150; and "A Word to Brotherhood," 75-77
Die Brücke, 128, 207-08, 217
Die Brüderlichkeit. See Brotherhood
Brüning, Heinrich, 106, 115, 117, 171-72
Bukharin, Nikolai I., 106
Burschell, Friedrich, 111, 134, 208, 217
Burschen heraus, 49
Burschen in Not (Wieprecht), 186
Burschenschaftliche Wege, 49

Campaign Committee for the Freedom of Literature (Kampfkomitee für die Freiheit des Schrifttums). See Kampfkomitee
Canonical Revelation, 21, 26
Caprivi, General Leo Count von (Reich Chancellor, 1890-94), 23
Cartel of German Lyricists, 98
Center party, 24-25, 190
Central Union of German Citizens of the Jewish Faith (C.V.), 72, 76-79
Christ (symbol of saving love in Brotherhood), 45, 73-75

Christian-Brandenburg Dining Society (Christlich-Brandenburgische Tischgesellschaft von 1817), 97-98, 143
Christian Democratic Union, 163
Christian Social Union, 163
Christianity, 4-5, 22-24, 36. See also Bloem, Walter: religious views of
Civil Peace (in Germany during W.W. IU.), 35
cologne (Köln), 190
Comintern (Communist or Third International), 106
Communist party (KPD), 86, 101-03, 106-10, 116, 128, 164, 202-03, 206-08, 211-13
Communist writers, 101-03, 108-09, 146-47. See also League of Proletarian Revolutionary Writers; Die Linkskurve; Opposition in the Protective Association of German Writers (OSDS)
conservatism: 22-26, 56; Bagehot's typology of, 24; of enjoyment, 24; Epstein's typology of, 25; of fear, 24; and Free Conservative party, 23-25; and German Conservative party, 22-26, 177; lack of principled German, 163; reactionary, 25; of reflection, 24-25; reform, 6, 25-26, 42-45; revolutionary, 6; völkisch, 6, 95, 139. See also principle, conservative
Contzen, Dr., 64
Courths-Mahler, Hedwig, 16, 18, 68, 133
CV-Zeitung, 1, 46, 75-79

Dahrendorf, Ralf, 20-21, 28
Dante, 19
Däubler, Theodor, 126, 131-32
Deak, Istvan, 107-110
Declaration of Independence, American, 22
Decree of the Reichspresident for Protection of the Volk and the State, 150
Dettman, Ludwig, 85
Deutsch-Österreiche Tageszeitung, 59
Deutsche Allgemeine Rundschau, 56, 81
Deutsche Allgemeine Zeitung, 85, 135, 173, 199
Deutsche Corpszeitung, 50
Deutsche Exilliteratur, 99
Deutsche Hochschul-Warte, 49
Deutsche Hochschul Zeitung, 50-51
Der deutsche Kaufmann im Auslande, 56
Deutsche Reichszeitung, 64, 190
Deutsche Republik, 70
Deutsche Roman-Zeitung, 70
Deutsche Zeitung, 12, 55
dialectical self-hood, 30-34
Dienemann, Rabbi Dr., 73-74
Dinter, Arthur, 1, 52, 56, 68-69, 98, 108, 162, 165, 185
Die Dithmarscher (Bartels), 108
Döblin, Alfred, 100, 107, 205-06
dogmatism, 28-29
Dovifat, Professor, 143
Dresdner Nachrichten, 187

Eichholz, Hans Joachim (Brotherhood hero), 42-45, 54, 57, 61-62, 71-72, 74
Elberfeld, 7, 46
Eleventh Party Congress of the KPD, 103
Elösser, Arthur, 112, 117, 208-09
Elster, Hanns Martin, 126, 130-33, 216
Emergency Decrees of 28 March and 17 July (1931), 117
Emig, Kurt, 50-51
Engel, Georg, 39
Engelbrecht, Hermann, 55
England, 10
Entente, 10
entertainment fiction (Unterhaltungsromane), 3, 15-19, 173-74
Epstein, Klaus, 25
Erzberger, Mathias, 190
Eulenberg, Herbert, 77-79
Ewers, Hanns Heinz, 146, 165, 222, 225
Existentialism, 21

Falkenhayn, General Erich von, 10-11
fallacy of certainty, 21, 28
Farben, I.G., 91
Federal Republic of Germany, 174
Feuchtwanger, Lion, 147
Field Press Office (Feldpressestelle), 10-11, 16, 83
First International congress of Revolutionary Writers (Moscow), 103
Fischer, Samuel, 3, 183, 196, 227
Fischer Verlag, S., 47, 227
Fluhme, Dr., 115, 210
Foreign Office, German, 87
France (the French), 8-10
Franco-Prussian War, 8
Franconia, 9
Franconia (dueling fraternity in Brotherhood), 42-45, 52, 57, 71, 181
Frankfurter Zeitung, 65, 69
Fränkische Volksblatt, 63-64
Frederick William IV (King of Prussia), 23
Freisler, Dr. Roland, 206
Freud, Sigmund, 29
Freytag, Gustav, 74
Fritsch, Theodor, 52, 185
Froberger, Dr. Jos., 64
Fulda, Ludwig, 39

Gabor, Andor, 104
General Staff of the Field Army, 10-11
Genosse Levi (Halbach), 77
German Democratic party (DDP), 67-68, 85, 191, 203
German Democratic Republic, 208
German Nationalist People's party (DNVP), 26, 55-57, 61, 80, 186-87, 227
German People's party (DVP), 55, 61, 136, 164
Germania, 64, 69, 190

Gestapo, 150
"The Gesture" (Wiechert), 1
Gläser, Ernst, 108, 206
<u>Die Glocke</u>, 208
Goebbels, Joseph, 2, 143, 146-47, 149, 150-51, 162, 222, 225
Goethe Festival, 128-29, 131, 215
Goldstein, Ludwig, 68, 71
<u>Der Gral</u>, 65
Great Depression, 91
Great Elector, 87
Great Main Headquarters (Charlesville; Pless), 11
Great War. <u>See</u> World War I
Gregor, Dr., 64-65
Grethlein und Co., G.m.b.H. (Bloem's publisher; Leipzig and Zurich), 15, 45, 47, 74, 82, 87, 142, 150, 162
Grimm, Hans, 95
Groener, General Wilhelm, 130
<u>Gross-Berliner neueste Nachrichten</u>, 71, 192
Grossmann, Stefan, 121
Grünberg, Karl, 103, 109

Haensel, Dr. Carl, 124
Hagemeyer, Hans, 150-51
Hagen, Hans W., 151
Hague Convention, 10
Halbach, Fritz, 77
Hallowell, John, 28
Hamburg, 86, 142
<u>Hamburger Nachrichten</u>, 87
Hanfstängel, Karl, 132
<u>Hannoversche Landeszeitung</u>, 51
Harper and Brothers, 90
Hauptmann, Gerhart, 205
Hauschild, Kurt, 47
Hayn, Dr. Georg, 65
hedgehogs and foxes in literature, 18-19
Hegel, Georg Friedrich, 30
Hegemann, Werner, 136, 219
Heimann, Moritz, 3, 227
<u>Heimgarten</u>, 54-55, 186
Helldorf, Otto von, 23
Helphand-Parvus, Dr., 208
Hemmingway, Ernest, 30
Herzfelde, Wieland, 209
Herzog, Rudolf, 15
Hesse, Hermann, 66
Heuss, Theodor, 101-02, 201-03
<u>Hildesheimer Allgemeine Zeitung</u>, 62
Hiller, Kurt, 205
Hindenburg, Field-Marshal Paul von Beneckendorff und, 11, 53, 89, 131, 134-35, 143-44, 150, 157, 221

Hirschberg, Herbert, 70
Hirschfeld, Magnus, 147
Historicism, 19, 21, 27, 29, 33, 176
Hitler, Adolf, 2, 4, 25, 35, 53, 68, 84, 113, 133, 139-40, 143-45, 151, 153, 157-59, 162, 167, 208, 220-21, 227
Hitler Youth, 152
Hochland, 65
Hoffmann, Theo, 63
Hohenzollerns, 36
Hohlbaum, Robert, 15, 160
Hohmann, Dr. (Brotherhood character modeled on C. Sonnenschein), 41, 44-45, 65
Holländer, Felix, 39
Hollander, Walther von, 131, 133-34
Holocaust, 28

Illustrierte Beobachter, 152
inflation, 46, 82-83, 197
Der Inflationsroman: Der grosse Betung (Scharrer), 107
Institute for Newspaper History, 143
International Office of Proletarian and Revolutionary Writers, 103
International Vereinigung revolutionär Schriftsteller, 104
International Worker's Novel, 105
Internationaler Arbeiterverlag, 105, 128, 215
The Iron Years (German title: Das eiserne Jahr; 1911), 8
Israelitisches Familienblatt, 46, 55, 71, 74-76
Israelitisches Wochenblatt für die Schweiz, 74

Jacobs, Monty, 121-22, 213
Jacobsohn, Siegfried, 136
Jäger, Hans, 108, 206
Jäger, Heinz. See Walter Kreiser
Jews: as first principle of evil to Nazis, 35; "national," 71-72, 91-95, 142
Jews of Kronburg (Püschel), 1
Johnson, Paul, 167
Johst, Hanns (SS Oberführer and Staatsrat), 149
Josephtal, Fritz, 77-78
Judaism, 4, 73, 94
Jüdisch-liberale Zeitung, 73-74
Jünger, Nathaniel (pseudonym for Johann Rump), 62, 189
Junkers, 22, 24-25

Kampfbund für deutsche Kultur, 224
Kampfkomitee, 118-19
Karlsruher Tagblatt, 68
Kartell Convent, 72
Kästner, Erich, 148, 205
Kattowitzer Zeitung, 62
Kazin, Alfred, 30
K. C. Blätter, 72
Keitel, General Wilhelm, 151
Kellermann, Bernhard, 172

Kerr, Alfred, 132, 136
Kesser, Hermann, 108
Kisch, Egon Erwin, 103, 109, 203
Kläber, Kurt, 103-05, 204
Klein, Alfred, 98, 118, 214
Klinnert, Ernst, 53
[K. F.] Köhler Verlag, 15, 90
Kohn, Hans, 22
Kollwitz, Käthe, 172
Kölnische Volkszeitung, 64, 190
Kölnische Zeitung, 8, 10
König, Johannes, 116-19
Königsberger Hartungsche Zeitung, 67-68, 71
Konrad, Dr. Karl, 49
Kösener Senioren Conventsverband (KSC), 39-42, 44, 50
Kreiser, Walter, 129
Kreuzburger Nachrichten, 186
Kühn, Karl Herbert, 67-68
Kyffhäuserbund, 135

Landsberger, Artur, 206
Langen-Müller Circle, 149, 222
Lania, Leo, 101
Lask, Berta, 101
Latvia, 152, 226
Law for the Protection of the Republic, 61, 117
lawyers, conserving attitude of, 20-21
League of Nations, 88
League of Proletarian-Revolutionary Writers: 127, 203, 205, 207, 211; and Bloem's election as SDS chair, 125; and Bloem, honeymoon with, 126-27; and censorship issue as weapon in SDS, 117-18; composition of, 104, 203; as core of SDS opposition, 108-09, 116-18; foundation of, 103-04, 203; literary monthly established, 104-05; and Marxists Workers' Library, Berlin, 106; and the Nazis, 106-08, 206; and proletarian mass novel, 105-06; purged from SDS, 120-21; regards the "Social Fascists" (SPD) as main threat, 106-07, 206
Leipzig, 15, 40, 45, 51-52
lending libraries, 15, 173
Lenin, V. I., 167
Leuchtturm, 63
Leyens, Erich, 71
liberalism, 29
Die Linkskurve: 109, 115-17, 204; attacks left-wing intellectuals, 107; attacks Nazis, 106, 206; attacks Social Democrats, 107; circulation of, 105; establishment of, 104-05; and proletarian mass novels, 105-06
Das literarische Echo, 70
Literarischer Handweiser, 70
Lohalm, Uwe, 6
Löwenstein, Justizrat (Brotherhood main character), 42-44, 54, 61, 67, 70-71, 73, 75, 193
Löwenstein, Ruth (Brotherhood character), 42, 44-45, 54, 70, 73
Löwenstein, Ludwig (Brotherhood character) 42, 44-45, 54, 70, 73
Löwy, Ernst, 139

Lübeck, 153
Ludendorff, General Erich, 11, 13, 87
Luftwaffe, 152
Lukas, Georg, 128
Lusatia in Leipzig (member corps of the KSC), 40, 51-52, 57, 78, 97
Lutz, Georg, 63

"M," 74
Magdeburg, 69
Magdeburgische Zeitung, 62
Mahraun, Artur, 84-85, 198
Main Executive Committee (SDS): 98, 102, 109-13, 115-17, 120-25, 127-29, 132-33, 146, 208, 211, 213, 215, 217; and Bloem's election as SDS chair, 123-24; misunderstands Nazism, 113-14; 123-24; purged from Berlin Ortsgruppe, leadership of, 116; purges SDS (1933), 146-47; suppresses SDS opposition, 120-21; Social Democrats as predominant group in, 112-13, 123
Majority Social Democrats. See Social Democratic party
Malik Verlag, 105
"Manifesto for the Freedom of Literature," 118
Mann, Heinrich, 135-37, 153, 199, 205, 222
Mann, Thomas, 29, 68, 107, 153, 205, 208
Mannheim, 68
"Die Mannschaft," (The Troops), 121-22, 150, 225
Mantua-Sdila, Hans Heinz, 146-47
Marburg, 40, 51-52
Marchwitza, Hans, 104-05, 107, 128, 205
Marcuse, Ludwig, 121
Maurina, Zenta, 139-42, 152
militarism, 22, 43
millenarianism, 4, 24-25, 34-36
modernization as source of insecurity, 33
Monatschrft für Geschichte und Wissenschaft des Judentums, 192
Montagsblatt, 54, 68-69
moral philosophy, 21, 155
moral relativism, 3, 21, 29, 155
morality in politics. See principle, political and moral
Moses (symbol of vengeful Judaism in Brotherhood), 45, 73-75
Mosse Concern, 65-66, 191
Mosse, George, 85, 182
Mühsam, Erich, 110, 147-48, 202, 207, 223
Müller-Jabusch, 108
München-Augsburger Zeitung, 56
Munich, 63
Münsterischer Anzeiger, 64
Münzel, Hermann, 52
Münzenberg, Willi, 110, 207, 213
Musil, Robert, 121

Napoleon I, 89
National Association of German Writers, 112
National Liberals, 21-26, 61

National Socialism. See Nazism
National Socialist German Workers' Party (NSDAP). See Nazism natural law, standards and rights, 21-22, 28-29, 155
Nazism: and Communist literature-politics, 106-08, 214; and dialectical selfhood, 30-31; and destruction of free literature, 145-49; and the disaster syndrome, 35; honors Theodor Fritsch as the "Old Master," 52; as millenarian radicalism, 25, 34-36; as National Fascism, 107, 214; and persecution of Jews, 28, 71, 141-43; and Stormtroops (SA), 54; in the Third Reich, 2-3, 139-53; totalitarian claims of, 113-14; utopian existences of, 34-36; and völkisch radicalism, 6, 43. See also Bloem, Walter; Hitler, Adolf
Neue badische Landeszeitung, 68
Neue Montagszeitung, 213
Neue Preussisch (Kreuz-) Zeitung, 56
Neukrantz, Klaus, 107
Nicolai, Major Walter, 10-11
Nietzsche, Friedrich, 33
November Revolution (in Germany, 1918), 13, 35, 43, 70, 83, 94, 144

"Old Nationalists," 2, 144-45
Old Testament, 4
Olden, Rudolf, 111-12, 115, 208, 216
Opposition in the Protective Association of German Writers (OSDS), 124-25, 213, 216; in Baden, 120; in Bavaria, 120; and Communist fraktion, 119, 122, 206, 209, 211-12; and Communist program, 116; composition of, 109-11; and defiance of Bloem, 127-29; emergence of, 108-09; in Hamburg, 120; in Königsberg, 102; manipulates censorship issue, 118-19; manipulates liberal-democratic principles, 133-34; "Program Declaration of the OSDS (Opposition in the Protective Association of German Writers)," 118-19, 211; in the provinces, 108-09, 119-20; and purge of SDS, 120-21, 125; revolutionary impulses of, 118-19; in Rhine-Main, 120; in Rhineland-Westphalia, 120; in Silesia, 120; submits petition for Ossietzky, 132
Oranieburg concentration camp, 148
Ossietzky Affair, 129-34, 217
Ossietzky, Carl von, 121, 129-33, 136-37, 205-06, 208, 216-17
Pan-German League (Pan Germans), 12, 23, 55, 70, 172
Papen, Franz von, 113
Pascal, Roy, 98
Patriotic Association of Jewish Front Soldiers, 91, 142
PEN-Club (German Section), 2, 3, 98, 125-26, 129-34, 217
PEN-Club (International), 125, 158
Pezold, Gustav, 95
Pfälzer Corpszeitung, 51, 184
Pfälzische Volkszeitung, 191
Philosemitism: definition of, 4-5; in nationalist fiction, 1; of Sonnenschein, Carl, 41; as treason to nationalist cause, 162-63. See also Bloem, Walter
Placzek, Dr. H. W., 79
Plato, 19, 24
Plessen, Colonel-General Hans von, 171
Pol, Heinz, 122, 127, 129, 212-13
Poland, 151, 226
Positivism, 21, 29, 33
Prague, 49, 68

Presber, Rudolf, 225
principle (transhistorical standards): 3-4, 21-30, 32-33, 176; Christian, 22, 36; conservative, 23-26, 33, 36; and the historian, 27-28; and the Holocaust, 28; as interpretive tool and object of study, 26-29; liberal, 5, 21-22, 26, 33, 36; rational choice of, 27; rejection in Germany of philosophic quest for, 21, 29. See also natural law standards and rights
Progressivism: 25; lack of principled German, 163-64
Proletarian Feuilleton News Agency, 103
proletarians, 41, 43, 174. See also League of Proletarian Revolutionary Writers
Protective Association of German Writers (Schutzverband der Deutschen Schriftsteller or SDS): 2-3, 98, 141, 201, 203, 208-12, 222; Bavarian Gau of, 208; and the campaign against the SDS opposition, 112-14; and censorship, 100, 108-11, 117-18, 127-28; coordination of in Third Reich, 139, 145-49, 223; establishment of, 201-02, 207; and general assembly of 9-10 January 1932, 124-25, 213; and the "Group Bohner-Breuer-Schendell," 112, 123; Marxist interpretation of Bloem's role in, 98-99, 213-14; and the "National Opposition," 121-23; and the Ortsgruppe Berlin-Brandenburg, 122, 124-25, 129, 213-14; political neutrality of, 100-01; and the politicization issue, 112-14; Rhine-Main district of, 108-09; right-wing role in the, 112; Socialist fraktion of the, 120, 123; structure of the, 99; as union, 99-100. See also Berlin Ortsgruppe (SDS); Main Executive Committee (SDS); Opposition in the Protective Association of German Writers (OSDS); Bloem, Walter
Prussia, 21-23, 25-26
Prussian Academy of the Arts, Sektion Dichtkunst, 222
Prussian Landtag, 22, 112
Prussian Pentegram, 22-23, 25-26
Prussian Upper Administrative Court, Third Senate, 128
Püschel, Ernst, 1

Rathenau, Walter, 46, 68
realism, literary and political, 21, 26
Realpolitik, 26
Red Group, 102-03
Red-One-Mark Novel, 105, 128, 204, 205
Reich Association of German Writers (Reichverband Deutscher Schriftsteller), 148-49, 223-24
Reich Commission for the Supervision of Public Order and News, 103
Reich Culture Chamber, 149
Reich Culture Chamber Law of 22 September 1933, 149
Reich Literature Chamber (Reich Schrifttumskammer or RSK), 2, 149-50, 224
Reich Literature Chamber, Group Writers, 149
Reich Ministry for Public Enlightenment and Propaganda, 143, 146, 149-52, 223, 225
Reich Office for the Furtherance of German Literature, 150, 224
Der Reichsbote, 12
Reichsguericht (Supreme Court), 129
Reichsschrifttumskammer. See Reich Literature Chamber
Reichstag, 102
Reichstag Peace Resolution (July 1917), 11, 170
Reichswehr, 129
Reinhardt, Max, 39
religious faith, decline of, 33
Remarque, Erich Maria, 59, 131, 205

Renn, Ludwig, 104, 109
Retallack, James, 22
Reventlow, Count Ernst zu, 100
Rheydt, City Theater in, 87
Rhineland, 78
Rhodes, James, 30-32, 34-36, 178
Richter, Hans, 146, 223
Riga, 151-52, 226
Rocholl, <u>Ministerialrat</u>, 52
Roda Roda (Sandor Friedrich Rosenfeld), 109, 113, 121, 127, 206-07
Rosenberg, Alfred, 2, 39, 55, 150-52, 165, 224-25
Rosseger, Peter, 186
<u>Die rote Fahne</u>, 123
<u>Roter Tag</u>, 55
Roth, Joseph, 206
Rousseau, Jean-Jacques, 20
Royal Theater (Berlin), 7
Royal Theater (Stuttgart), 7
Ruhr, French occupation of, 46
Rust, Bernhard, 222

Schafflingen (University in <u>Brotherhood</u>), 42, 181
Schaffner, Jakob, 116, 118, 120, 134
Scharrer, Adam, 107
Schendell, Werner, 108, 112, 115-16, 118, 210
Scherl Verlag, 15
Scheuer, Dr. O. F., 49
Schiller Foundation (Weimar), 130, 151
Schirach, Baldur von, 162
Schlageter, Albert, 143, 221
<u>Schlesische Zeitung</u>, 57
<u>Schmutz- und Schundgesetz</u> (Filth and Trash Law), 102, 202
Schönlank, Bruno, 113, 202
<u>Der Schriftsteller</u>, 115
Schultheiss, Wilhelm, 40, 42
<u>Schutzverband der Deutschen Schriftsteller</u> (SDS). <u>See</u> Protective Association of German Writers
<u>Schwäbische Tageszeitung</u>, 56
SDS. <u>See</u> Protective Association of German Writers
Second Reich, 13, 22, 26, 35, 41, 83, 85, 137
Seldte, Franz, 85
<u>Sin Against the Blood</u> (Dinter), 1, 52, 56, 68-69, 108, 185
Sinn, the (river in Franconia), 9, 81, 91
Snell, John L., 227
Social Democratic party (SPD): 13, 25, 67, 69-70, 105, 164, 202-203, 206, 208; as Social Fascists, 99, 106-07, 205, 214
social science, 26-27, 29, 33
society: estates, 25, 32, industrial (class), 25-26, 32
"Solidarity Declaration for the Opposition in the SDS," 121
Sonnenschein, Carl, 41, 63
Speckert, Heinrich, 51

Speer, Albert, 162
Spengler, Oswald, 76, 174-75
[L.] Staackmann Verlag (Leipzig), 15
Stahlhelm, 85, 135
Stalin, Joseph, 106
Stapel, Wilhelm, 95
State party, 85
Stimmen der Zeit, 65
Stinnes, Hugo, 173
Stoffregen, Götz Otto, 147-48, 223
Stölting, (Joseph?), 56
Strauss, Leo, 26, 177
"Strength through Joy," 151-52, 226
Ströbel, Hermann (Brotherhood character; representative of radical völkisch movement), 42-44, 56, 185
Strobl, Karl Hans, 15, 59, 160
Strothmann, Dietrich, 148, 223
student corps: as crucibles of future national leadership, 39, 41, 43-45, 60; völkisch radicalism in, 39-45, 50; in Würzburg, 53, 185
Sturm auf Essen (Marchwitza), 105, 107, 128, 204, 215
Stuttgart, 12, 56
Süddeutsche Zeitung, 56
Supreme Command, 10-11, 87, 170

Der Tag: Die grosse national Tageszeitung, 186
Das Tagebuch, 136
Tegel Prison, 130
Teutonia in Heidelberg (member corps of the KSC), 52, 78
Teutonia in Marburg (member corps of the KSC), 40, 51-52, 57, 97, 181
Thälmann, Ernst, 116
Third Reich, 24, 35, 71, 98, 134, 136-37, 139-53, 162, 164, 216
Tivoli Program (1892), 22-23
Tocqueville, Alexis de, 155
Todt, Fritz, 151, 226
Toller, Ernst, 101
Tolstoy, Leo, 18-19, 175
transhistorical standards, See natural law, standards and rights; principle
Treaty of Versailles, 46, 129-30, 144
Trebitsch, Arthur, 54
trivial literature (Kitsch), 16
The Troops, See "Die Mannschaft"
Tucholsky, Kurt, 100, 211
Der Türmer, 134
Twelfth Grenadier Regiment, 9

Ullstein, House of, 47, 190
United States of America, 87, 90

Verdun, Battle of, 10
Verlag Reimar Hobbing, 85, 135, 173
Vesper, Will, 222

Vienna, 126
Vivos Voco, 66
Voegelin, Erich, 26, 30, 177
Volk. See völkisch
völkisch, definition of, 6
völkisch conservatives. See conservatism
völkisch radicalism, 6, 25, 42-45, 53-55, 80, 155, 177, 186, 206, 223
Völkischer Beobachter, 55, 147
Die volkshochschul-Gemeinschaft, 50
Volksstimme, 69
Vorwärts, 13, 69, 87, 203
Vossische Zeitung, 8, 65, 69, 112, 122, 213

Walter, Hans-Albert, 99, 111-12, 146, 164, 214
War Ministry, 11
War Press Bureau, 11-12, 16
Wassermann, Jakob, 205
Weber, Max, 27, 29, 155, 158
Weimar, 130, 132
Weimar Coalition, parties, of, 61
Weimar era, 22, 82, 159
Weimar Poets' Congress, 151
Weimar Republic, 9, 20, 34, 39, 43, 46, 53, 58, 69-70, 83, 85, 87, 89, 94, 110, 123, 125, 134, 143-45, 147, 158, 160, 224
Weinert, Erich, 104
Weiss, Georg, 51-52, 185
Die Welt am Abend, 133, 213
Weltbühne, 100, 129-31, 136, 213, 216-17
Weltbühne Circle, 109-10, 118, 207-08
Der Weltkampf, 55, 75
Weltman, Dr. Lutz, 111-12
Werfel, Franz, 205
Weser-Zeitung, 57
West-Elbian Germany, 22-25
white-collar workers, 25
Wiechert, Ernst, 1, 121
Wieprecht, Erich, 186
Wiesbaden, 61
Wiesbadener Zeitung, 61-62
Wilhelm II (German emperor, 1888-1918), 8, 11-13, 17, 43, 52, 89, 171, 198
Wilhelmine era, 20, 23
Wilhelmine Order, 10, 56
Winckler, Wolfgang, 54, 220-21
Wirth, Joseph, 190
Wismann, Dr. Heinz, 223
Wittfogel, Dr. K. A., 127
Woltereck, Richard, 66
Working Community for the Freedom of Spiritual Creativity (Arbeitsgemeinschaft für die Freiheit des geistigen Schaffens), 119
Working Committee of Nationalist Writers, 146
World War I, 4, 9-13, 16-17, 25-26, 34-35, 39, 42, 70, 76, 83, 85, 88, 98, 155, 157, 198

World War II, 141, 151-53, 164
Wotan (symbol of intolerant nationalism in Brotherhood), 45, 73-75
Wuppertal, 7, 39, 46
Württemberg, 23
Würzburg, student corps in, 53, 185
Würzburger, Karl, 66
Young German Order (Jungdeutscher Orden or Jungdo), 84-85

Zionism, 72, 74
Zweig, Arnold, 100-01, 205, 208

STUDIES IN GERMAN THOUGHT AND HISTORY

1. William A. Pelz, **The Spartakusbund and the German Working Class Movement, 1914-1919**
2. Ruth Richardson, **Dorothea Mendelssohn Veit Schlegel: The Berlin and Jena Years 1764-1802**
3. Eric von der Luft, **Hegel, Hinrichs, and Schleiermacher on Feeling and Reason in Religion: The Texts of Their 1821-1822 Debate**
4. Karla Poewe, **Childhood in Germany During World War II: The Story of a Little Girl**
5. Bruno Bauer, **The Trumpet of the Last Judgement Against the Athiest and Antichrist: An Ultimatum,** Lawrence Stepelevich, (trans.)
6. Fanny Lewald, **Prinz Louis Ferdinand,** Linda Rogols-Siegel, (trans.)
7. Rodler F. Morris, **From Weimar Philosemite to Nazi Apologist: The Case of Walter Bloem**
8. Marvin Thomas, **Karl Theodor and the Bavarian Succession, 1777-1778**
9. Peter Petschauer, **The Education of Women in Eighteenth-Century Germany: New Directions From the German Female Perspective**
10. Eric von der Luft, editor, **Schopenhauer: New Essays in Honor of His 200th Birthday**